Advance Praise for *Managing Virtual Projects*

"Goncalves' new book *Managing Virtual Projects* provides project managers with all the necessary information to manage projects virtually. The book does a great job in outlining best practices, real-world examples from his own practices, and alignment with PMI's PMBOK. The book is a must have."

John J. Cirignano, PMP
President, Patriots Technology Consulting and the Microsoft Project Users Group—Global
Boston Chapter

"Those new to project management and those with many years of experience will find *Managing Virtual Projects* to be filled with strategies for managing projects in the today's global, virtual, culturally diverse, schedule-challenged world. Marcus Goncalves covers all aspects of project work, and balances theories with a practical approach to planning and execution. Virtual management and virtual project management are exciting and evolving fields—Marcus gives us a blend of examples and courses of action that can be immediately applied to current work."

Pamela Campbell
Senior Manager, BEA Systems and Lecturer
Boston University

"The experienced project manager will be able to use this book immediately as a reference on how electronic project management can be done successfully. It has examples of real-life projects and it is based on current project management models and tools. Command and control doesn't work in a virtual world; going over thousands of miles dissipates incentive and power. Instead, alternative ways must be instilled into project managers if they want to be successful in the virtual arena. The case studies provide for interesting discussions and insights."

Star Dargin—Founder SDC Consulting
Facilitator for HeiterConnect
Virtual Leadership Workshop

"Marcus Goncalves, in his new book, *Managing Virtual Projects*, describes the process of managing projects in the new, more loosely coupled, high-pressure business world in which we all operate. Even for smaller companies that are not dealing with "globalization issues," this book is a must read for all managers—the wizards of odds. With reduced work forces that necessitate dotted-line teams, increasing partnerships to provide best of breed solutions, added pressure to bring products to market faster, and acquisitions abounding that create disjointed teams of people, this innovative, practical, manage-the-boundaries framework will ensure that teams communicate, continue to work with the local tools that make them effective, and meet overall project goals."

Kerri Apple
VP Development and Operations
bTrade, Inc.

"Goncalves's book *Managing Virtual Projects* provides excellent insights and best practices in managing project and business processes from afar. Having worked with him before on management of early-stage companies, I am aware of his effective style and believe this book to be an essential tool for virtual project managers and executives operating their organizations in a global scale."

Gregory S. Baletsa
President of Azonix Corporation

"Managing a major virtual project such as our digital cable television and interactive services (TeleMedia Group) in Istanbul, Turkey (our resources are scattered all around Turkey and the world, including Boston, Miami, Genoa, and Amsterdam), I appreciated the virtues of Marcus Goncalves in his book on ePM. As Marcus Goncalves recommends, we use the Web as our infrastructure for communication and remote collaboration between our virtual project teams. There are some obstacles, but e-mails, voice mails, video conferencing, Groupware, and Workflow tools enable us to meet our business and project objectives and save us time and money in the long run."

Semih Arslanoglu,
CEO TeleMedia Group
Istanbul, Turkey

"*Managing Virtual Projects* is a very important and timely book due to globalization. Corporate America is depending on outsourcing to speed innovation and generate growth—therefore there is a need for skills in managing projects virtually. At Boston University this will be required reading for our students, as it will provide our project management students with the latest skills."

Professor Vijay Kanabar
PMP, Head of BU Global Project Management and Associate Professor
Boston University

"There are a lot of theories and opinions about how to manage virtual teams and virtual projects. Marcus Goncalves screws the lid off the traditional concepts of project management and describes in detail the way to get projects done in less time utilizing tools, timing, and trust. His descriptions are entertaining and enlightening. His loose, no-rigid-boundaries approach to ePM is exciting. He has truly defined a framework and set the bar for the tools manufacturers. The book describes organized chaos at it's finest and is an absolute must read for senior executives and managers as well as project managers."

Bob Stalcup
PMP, Principal Architect/Infrastructure Data Service
American Electric Power

"More than ever before, project management is being looked to as the mechanism that ties the corporate vision to work performance. Acting as the primary bridge between management and workers, project managers are facing new and extreme communication and time management problems resulting from globalization, outsourcing, or more simply a geographically challenged organizational structure. *Managing Virtual Projects* provides an accurate assessment of these emerging problems and offers a sound starting point for discovering situation-specific solutions for your organization. Functioning on the front line of cutting-edge technology, Goncalves leverages his technological expertise and management experiences to package together a collection of lessons learned within the emerging and changing field of virtual project management."

Stephanie Pawlowicz
PMP, PMO Director
State of New Hampshire

"As a shareholder in a large law firm with multiple offices and an international client base, I am fascinated with the potential benefits to be derived from the application of Marcus Goncalves' innovative theories regarding ePM to 'projects' being undertaken by professional service firms. For law firms, and for accounting firms as well, the management of complex litigation, with attorneys, witnesses, consultants, and experts in disparate locations; and the implementation, from a legal/accounting standpoint, of large-scale mergers and acquisitions or financial transactions come readily to mind as potential applications. Since most large professional service firms today have the technological capabilities to support ePM, why should its competitive benefits be limited to the corporate world? *Managing Virtual Projects* contains many innovative ideas that are ripe for exploration in a professional services firm context."

Mary Jane Augustine
Partner, Attorney at Law
Budrovran Ingersol

Managing Virtual Projects

MARCUS GONCALVES

McGraw-Hill

New York   San Francisco   Washington, D.C.   Auckland   Bogotá
Caracas   Lisbon   London   Madrid   Mexico City   Milan   Montreal
New Delhi   San Juan   Singapore   Sydney   Tokyo   Toronto

1 2 3 4 5 6 7 8 9 0 DOC/DOC 0 9 8 7 6 5 4

ISBN 0-07-144451-3

McGraw-Hill books are available at special quantity discounts to use as premiums and sales promotions, or for use in corporate training programs. For more information, please write to the Director of Special Sales, McGraw-Hill, Professional Publishing, 2 Penn Plaza, New York, NY 10121-2298. Or contact your local bookstore.

This book was printed on recycled, acid-free paper containing a minimum of 50% recycled, de-inked fiber.

Library of Congress Cataloging-in-Publication Data

Goncalves, Marcus.
   Managing virtual projects / by Marcus Goncalves.—1st ed.
       p. cm.
   Includes bibliographical references.
   ISBN 0-07-144451-3 (hardcover : alk. paper)
  1. Project management—Automation.   2. Project management—Data processing.   I. Title.
   HD69. P75. G648 2004
   658.4′04—dc22

                                   2004015434

To my loving and merciful wife, Carla,
my son and friend, Samir,
my princess and daughter, Andrea,
and my little prince and young son, Joshua.
These are the real treasures of my life.

Eternal gratitude goes to my beloved brother in Christ, John
Howard, who passed away during the development of this book, for
his friendship, advice, love, and support in many ways.

To God be the glory.
Marcus Goncalves

CONTENTS

CHAPTER 8

Integrating Speed, Change, and Radical Innovation with ePM   273

CHAPTER 9

The ePM Office   311

CHAPTER 10

Concurrent Projects and Change Management   345

FOREWORD

I am a skeptic. Years of hard work have led me to theorize that there are seldom quick fixes or easy solutions to life's problems. And years as a project manager, working in the highly concentrated test lab of life—projects—have done nothing but confirm that theory. I have discovered that problems come in all shapes and sizes and unfortunately solutions are not "one size fits all."

To combat this phenomenon, I make a habit to absorb as much information about lessons learned, new tools, emerging problems, new solutions, and trends from my projects, peers, mentors, experts, and not-so experts. All is fair in love, war, and yes—project management.

Over the past two decades, American businesses have experienced an expansion of worldwide proportions. Literally. Cross-town customers that were never before accessible by the corner grocer are now only a small percentage of a national eCommerce Grocery market. Geographically dispersed vendors, suppliers, laborers, and customers are becoming the norm within projects and are contributing to the latest outbreak of project problems; these virtual teams are challenged by the increased need for unique communication tools, techniques, processes, and procedures.

Adapting existing project management practices and creating new tools for use within virtual projects is quickly becoming a necessity. Businesses that choose to take an ePM approach to the management of these projects will find that they have an edge; their solid understanding of the virtual project management landscape will better position them to capitalize on the opportunities that, such as a 24-hour labor force at 1st-shift rates.

Businesses who fail to acknowledge and take steps to address virtual project management through training, adaptation, and creation of methods will sink beneath the weight of the more complex communication structure. Tools that were once adequate to control and handle project communication will fail as traditional project managers attempt to fill the larger opening with a larger window. What they will fail to see is that the landscape has changed so much that a door is now required.

At the heart of the problem is that communication as we know it, and have previously defined it, has not just grown in complexity, but has changed altogether. Communication management is not just about communication. It has expanded to include:

- Information, the raw data
- The knowledge extracted from that information
- The trust necessary to obtain that information
- The information network, whether automated or manual
- The infrastructure to support information sharing, capturing, and promotion of the generation of more/new knowledge

From my perspective, that is the true value of ePM: management of virtual projects—the redefining of project management communication brought about by globalization. This book provides a new perspective on the changing landscape of project management, communication, and virtual teams. Solutions are presented as possible approaches, lessons are captured in case studies, and various scenarios are presented for contemplation. A step-by-step guide or cookie-cutter approach to virtual project management would have evoked the skeptic in me; this thought-provoking book supplied the right amount of trend analysis, problem identification, and tool presentation for any project manager or business to establish a solid foundation for addressing this complex project management area.

Stephanie Pawlowicz
PMO Director
State of New Hampshire

ACKNOWLEDGMENTS

I have been incubating this book in my mind for quite some time, taking notes here and there and dreaming about it a lot. Much of the book is a result of my curiosity throughout my professional life as a knowledge and project manager. Thus, I have tried to convey what I've learned in my consulting practices over the last 14-plus years as well as my reading and research on the subject. I have also talked to a lot of people and learned from many people as well.

To thank every single one of them here would be impossible, so if I miss some of their names, please forgive me. I would like to start by thanking the Boston University Administrative Science and Computer Science departments, where I've lectured for several years, but mainly I'd like to thank professor Kip Becker, Ph.D., chairman of the Administrative Science Department, for all his support; he has been a source of excellent information and a fine resource. I also would like to thank Professor Vijay Kanabar, Ph.D. and PMP, for his extensive knowledge of project management and full support in this project.

My expression of gratitude goes to Semih Arslanoglu, CEO of TeleMedia Group and lecturer at Boston University, for his international business management advice and support; Carla Carter, for her change management expertise and contribution to Chapter 10; John J Cirignano, PMP and president of the Microsoft Project User Group (MPUG); Star Dargin, president of Star Dargin Consulting; Pamela Campbell, vice president of product development at BEA; Doug Sinclair, senior partner at Atlantic Information Systems, Inc.; Yogesh Malhotra, Ph.D., founding chairman and chief knowledge architect of BRINT Institute (www.brint.com); and Dorothy Leonard from Harvard Business School, author of *Wellspring of Knowledge*, for her insightful feedback and permission to use some of her references.

I would also like to express my appreciation to the many corporate leaders who shared with me their views of and experiences with management in the knowledge economy. My special thanks go to the following leaders: Steve Fisch of Iona; Kerri Apple of Crossmark; Gregory Baletsa of Azonix Corporation; Andy Chatha of ARC Advisory Group; Vijay Kanabar, Ph.D., of Boston University; Dan Bathon of WindSpeed Ventures; Mark Lukoviski of Microsoft; Carla Dimond of Sun Microsystems; Donald Eastlake III from Motorola; Jeremy Epstein from WebMethods; Luis Ferro from SAP Brazil; Jack Genest from YankeeTek Ventures; David Webber from XML Global; David Mellor from Oracle; Tarek Makansi from IBM; Hans Holmstrom from ABB; Arthur Butt from AOL; Steve Carpenter from BAAN; Susan Osterfelt from Bank of America; Jeffrey A. Studwell from BASF; Bill Kirkey from Dupont; Mark Mueller from DynCorp; and many others.

I would like to thank Lisa O'Connor at McGraw-Hill for her patience with me during trying times as well as her confidence in entrusting this topic to me. Many thanks also go to my

spiritual leaders at the Boston Church of Christ, Mike Van
Auken and Ken Ostrowski, for their continuous spiritual support and friendship. Last but not least, my deepest gratitude to
my wife, Carla, and kids, Samir, Andrea, and Joshua, for their
unconditional support during the many hours it took to write
this book.

To God be the Glory!

PREFACE

During the last 10 years, the demands and scope of project management have continued to broaden on a global scale. Whether it's a global construction project, a worldwide research and development initiative, or a new overseas strategic alliance, the complex dynamics involved in today's global projects require project managers to have a certain skill set and a global knowledge base unlike what was required for their previous work on local projects.

Project managers increasingly are finding themselves having to work across multiple cultures under the extreme pressure of deadlines and budget constraints. Although this business model is exciting, it is unfamiliar to many technically talented project management professionals from all areas, including but not limited to information systems and technology, engineering, financing, and marketing experts.

These managers often discover that they are ill equipped to deal with the challenges presented by working with colleagues and clients from different cultures and managing projects from a distance. Thus, a critical need has arisen in project organizations to ensure that these key individuals acquire the core cross-cultural management competencies to develop into global and virtual project managers who will succeed with a multinational virtual project team and clientele, as they have already done in their local environments.

At MGCG we recognize that today's global economy brings with it the need for a new breed of project manager capable of managing complex projects from a distance while being aware of the many facets a project can adopt based on the mix of disparate communication and collaboration technologies, heterogeneous virtual project management environments, languages, culture, religion, and politics.

This book aims to help project managers understand the challenges of virtual project management (ePM) and supply vital information to help them become better virtual project managers (ePM managers) by providing

- Awareness and recognition of cultural differences
- Knowledge of how to manage projects across borders (i.e., across time zones, functional lines, distances, and national boundaries)
- A sound understanding of the available collaboration and telecommunication/Internet technologies to aid in ePM, as well as the technologies ePM managers and their virtual teams and remote project management offices (ePMOs) must have

How This Book Is Organized

This book is divided into three parts. Part I is a business case and conceptual overview of project management today and its fundamental disciplines. Part II has a practical focus on ePM, the differences between virtual and conventional project management, the must haves, and the challenges and additional resources, such as a change and knowledge management approach to ePM. Part III provides a full focus on the management and execution of virtual projects as well as a comprehensive glossary. More specifically:

Chapter 1, "A Business Case for ePM," provides an overview of the world's sociocultural and economic landscape in the last 10 years, more specifically in the last 5 years in the United States, and characterizes a virtual project management approach as a necessary evolution from the conventional methods.

Chapter 2, "Introduction to ePM," depicts the evolution of ePM from the conventional approach, emphasizes its applicability (and when it's not applicable), discusses the importance of the CMMI model, and outlines an ePM methodology.

Chapter 3, "ePM versus Conventional Project Management," deepens the discussion of conventional versus virtual project management in all the main aspects, including project focus, the *formal* inclusion of change management, the project life cycle, and the technology factor.

In Part II, "The Project Management Foundation," an in-depth discussion of ePM practices and scenarios aided by insightful case studies at the ends of chapters is presented.

Chapter 4, "The E-Project Management Process," describes the ePM staff, a new breed of professionals, as well as the structure of virtual project teams, the challenges, and how the conventional approach and techniques such as PERT, CPM, and measurable probes are important for ePM's success.

Chapter 5, "Techniques for Keeping an E-Project on Course," is a very practical chapter, providing step-by-step best practices for managing ePM and the needed collaboration technology.

Chapter 6, "Virtual Project Management Controls," provides virtual project managers with tools and techniques to measure a project's performance, quality, and earned value.

Chapter 7, "E-Tools for Quality Control," provides an overview of tools and procedures to control project quality as well as collaboration techniques.

Chapter 8, "Integrating Speed, Change, and Radical Innovation with ePM," identifies the need for the integration of speed, change management, and innovation as catalysts of virtual project management success. The chapter also depicts a customer-driven approach to ePM and the importance of such an approach, especially when one is managing virtual projects where clients as well as deliverables may be virtual.

PART III, "ePM Execution," focuses solely on the execution of virtual project management.

Chapter 9, "The ePM Office," provides comprehensive information on developing a virtual project management office (ePMO), discussing the structure, environment, and technology necessary.

Chapter 10, "Concurrent Projects and Change Management," explains what concurrent e-project management is, the rational for it, and how to implement it. It also discusses the need for change management in this process, the advantages it brings, and the many obstacles one should be aware of.

Who Will Benefit from This Book?

This book is geared toward project managers, project leaders, and project workers involved with virtual execution of their projects who would like to understand the virtual project management approach as well as the communications and collaboration technologies available to support it. This book assumes the reader is familiar with the traditional project management body of knowledge, approach, and techniques. Some of these concepts are discussed in the book, but mostly as part of an overview of virtual project management from a distance.

CHAPTER

A Business Case for ePM

Although project management is one of the oldest accomplishments of humankind, dating back to the extraordinary achievements of the builders of the Egyptian pyramids, the Babylonian hanging gardens, and the Great Wall of China, the great majority of companies do not employ a structured form of project management. Managing by walking around is still very common: Popping one's head into a team member's office and asking, "Hi, Joshua. How's it going?" can be an efficient and informal way to manage projects. If you do this across the team a few times a month, you will find either that your project is performing well or that you need a new team.

The problem is that you need more specific information about the project, something that informal management without resource scheduling tools, performance measurements, and baselines cannot deliver. In addition, today's projects often have several teams, making it nearly impossible to walk around and visit project leaders. Furthermore, these professionals may be scattered across the city, state, and continent. Thus, you are forced to review these project resources *virtually* rather than *physically*, a variation that might be called project management by *cybersurfing* as the walking around occurs in cyberspace, without having to leave the office to do it. Say hello to virtual project management (VPM), or electronic project management (ePM).

Although VPM and ePM are considered the same, the word *virtual* makes me nervous when it refers to project management. As a discipline, project management relies on very specific data to be successful, and having a virtual approach to it—if by that you mean abstract—can be dangerous. I see no problems with virtual reality and virtual friends, but project status reports must be concrete, that is, real, not virtual. Of course, I am exaggerating the importance of semantics here, but if we call it VPM or ePM, information about the project must be available in cyberspace so that all teams, all members of the project, can access and update it. This should be done electronically, thus the term *ePM*.

As Figure 1–1 suggests, electronic project management is the Information Age equivalent of management by walking around. It does not replace conventional project management

FIGURE 1–1

Electronic project management (ePM) is the Information Age equivalent of management by walking around.

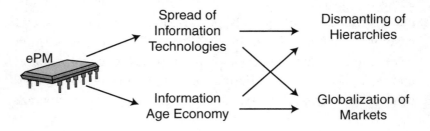

practices; rather, it has evolved from them. Globalization, compression of product life cycle, global competition, and many other factors have contributed to a transformation in project management to a more ubiquitous and pervasive approach. Recent Internet-based collaboration tools have also contributed to new possibilities for Web-based project management. Thus, understanding twenty-first-century project management challenges and how ePM can support and mitigate those challenges can be advantageous to any project manager.

THE GLOBALIZATION OF MARKETS AND PROJECTS

The rapidly growing integration of economies and societies around the world has been one of the most hotly debated topics in international economics over the last few years. To be competitive in the twenty-first-century, global and knowledge economy organizations must be able to provide cost-effective products and services while maintaining their level of quality, if not exceeding it. Hence, management of virtual projects becomes a very important factor for the success of such ventures, as it enables project managers to assess and control projects from a distance.

Globalization has enabled rapid growth and poverty reduction in countries such as China and India, among many other nations that were poor 20 years ago. But globalization has also generated significant international opposition because of concerns that it has increased inequality among nations and led to environmental degradation. The main opposition, however, has been to the sharp increase in project outsourcing, in particular in the United States. Organizations are moving many of their production activities overseas, taking advantage of lower-cost labor markets, favorable taxation laws, and the availability of highly skilled professionals.

I believe that in the long run this trend will be beneficial to the world economy as a whole; an example is the outsourcing of blue-collar jobs in the United States, which has generated white-collar jobs. But to be successful these projects need to be well managed regardless of geographic distances, cultural diversity, and time zone limitations. By having ePM expertise, project managers will be equipped to deal with the unique challenges of managing virtual teams and handling cultural and political issues that often are unfamiliar. In talking about the challenges ePM poses, not only technically but in terms of financing, project managers and executives should also recognize and be brave enough to admit that project development and execution is not just a question of economics; it's also a question of belief, morality, ethics; and spirituality. Wherever your project is or wherever you decide to build a virtual team—in Brazil, Argentina, or India, in slums or in villages throughout the world—you will realize the importance of spirit, culture, and the environment in which people live. I am not sure what the next collar color will be after the outsourcing of the white (how about gray?), but I am certain that it will take place only if projects are well managed and successful.

According to the Project Management Institute (PMI), the average project tends to experience a 168 percent cost overrun and only 22 percent of such projects are successful—finished on time and under budget. Who is to blame? Certainly not the sponsors and project managers, for their decisions to push for cost-cutting measures are one of the main reasons given for outsourcing. Certainly not the fact that we do not have enough qualified professionals with the right expertise, in particular for information science/information technology (IS/IT)-oriented projects, which is another reason given for outsourcing.

The reasons for such discouraging statistics are many, and while globalization and outsourcing are at the core of most of those reasons, the lack of good project record keeping and good measuring of project performance and results is at the core of the problem. According to Microsoft, more than 60 percent of project managers are still using Lotus/Excel spreadsheets to manage and keep track of their projects. Although these applications do a great job in tracking results, they are a far cry from a minimum set of features project managers need to manage their projects, as we will discuss later in this book.

These challenges have led to the emergence of quality movement across the world, with ISO 9000 certification a requirement for doing business. ISO 9000 is a family of international standards for quality management and assurance that covers design, procurement, quality assurance, and delivery processes for everything from banking to manufacturing. Of course, quality management and improvement invariably involve project management.

THE RAPID DEVELOPMENT OF THIRD WORLD AND CLOSED ECONOMIES

There has been an ever-increasing demand for managers of consumer goods and infrastructure development since the fall of the Soviet Union and the gradual opening of the Asian markets. As western companies rush to establish a presence in those markets and capitalize on it, many are taking advantage of project management techniques to develop supply chains and establish distribution channels and foreign operations in those countries.

This rapid development of third world markets and closed economies will continue to increase geometrically, pushing the adoption of ePM to much higher levels. Saying that India once had "one of the most closed economies of the world," U.S. Trade Representative Robert Zoellick has called on more competitive developing countries such as India, China, and Brazil to open their markets to sustain support in the United States and elsewhere. Zoellick insists that more competitive developing nations such as Brazil and Argentina should not expect to get the same kind of special and preferential treatment—such as longer implementation schedules—that the poorest countries get in agriculture and other sectors. Nonetheless, these economies are very attractive for outsourcing because of their highly skilled professionals, affordable labor, and manageable time zone restrictions.

For instance, at Marcus Goncalves Consulting Group (MGCG), 80 percent of systems development projects are executed in Argentina. Although that strategy is a form of outsourcing, we do not consider it as such, as we have a presence in Buenos Aires as well as in Brazil. From the start, our tactic was to incorporate the skill set from abroad into our internal corporate operations, allowing them to be an integral part of process and project management. By tapping into ePM techniques, we can pull those resources in, transparently, to the whole organization. To the staff and mainly to our clients, our information systems and technology (IS&T) group appears to be *in the next building* or *across town*, not thousands of miles away, except early in the morning or late in the afternoon during the winter months, when the time zone difference is three hours. But that is not a problem for us, because in the United States we have become accustomed to the three-hour difference between the West Coast and the East Coast. For the most part, working with our Brazilian and Argentinean counterparts is actually more productive than working across the country in the United States, as for the most part the time difference is of only one hour or a maximum of two hours for the greater part of the year.

The reason many outsourcing projects fail is precisely the fact that these outsourced tasks are decoupled from the overall process management of a project. I believe that much of this is due to poor use of measuring and controlling tools and practices that are available or known in managing virtual projects.

CORPORATE DOWNSIZING

In 2000, General Motors (GM) laid off about 20 percent of its Wilmington, Delaware, assembly plant owing to poor sales of some of its new automobile models. The employees in Delaware received 95 percent of their pay for the next six months before being put in a GM job pool to become eligible to work in other company facilities.

In February 1998 the Boeing Company cut down its number of employees from 238,400 to 191,500 after spending the major part of the two years preceding the layoffs in corporate restructuring. By the end of 1999 the company was still not done with its business process improvement (BPI) project and was planning to cut 5000 more jobs than intended during the year 2000.

This phenomenon affects not only large companies but small ones as well. ThirdAge Media laid off more than 30 employees in 2002 in an attempt to increase the focus of its website on areas of interest for baby boomers. To name only a few others, Petstore.com, Iexchange.com, Corel, and Coke have all gone through business process reengineering (BPR) and BPI, which resulted in corporate downsizing and pink slips.

A company cannot have constant growth without proper management. What this means is that at some point companies must take time out from their hectic schedules and start crossing out the names of employees they can do without. Despite the fact that you may be an excellent employee, there is no guarantee that you will make it past the downsizing/rightsizing in many companies. You may not lose your job, but you may become responsible for double the number of your original tasks. Nonetheless, the reorganization of a company's employee layout does not simply involve firing employees; it also presents opportunities for increased responsibility, a higher salary and advancement. Again, ePM can minimize this Darwinian approach by enabling professionals to be engaged in several projects at the same time, around the globe, minimizing overhead costs, increasing the level of effort (LOE) of professionals, and keeping them busy, which reduces the chances of their no longer being needed.

The last 15 years has seen a remarkable restructuring of organizational life and business processes. These BPR and BPI projects have generated a chain of corporate downsizing, or rightsizing if one is still employed, calling for a return to the core competencies necessary for survival in many organizations. The middle manager disappeared and began to be replaced by project management as a strategy to ensure that tasks would get done. Organizations became flatter and leaner, realizing that change was inevitable and therefore had to be managed.

It was also at that time that as a result of downsizing, companies began to outsource, promoting a major paradigm shift in the way projects were managed. More than ever before project management techniques and best practices became vital to successful project execution. The challenge—and we are dealing with it today more than ever before—was that companies were outsourcing a significant proportion of project work, but project managers had to manage not only their own staff but also on their counterparts in different organizations, often outside the company, the building, the state, and the country.

Effects of Corporate Downsizing in Project Management

The long-term effect of corporate downsizing has affected the way projects are managed, especially when downsizing entails mergers. In my last major project with Virtual Access Networks, we successfully completed phase 1 when our product was launched at Comdex Fall 2000 and was awarded the Best Enterprise Product there.

A reevaluation of a company's assets and expenses does not mean that the company is heading for disaster; in fact, it can signify the opposite. It usually indicates that the corporation has reached a level of maturity that requires serious decision making so that the board of directors and the shareholders will remain pleased. These cases are the ones that should encourage workers to keep their positions within the company because of its growth and savvy regarding the allocation of its funds.

Therefore, we thought our project was going to enter phase 2 as we became profitable and were getting ready to expand the business. Instead, the company was acquired, and as a result of the merger, the newly established strategy morphed the project into the buying company's current product. In other words, the project was killed, and the members of the team were dispersed in the name of cost-efficient operations.

The competitive global marketplace is assuring that downsizing is here to stay. As a result, companies have to run their businesses with efficiency and cost-effectiveness, and project management—virtual project management, as most projects are no longer local to organizations—is an important technique in this process. Companies are no longer downsizing because of *general economic conditions* but as a result of better staff utilization, outsourcing, plant closures, mergers, automation, and the use of new collaboration and communication technologies.

The adoption of ePM is a strong business justification to mitigate the effects of corporate downsizing. By their nature, virtual teams can be formed quickly and are agile. They can help organizations shorten their response time to changes in today's hypercompetitive markets. Organizations are also able to leverage expertise that is dispersed over geographic areas that previously were untapped. Furthermore, virtual teams can benefit employees as they lessen the disruption of an employee's life by requiring less travel time to meet with dispersed teams. Additionally, team members have the opportunity to broaden their experience by working across organizations and cultures.

As in the Virtual Access Networks example, professional individuals are also affected. It is a sad scenario when projects need to be shut down because of poor performance, in particular when excellent professionals are let go. Research shows that being let go is likely to mean the loss not only of upward career movement but also of economic stability and self-respect. As a management consultant, I have seen this situation too many times: Projects are killed, and the members of the teams feel they are being sacrificed not because their projects were in serious financial trouble but because the cost performance index (CPI) or the profits being made were not high enough.

Another consequence that many project management professionals have to address on a failed project is the low morale among the teams left after the disengagement or downsizing process. Companies that help the project team members get new jobs and provide outplacement services end up much better positioned than companies that simply wield the ax. This is the case because they have a better chance of retaining the loyalty of the surviving professionals. This is particularly true in virtual project management, as we'll discuss in later chapters. Trust is one of the most valuable yet brittle assets in any project, especially with ePM, in which you don't have the level of interaction characteristic of conventional project management.

Project managers should remember that they are artificial creatures chartered by the sponsors and the stakeholders. As such, those managers are subject to their values, and their approvals can be withdrawn at any time. Hence, efficiency and cost-effectiveness are becoming more paramount than ever before.

ePM Can Mitigate Project Downsizing

In our practice we have been advocating the use of virtual project management techniques as an alternative to project downsizing and change of scope to control costs. In particular, ePM can address problematic projects at several levels, including the following:

1. Decisions by project sponsors to downsize or dramatically reduce the scope of a project
2. Mitigation of morale problems affecting a project after the scope reduction or downsizing decision
3. Development of ePM procedures for reallocation of resources with a minimum impact to the current project organization breakdown structure (OBS) and work breakdown structure (WBS)
4. Long-term effects of the project's downsizing or change of scope efforts

The Determination by Project Sponsors to Downsize or Dramatically Reduce the Scope of the Project

Typically, project sponsors downsize or reduce the scope of projects to cut cost, improve efficiency, and maintain a CPI level acceptable to their stakeholders and shareholders. This phenomenon in both the United States and other countries is here to stay. Every day we hear and read about projects that are being abandoned or having their scope reduced for many reasons, all of which point to the financial aspects of a project. But there is a difference between reducing scope and terminating projects, and it is important to understand those differences as one attempts to mitigate those risks and perhaps rescue a project.

The reduction of a projects scope, if not done for a technical reason, usually involves a decision to reduce the amount of resources, or workforce, that is intended to improve project performance. At MGCG we view this approach as part of a larger plan in which sponsors analyze their core business and develop it to its fullest extent. In other words, the organization often goes *back to the basics,* making the original scope of projects suddenly no longer desirable. When reduction of project scope needs to occur, we recommend that sponsors and project managers look at whether such a reduction is proactive, intended to obtain efficiency and market share, or reactive, resulting from deep financial trouble within the project. In my view, reduction of project scope, when it is not done for technical reasons, occurs because of the following:

1. An intentional decision by project managers and/or sponsors
2. A reduction of project resources (personnel), often disproportionately in the management ranks

3. Improvement in efficiency and/or effectiveness

4. Changes in work processes often caused by dangerous delays in the schedule or budget overruns

Again, reduction of project scope usually equates to lowering operating expenses, mostly direct costs, after crashing has proved not to be effective. After all, in recent years emphasis on time to market has taken on new importance because of intense global competition and rapid technological advances. The market imposes a project duration date. Such analysis becomes even more serious during recessionary periods, such as the one experienced since 2000 in the United States and throughout the world, when cash flows are tight.

Reductions in project time or scope also occur when unforeseen delays caused by adverse weather, design flaws, and equipment breakdown result in substantial delays midway through a project. The adoption of ePM in many of these cases can be an excellent alternative method to reduce cost, improve efficiency, and realign project goals.

How ePM Can Mitigate Morale Problems After Scope Reduction or Downsizing

Countless projects have seen the negative effects of downsizing or reduction in scope. Morale suffers, which equates to lower productivity and cost-efficiency for the project. Project managers tend to complain about the morale-sapping character of most downsizing efforts and reductions of scope and about how low morale creates anxiety and paralysis in their project teams, to the detriment of productivity. When a professional loses his or her job, confusion and anxiety set in. Many professionals are thrown into unexpected transitions with extended middle periods characterized by confusion and a lack of ability to move forward. This can have long-term consequences for the project at hand.

In my 14 years of experience managing projects both in United States and abroad, I have found that a 10 percent reduction in project personnel results in only a 1.5 percent reduction in costs. In addition, I have found that project workers' trust and empowerment are shattered after downsizing or significant reduction of scope for nontechnical reasons. This caused workers who stayed after the restructuring to show less initiative in getting the work done. Their feeling was that they would terminated next, and so their attitude was "Why try to do the job since I am going to be the next one laid off?"

Again, ePM practices can help in this process by providing a more creative way to deploy human resources, such as through telecommuting, where a significant amount of money can be saved through reduction in physical space, more flexible hours of work, more efficient multitasking and splitting activities, and so forth. Other ways include the use of SWAT (highly specialized) teams with very focused and specialized know-how, without the overhead cost of engaging them full-time or relocating them to a project's site.

Development of ePM Procedures for Reallocation of Resources with a Minimum Impact on the OBS and WBS

When a project manager decides to downsize or reduce scope, a detailed and well-planned program has to be implemented. Unfortunately, many project managers restructure their projects without looking at the negative repercussions, whether the order came from sponsors or not. Some project managers are able to increase profitability and/or productivity on their projects, but in many restructured projects the results have been disappointing. There are at least six reasons why project downsizing or reduction of scope does not work in many projects:

1. Project managers fail to set up retraining policies and do not foresee the human resource problems that develop when downsizing/scope reduction takes effect. ePM can be used to reach out to project teams and mitigate those adverse results.

2. As project managers downsize/reduce scope of projects, they often overuse consultants and third-party providers instead of retraining the retained staff. They end up relying too much on the consultants and third-party providers to do the work. E-learning, Web conferences, instant messaging, and groupware tools can mitigate many of the adverse effects of the restructuring process.

3. As the project is downsized or has its scope changed, the added work is thrown to line or project leaders with limited time to do the job and limited expertise in that field.

4. As projects become flatter, the communications that once worked well are gone. No communication between the different levels within the organization takes place.

5. As was mentioned earlier, often productivity and quality suffer because there is no plan for how the work is to be done with a reduced staff.

6. Project restructuring eliminates job security, the sense of belonging. When this happens, project workers show no loyalty to the project and will move to firms that pay them more. They become "guns for hire."

To have a successful program for downsizing/scope reduction efforts, various points have to be addressed. The development of a well-detailed plan to train each retained worker is a major one. When this is done, rehire "creep" will not take place. In other words, hiring consultants or rehiring new project workers to do the work once done by the laid-off staff will not be mandatory. Another part of making a restructuring program a success is to keep the severance-related costs low. To do this, a project manager should use nonvoluntary programs that identify who will be affected rather than using a voluntary program. When voluntary programs are implemented, they are often overused by people who have high severance packages.

Of course, keeping up communication with each member of the team is very important for success in restructuring efforts. As depicted in Figure 1–2, ePM can help by establishing a virtual team management system, which will be discussed in more detail in later chapters. The full integration of virtual team leaders and members with a well-defined technology structure process facilitation system and the project problem and tasks at hand can be a catalyst for generating ideas, collaborative decisions, and actions that otherwise would be impossible to achieve.

Another important area where ePM can help mitigate problems in restructuring projects is the hidden costs, such as the increase in the costs of quality caused by rework and scrap and overtime payments to the project workers retained because of an increased workload, which can be lowered by effective (read real-time) scheduling and the handling of project workers' concerns with openness and in a timely fashion. A way to make a project restructuring effort effective is to track its cost efficiently. Without controls set up within the project information systems to track the payroll, overtime, and cost overruns

FIGURE 1–2

Virtual teams management system.

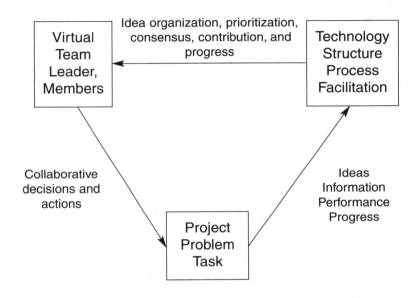

(Based on Kurstedt's Management System Model)

caused by the restructuring efforts, the effort would be futile. The adoption of Web-enabled tools such as Microsoft Project EPM (Enterprise Project Management) can help in this process, as all project parties, from sponsors and stakeholders to project managers, leaders, and workers, can receive up-to-date information on the status of any task.

Mitigating Long-Term Effects of Downsizing/ Change of Scope with ePM

Whether project downsizing/change of scope is implemented successfully over a long period depends on how the implementation takes place. Again, ePM can aid in this process. Project managers should never see project restructuring as a short-term fix. Instead, they must integrate the decision to restructure into a well-crafted, credible vision that makes it clear how the restructuring will create a competitive advantage. This will set the tone of the restructuring effort as well coordinated and planned; otherwise, its success in the long term is questionable. Of course, when project teams are colocated, often the alternative is to eliminate (downsize) the resources that become unnecessary for project execution. By having ePM expertise, ePM managers have new alternatives to downsizing. They can reassign some of the idle resources to distant projects as well as enable those professionals to virtually multitask in one or more projects. The simple elimination of idle resources tends to emphasize the nature of work for hire that is not desired in a well-integrated project team. In these cases, what develops is distrust of management, and the group that remains in the project will question the validity of the restructuring effort.

Getting a formal group together to implement the project's restructuring efforts is key, and ePM can help here by providing tools and techniques for a smoother transition. By relying on the techniques and collaboration tools discussed throughput this book, project managers can better plan and implement the restructuring of a project to represent all members' interests. It is important that project workers see that management is looking carefully at everyone's needs and concerns, not only the project's objectives.

For instance, in the 1980s Xerox lost market share. The problems within the organization's projects were, however, minimized when the executives effectively communicated the dire situation of the company. Those executives received from the employees greater understanding and a willingness to follow management's lead in saving the company. Without loyalty from each employee, the implementation and success of project restructuring effort become questionable. The timeliness with which such communication occurs is also critical, and again, ePM can expedite such communications and promote consensus by allowing a greater expression of opinions from all levels via electronic means such as e-mail, instant messaging (IM), and bulletin boards, including anonymous ones for those who fear retaliation for delivering bad news or unpopular opinions.

Failure to attend to this transition with caution and open communication can have a tremendous impact. As a project leader for a bridge construction project in Brazil in the early 1980s, I witnessed my project manager going through a very hard and uncertain time for failing to observe the points outlined above (unfortunately, ePM was not an option back then):

> Shortly after the project reorganization, we started to lose employees because someone decided we didn't need as many people. No one seems to know how they figured out how many employees we needed, and we simply did not have enough people to do the job that was demanded of us. This was not a good place to work anymore. When the right job comes along, and it will, I'll leave my current position.

A client of mine in the financial industry shared his frustration during our attempt to mitigate the negative results of poor communication in a project restructuring that involved three different sites spread across United States, where most of the background information was withheld from project leaders as a way of minimizing the impact of those changes. Memorandums communicating the changes in the project were sent by FedEx but arrived after the fact, did not provide background information for the decisions that were made, and did not provide a way to communicate with the channels responsible for those decisions, which included not only the project manager but also sponsors and third-party consulting firms:

> I have experienced a series of three mergers and acquisitions during the last six years, which has resulted in declining levels of my personal responsibility and authority in these projects. Changes in corporate culture disrupt many projects and career paths, generating concern about job security, and often result in a reduced inner sense of loyalty to the company.

In summary, it is apparent then "getting smaller" is not enough when it comes to project management. Downsizing or reducing scope is the equivalent of project anorexia, as it can make a project thinner, not necessarily healthier. Unfortunately, there are times when such restructuring is necessary, especially in cases of technical constraints or market shifts. Nonetheless, project managers should always proceed with caution when contemplating restructuring and look at the relationship of restructuring and productivity as well as project management effectiveness after the fact. Just because the project is now leaner and the critical path has been crashed, that does not necessarily mean it is more efficient and cost-effective. Research also shows that over the long term the financial health of many projects diminishes with the downsizing/crashing efforts, especially for long-term projects and those not experiencing technical constraints. Some projects increase profitability and productivity, but for many, downsizing/reduction of scope has been disappointing.

TELECOMMUTING: A STEP IN THE "VIRTUAL" DIRECTION

In 1989 the mayor and the city council of Los Angeles approved a telecommuting pilot project to be conducted between 1990 and 1993. The analysis suggested that as many as 15,000 city employees could telecommute. As a result, the mayor and the city council approved a pilot project that involved working, at least part-time, either from home or from a satellite telework center closer to home than the primary office.

Telecommuting (Figure 1–3) is not new, yet many companies are still resisting the idea, particularly project-oriented ones, because conventional project management approaches do not provide effective tools for managing and monitoring the performance of the tasks being executed. The functions assessed as appropriate for telecommuting (ePM is ideal for such an environment), include the following:

- Monitoring tasks
  - Fact checking
  - Project management
  - Analyzing
  - Auditing
  - Reading/studying (e-learning)
  - Record keeping
- Development tasks
  - Thinking
  - Research
  - Planning
  - Designing
  - Computer programming
  - Data entry
- Communications tasks
  - Correspondence
  - Telephone answering
  - Typing
  - Writing

FIGURE 1–3

Telecommuters tend to be more productive and effective when working at home and avoiding the hassles of commuting to work.

Like ePM, telecommuting is not for everyone. Both are generally suitable for project workers who are self-motivated, well organized, and conscientious about work time; require minimal supervision; prefer a home environment; have strong time management skills; exhibit a positive attitude toward telecommuting; and have a trusting relationship with their supervisors.

In addition, telecommuting, like ePM, can be very cost-effective. In the example of the project in Los Angeles, according to project managers, the following results occurred:

- *Effectiveness.* The effectiveness of the telecommuters increased by an average of 12.5 percent relative to nontelecommuting coworkers. The annual economic impact was about $6100 per telecommuter.

- *Retention of personnel.* Eighteen percent of telecommuters said the ability to telecommute was a moderate to decisive influence in their decision to stay with the city rather than take jobs elsewhere. The estimated benefit in 1992 was $200,000.

- *Low (or no)-cost trip reduction strategy.* By having its employees telecommute, the city could achieve air quality trip reduction mandates without other costly incentives. The potential annual savings was $898,000.

After the success of the pilot project, the mayor and the city council approved a permanent telecommuting program in 1994. Other full-scale telecommuting programs are being implemented in the county of Los Angeles, the Metropolitan Water District, the city of San Diego, the city and county of Denver, the state of Oregon, and the state of Arizona.

The reason for using these outdated numbers is to convey the fact that telecommuting and ePM are not new. Using more up-to-date data from IDC, according to its more conservative information about telecommuters working at home at least three days per month, there is today a population of 8.7 million in United States alone. To be effective, these telecommuters are traveling back and forth from office to home with laptops and have Internet access, preferably broadband instead of dial-up; fax machines; and a growing range of corporate-based software applications accessible from home. Despite the fact most of these telecommuters have family members, dogs, and even the plumber to distract them at home, their productivity is still higher than it was at the office, and they don't have to commute every day, saving time that is being used to "catch up with e-mail." This fact alone should provide a convincing argument for the use of ePM.

The issues that are preventing a more aggressive growth of telecommuting are in many ways the same as those for ePM: human behavior and change management. Despite the fact that telecommuting can produce real savings, employees are reluctant to cut the cord with their organizations. Many feel that way because of insecurity, fear that their supervisors and project managers will realize they are not needed, and the "vacuum" feeling of disconnect many of them experience.

Not Convinced Yet about the Benefits of Telecommuting?
In 2003 Sun Microsystems reported a $71 million reduction in or avoidance of office space expense as a result of telecommuting.

As a project manager in these uncertain economic times, imagine saving $4500 per project worker per year. How about adding to that sum an average of $71 millions off your real estate bill, as Sun Microsystems reported? How about a 4 to 12 percent boost in employee productivity? These numbers may be optimistic, but they are not far off the mark. One of the major issues is how to equip a remote worker; another is deciding whether the investment truly pays off. But four companies that employ large numbers of telecommuters—Cigna, Hewlett-

Packard, AT&T, and Sun Microsystems—report that the strategy is beneficial for cost and productivity.

Telecommuting and Virtual Project Management at MGCG

At MGCG, at any given time we may have 30 to 50 professionals engaged in projects, both internal and external, in the United States and abroad, mainly in South America and Germany. From that pool, only about three people are based in our headquarters. All the others are somewhere else: in their cars, their remote offices, their homes, their client sites, at the airport, and, every now and then in their bathrooms.

As Figure 1–4 illustrates, currently I am responsible for a project in Brazil (customer headquarters), another one in Argentina, another in Germany, and three others in the United States (customer field operations). But I am located at our headquarters, in Hopkinton, MA, not where my IS/IT developers are (Argentina) or one of our newest major client (Brazil) and our newest project (Germany) are. With the aid of an Intel Centrino wireless networking laptop computer, a global system for mobile communication/General Packet Radio Service (GSM/GRPS)-enabled cell phone that is operable worldwide with a full keyboard for quick IM, and a Palm wireless-capable PDA (personal digital assistant), I maintain an active personal area network (PAN) that is in sync at all times, giving me access to my MS Project files, contacts, database, and accounting system, as well as printers and other devices (both Bluetooth and wireless-enabled) for effective communication and exchange of timely and vital data.

These technologies, applications, and collaboration tools enable me to manage a workforce that lives and works on

FIGURE 1-4

At MGCG, ePM begins at our headquarters in Hopkinton, MA, and
spreads across three continents.

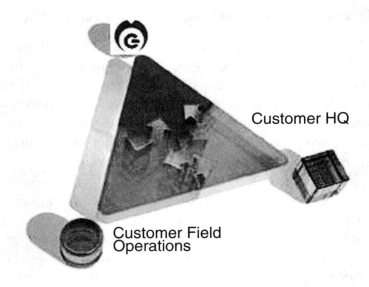

Customer HQ

Customer Field
Operations

different continents. I receive and respond to about 200 e-mails
a day. The technology helps, in particular hub-and-spoke ones
such as the one used at MGCG (Figure 1–5), but that is not
enough to lead my team. I have to travel frequently to spend
real time with those people. Telecommuting is great, but face-
to-face time with a team is essential to provide appropriate
coaching and offer real support to the field. We will discuss
these ePM techniques in later chapters.

GLOBAL COMPETITION

Today's global economy is demanding not only feature-rich
products and services but also cost-effective ones. This trend
has led to the emergence of the quality movements around the
world with ISO 9000, a family of international standards for

FIGURE 1-5

Hub-and-spoke technologies are key for the support of ePM systems.

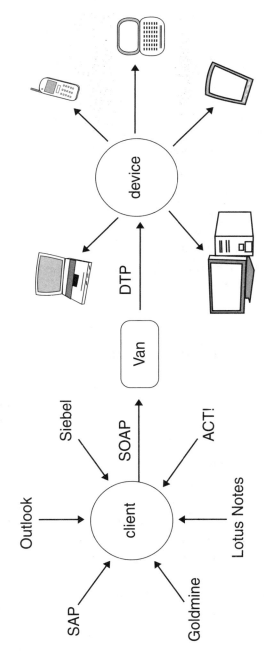

HUB and Spoke

ePM Information Exchange System

quality management and assurance; certification is a requirement for doing business. The standards cover design, procurement, quality assurance, and delivery processes for everything
from banking to manufacturing. For that reason, bodies of
knowledge (BoKs), as discussed next, have become a fundamental part of project management.

But what are they, why are they important, what are the
issues in creating a valid (universal) BoK, and what is the Association for Project Management (APM) doing in this area?
Later in this chapter, Peter W. G. Morris, vice president of
APM and vice chairman of the International Project Management Association (IPMA), explains. Figure 1–6 shows the
APM's website, which I recommend that you visit (http://
www.apm.org.uk).

The Project Management Bodies of Knowledge[1]

Project management bodies of knowledge (PMBOKs) have
been around for 10 to 15 years. They have come to represent
one of the most important features of project management.
They are used by many organizations as the basic template on
which project management competency is defined and
assessed.

But not many project management professionals, except
maybe those who are project management professional PMP-
certified, know what a BoK is, why it is important, how a BoK
differs from a body of competence (BoC), how many BoKs
there are, what the issues are in creating a valid (universal)
BoK, and what APM is doing in this area. In addition, I believe
it is important to understand the role of BoKs in project management so that we can rely on it for ePM. PMI is researching
the subject extensively and routinely adding the topic of managing virtual projects to its best practices.

FIGURE 1–6

The Association for Project Management website is an excellent source of information on BoKs and project management in general.

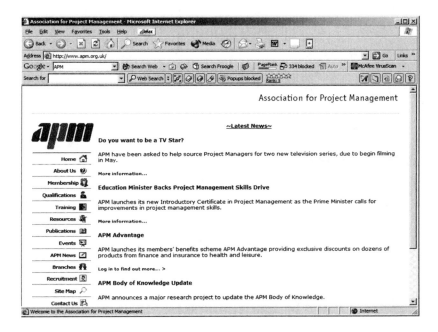

What Is a BoK?

All project management society BoKs except PMI's, (Figure 1–7), are misnamed: They are not bodies of knowledge as such but guides to the topics a project management professional ought to be knowledgeable about to some degree. APM's BoK simply describes the nearly 40 elements it believes a project management professional should be knowledgeable about. To be precise, it describes three different levels of knowledge for each of these elements. The APM BoK was developed for candidates for the Certificate Project Manager (CPM) qualification to assess their level of knowledge in preparing for the

FIGURE 1–7

PMI's website is a good place to research all topics in project management, with extensive information on the PMBOK.

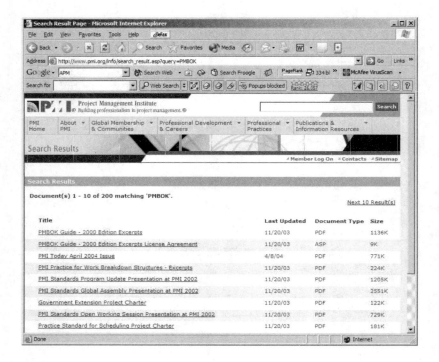

CPM qualification. It is now used by APM as a general norma-tive guide in accrediting courses, in its continuing professional development (CPD) program, and as the basis of its Associa-tion for Project Management professional (APMP) qualifica-tion, the equivalent of PMI's project management professional certification.

A BoK, then, is not an all-encompassing textbook in which all project management knowledge is defined. It is doubtful that such a thing could be written. For this reason PMI has termed its version, the *Guide to the Project Management Body of Knowledge*.

Why Is a BoK Important for ePM?

Almost everyone working in project management is interested in knowing what he or she needs to know to be considered a competent project management professional. These managers look to the professional societies to tell them, and typically they value a certificate or qualification that says they have attained a required level of knowledge. Many organizations use a BoK as the project management component of their more general company-specific definitions of competencies. The same is true for ePM, especially when you don't know the members of your virtual team personally. Knowing that they have been certified under the same standards you abide by is very important.

In our project management practice in Brazil, 80 percent of our project staff is PMP-certified. Despite language and cultural differences, it is comforting to know they all are certified by PMI under the same BoK (PMBOK); as with ePM, we all speak the same language.

How Is a BoK Different from a Body of Competencies?

Competencies are the things one needs to perform a function competently. The key point about competencies is that they are based on measures of the ability to do a task. They relate primarily to how one performs. They say, for example, that to perform effectively as a project management professional one needs to have knowledge, skill, and experience in certain technical and commercial areas; have certain personal qualities and

organizational skills; and have certain knowledge about the
organization—and be experienced, knowledgeable, and skilled
in project management.

The difficulty comes in defining what the areas of project
management knowledge should be. Almost always the actual
definition of competencies is not just company-specific but
role-specific. Companies find professional BoKs (APM's,
PMI's, etc.) useful because they provide an authoritative international template that helps them answer this question.

The guides to knowledge do not represent competencies.
Competence is demonstrable only by being able to prove one's
ability to perform in a given role. The nearest the BoKs come
to this is when candidates demonstrate that their level of
knowledge, experience, and skill qualifies them to be recognized as having attained either a company-specific standard or
a national or international standard such as a PMP, an APMP, a
German Fachman, or a CPM.

How Many BoKs Are There?

Knowing how many BoKs there are may not be relevant to
local execution of projects where all professionals are colocated. However, awareness that there is more than one BoK,
that PMI's BoK is not the only one, will also make you aware
of the fact that some international project management professionals have different approaches or techniques in executing a
project, aside from technical terms that may have different definitions. For instance, PMI's PMBoK defines the amount of
time a task can be delayed without delaying the project completion date as a *float*. Other BoKs may define this as *slack*.
When interacting with project managers who do not have
PMBoK's knowledge, you may find that some of them do not
know what you mean by *float* even though they understand the

concept of *slack*, and vice versa. The same goes for project initiation versus project definition, and so on.

The oldest and, in the number of people and countries affected by it, the most influential BoK is PMI's, followed by APM's. There are no other significantly different BoKs, though the French project management institute uses a scaled-down version of APM's and the German and Swiss use their own modified versions of the APM BoK. The Dutch basically use APM's BoK. The Australian Institute for Project Management uses PMI's. Many national chapters of PMI of course use PMI's. IPMA is attempting to harmonize the BoKs of its member associations.

What Are the Issues in Creating a Valid (Global) BoK?

The creation of a global BoK is vital for ePM management, as it would standardize the taxonomy and practices of project management across the globe. There are, however, a number of challenges in creating such a global standard: What should the elements be? What is a proper definition of each of these elements? How should the elements be structured? PMI has 47 elements divided into three levels of a product breakdown structure. APM has 44 at two levels. The APM's set is much broader than the PMI's. Fifteen of APM's elements represent all 44 of PMI's.

There are three core issues in defining the elements. The first two are agreeing on whether the project management professional's remit begins before the project definition is agreed on and how far into operations it should go. The third is deciding how much the PMBoK should reflect the broad range of issues, skills, and knowledge—the management of technology and design, for example—that a project management professional will encounter in managing a project.

Deciding to what extent these BoKs are industry-specific is another issue with a global perspective. Deciding what are the elements in any professional guide to a project management (PM) body of knowledge is critically important. We are still a fair way from having accomplished this. Deciding on authoritative definitions is equally hard.

Language is another issue as it varies not just between nations but even within those which speak English. It can vary between industries. Some industries have different conceptions, for example, of what words such as *systems engineering, configuration management, procurement, mobilization,* and *logistics* mean. One of the challenges for a BoK writer therefore is to strike a balance between creating a genuinely useful general language of project management and putting people off by using unfamiliar words.

For some people the first discussion regarding a BoK involves its structure. Indeed, there have been many debates about the relative merits of PMI's process-based BoK and APM's four functional columns. Actually, although structure is very important, if only from a communications viewpoint, logically it is not central. Once the elements and their definitions are agreed on, they can be structured and restructured as required. This is not to say that discussion of structure is not important, but it can be disconnected from discussions about content.

What Is APM Doing in This Area?

In the last few years APM, together with a number of companies, has commissioned research by the British University of Manchester Institute of Science and Technology (UMIST) Centre for Research in the Management of Projects to investigate the BoK elements that the industry and practitioners consider appropriate. The list of elements and their definitions was reviewed critically. It was seen that inadequate recognition had been given in the previous BoK to a number of elements, for example, the "set up and definition" phase of the project: design and development, procurement, testing, and organization and methods (O&M).

As a result, new definitions were developed, which were checked through an extensive interviewing program. Additional research investigated the extent to which those BoK elements were used in practice rather than merely accepted in theory. The results of this research were published in early 1999.

In addition, surveys have been carried out of the papers published in the *International Journal of Project Management* going back 15 years and in the *Project Management Journal* to map the match between articles and BoK elements in an attempt to identify gaps and look for trends. Also, polls have been conducted of practitioners and academics to determine preferred reading lists for individual elements. Therefore, it is extremely difficult to find authoritative guides to many of the elements and indeed to the BoK as a whole.

The Future

The outlook for good work in this area is encouraging. PMI has been working on updating its Guide to the PMBoK. In doing so, it is paying explicit attention to other work, such as that at UMIST and the IPMA and in Australia and Holland, on the BoK.

There is increasing recognition that this kind of normative research needs to be extended to give better guidance on what best practice is, especially in the global perspective, or, rather, what best appropriate practice is. Many companies want to pick up the best of PMBoK practice and, where appropriate, emulate it. Work on this best appropriate practice is beginning.

Before long we might, have some empirically validated guides to what constitutes good, and best, practice in the management of projects, what the best writing and teaching has to say, and where help can be found. All this will be Internet-based and available at the touch of a button. At the heart of it will be the BoK.

We are, I believe, about to enter the second generation of project management bodies of knowledge: a maturing of project management.

IMPROVING TIME MANAGEMENT WITH ePM

Time management skills are essential for successful project managers and workers. These are the practical techniques that have helped the leading people in business, sports, and public service reach the pinnacle of their careers.

The same is true in ePM. Professionals who use time management techniques and technology and take advantage of the world's time zones routinely are the highest achievers in all types of project execution. Time management is essential for a successful ePM strategy, and throughout this book there are several examples that explain why. If you use these skills well, you will be able to function effectively, even under intense pressure. At the heart of time management is an important shift in focus: Concentrate on results, not on being busy. Many project managers and workers spend their days in a frenzy of activity but achieve little because they are not concentrating on the right things.

The 80:20 Rule

This observation is neatly summed up in the Pareto principle (Figure 1–8), or the 80:20 rule. This principle argues that typically 80 percent of unfocused effort generates only 20 percent of results. The remaining 80 percent of results is achieved with only 20 percent of the effort. Although the ratio is not always

FIGURE 1–8

The Pareto principle (the 80:20 rule) was named by the statistician J. M. Juran in the late 1940s after Vilfredo Pareto, an Italian economist.

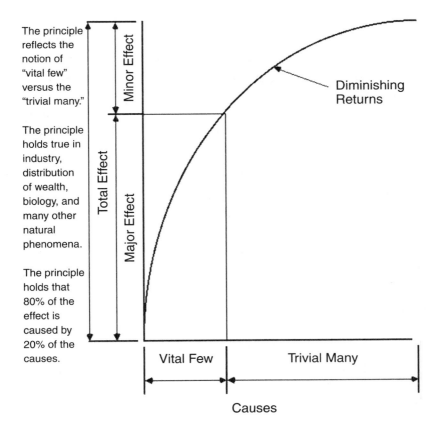

80:20, this broad pattern of a small proportion of activity generating nonscalar returns occurs so frequently that it is the norm in many areas.

The Essence of ePM: How Much Your Time Is Worth

For ePM to be successful, one should always focus on results. The first part of a focus on results should be to work out how much your time and that of your peers and team costs. This helps you see if you and your project team are spending time profitably.

As you work for an organization, calculate how much it costs you each year for that project. Include your salary, payroll taxes, the cost of the office space you occupy, the equipment and facilities you use, expenses, administrative support, and so on. If you are a self-employed project manager, work out the annual running costs of your business.

To this figure add a "guesstimate" of the amount of profit you generate by your activity. If you work normal hours, you will have approximately 200 productive days each year. If you work $7\frac{1}{2}$ hours each day, this equates to 1500 hours in a year. From these figures, calculate an hourly rate. This should give a reasonable estimate of how much your time is worth; it may be a surprisingly large amount.

Next time you are contemplating whether to take on a task, think about this value. Are you wasting your or your organization's resources on a low-yield task? Are there tasks that can be automated? Calculating how much your time is worth helps you work out whether it is worthwhile doing particular jobs. If you have to spend much of your time doing low-yield jobs, you can make a good case for employing an assistant or investing in technology to automate some of those tasks.

To Clone or Not to Clone: Technology
May Help Organize Tasks

In the movie *Multiplicity*, Doug Kinney (Michael Keaton) is an overworked professional who allows himself to be cloned so that he can accomplish collectively what he can't do individually. It doesn't work out, but with ePM you might be able to pull it off. Many tasks can be automated, and several people can work in parallel as long as, much like a conductor, you keep the orchestra in sync.

If it is not planned well, ePM can backfire and won't work, as in the movie cited above. Technology analysts predict something similar for the typical office worker, only in this case multiplicity pertains not to people but to the gizmos we all rely on. By 2007, says Meta Group Inc. analyst Steve Kleynhans, a knowledge worker will depend on at least four different devices: a home personal computer, a corporate computer, a mobile information device, and a "smart digital entertainment system."

As in my example at MGCG, (Figure 1–9), the idea of equipping project workers with multiple gadgets may sound expensive, but Kleynhans claims that if companies study the options coming into the market, they will be able to reduce overall IT expenses and make workers more productive. Today Microsoft, through its .Net Platform, enables a multitude of devices and platforms to be integrated over the Web, facilitating the process of information exchange.

THE INCREASE OF OUTSOURCING IN THE VIRTUAL WORLD

Take the example of Cessna Aircraft Co, which announced in fall 2003 that it was in the beginning stages of determining whether to increase the amount of manufacturing work it has done outside its Wichita plant. The company has been

FIGURE 1-9

Microsoft, through its .Net Platform, enables a multitude of devices and platforms to be integrated over the Web, facilitating the process of information exchange.

outsourcing parts-manufacturing work for some time, and this latest examination is part on an ongoing evaluation of whether additional work could be outsourced cost-effectively.

As part of sweeping cost-cutting efforts, GM's manufacturing arm plans to increase the number of white-collar workers in Canada and overseas, according to an internal company report.

Another of many examples is GM's spending plan announcement during the spring of 2004 of its decision to outsource more white-collar work to cut costs. In 2003 the company began offshoring activities, moving $3.5 million of work to lower-cost locations, and GM plans to increase that to $48 million in 2004.

One way to create a kind of distributed project or organization is to outsource some services. Creating a good outsourcing deal isn't easy even in one's home country. Offshore outsourcing, with all its legal and cultural problems, is even more difficult. There will be times you probably will need the services of offshore outsourcing brokers who can lower the effort and risk involved in these deals. Although global organizations always had the opportunity to outsource work, the risk and effort involved were almost always too much for middle-size or small companies.

Outsourcing—even offshoring—is necessary and is not evil. It is an absolute necessity if you are to serve a choice-and competitive-minded public, and without it many companies, including auto companies, would be gone. Furthermore, outsourcing is not a new trend: It's actually part of socioeconomic evolution. It happened at the end of the industrial revolution, when many blue-collar jobs were outsourced overseas. The phenomenon, although painful at the time, provided the economy and the workers with incredible long-term business perspectives. The white-collar class was born out of the outsourced blue-collar one. Whatever color the new "collar" will be, I am certain that it will be bring long-term booming results to the economy.

Thomas Friedman, the *New York Times* reporter-columnist, supports my point of view. Recently he went to India to check out the outsourcing business. He wrote on February 28, 2004:

> So when I came to the 24/7 customer call center in Bangalore to observe hundreds of Indian young people doing service jobs via long distance—answering the phones for U.S. firms, providing technical support for U.S. computer giants or selling credit cards for global banks—I was prepared to denounce the whole thing.[2]

But then he interviewed 24/7's founder, S. Nagarajan, who provided him with a completely different perspective on this outsourcing business. He was told that Mr. Nagarajan had bought all his computers from Compaq, his software from Microsoft, and his phones from Lucent. He was using air-conditioning from Carrier and bottled water from Coke. In other words, while Indians were benefiting from this outsourcing business, Americans were benefiting even more.

Most revealing was the surprising fact that 90 percent of the shares in 24/7 were owned by American investors. U.S. exports to India grew from $2.5 billion in 1990 to $4.1 billion in 2002. It is American technological superiority that has made outsourcing possible. Effective project management controlling tools are necessary, as the conventional approach hardly meets the need; ePM, tapping the communications revolution that has made global telephoning as cheap as making local calls and the abundance of broadband technologies worldwide, is the solution for catching the wave of ever-increasing outsourced projects, mainly for those abroad or in disparate geographic locations.

I believe, that the view that project managers' unemployment levels are due to corporate America moving its operations abroad is shortsighted. Americans will always be able to do well economically because of this country's capitalist reliance on the individual for economic improvement. According to the SBA (Small Business Administration), 80 percent of all businesses in America are small businesses with fewer than 12 employees. In my view, it is these thousands of small businesses created every year that provide Americans with the jobs and wealth that keep this country in a dynamic economic mode.

It is true that the last four years have been hard economically, but it was the success of the many businesses that are created in America all the time that promoted the biggest stock market bubble in history. Many young brokers began to believe that a stock market crash could never happen again. But note that when the bubble burst, we didn't go into a depression. We went into a recession. And now we are slowly coming out of that recession, with companies leaner and more efficient, with everyone being more than ever interested in projectizing his or her organization, in staffing it with knowledgeable project managers. That is why job creation has been slow. But as economic activity increases, there will be more jobs. Look at PMI's growth rate and you will get the picture.

Perhaps no city in the United States has undergone as dramatic an economic revolution as Boston. It used to be a manufacturing town, but after World War II the manufacturers began heading south. Today Boston is bustling with high-tech hospitals, labs, universities, conventions, restaurants, high-fashion malls, publishing houses, art galleries, insurance and finance companies, and tourist attractions—all greatly aided by the computer revolution. What we need is a better way to manage these outsourced projects. We can no longer live with statistics such as the one recently released by PMI that showed that on average projects tend to experience 168 percent cost overruns, and that only 22 percent of those projects are successful. Such data come as no surprise. How can project managers oversee and control a project abroad with conventional tools? At best, they will have to be on airplanes a lot, flying from their offices to the field and back, and that alone will not guarantee effective project management. ePM may be the solution to this problem.

2 CHAPTER

Introduction to ePM

In today's fast-paced world, people should be able to run their businesses without being physically present. The same goes for professionals who need to tell their peers to take action on a project; they should be able to do that immediately without regard to project location.

Let me illustrate what I mean by using a real-world example. Not long ago the Marcus Goncalves Consulting Group (MGCG) had a great RFP (request for proposal) presented to us from one of the major semiconductor companies in the world to develop a full Web portal for its worldwide sales organization. We decided to bid on it and felt pretty good about winning and delivering a quality project, which, using conventional project management techniques and a traditional approach, we budgeted about 24 weeks to execute.

What we didn't know was that we were competing with one of the major Web development companies in the United States, Razorfish, a publicly traded organization with at least 10 times more resources at its disposal. When the prospective client came back and asked for our final review of the proposal, we knew we could not win the contract through conventional project management methodologies, as our contender was already known for its adoption of that system. We realized that, as we will discuss in more detail later, the conventional approach to project management is more predictable and reliable but also more expensive and time-consuming than a virtual project management approach.

Furthermore, we realized that we could use ePM not only as a project management methodology but also as a strategy to gain competitive advantage by increasing quality and reducing development cost and time (Figure 2–1). Since MGCG's inception, my premise has always been that it is not the big that eat the small but the fast that eat the slow. We decided to adapt the original proposal to an ePM approach.

FIGURE 2–1

ePM can help reduce development time and cost while increasing quality.

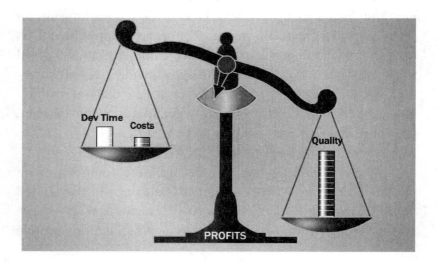

We adjusted (read: reduced) the schedule, the resources, and the cost but kept the scope and quality intact. To our prospective client's disbelief, we won the bid. Not that they were comfortable with our approach and ability to deliver on time and under budget, but in their view our proposal was so absurd that even if we failed, they would still be able to deliver the project on time, under the original timetable and within the forecasted budget, by using our competitor and their original proposal. To illustrate the impact of ePM on projects, Table 2–1 lists some of the key areas of our proposal and deliverables compared with those of our competitor, which chose to abide by the client's RFP. Unfortunately, we can't disclose the name of the client. If you are familiar with the biblical story of David and Goliath, you will be able to see the parallel.

How can we deliver scope of work (SOW) in such a short period? Yes, we did deliver a day early and within the budget! The answer is ePM. While our people took care of the whole site architecture in the United States and interacted with the client on a regular basis, also virtually, from beginning to end (we never met even to sign the contract), our branch in Buenos Aires did most of the coding and database integration. The logo, look and feel, and branding were outsourced to a partner in Hong Kong. Not only did we save on cost, we purposely chose that area of the world so that we could take advantage of different time zones and have virtually a 24-hour development time without having to pay for overtime, implement second or third shift working hours, and stress our staff.

On any given day, our staff members in Argentina (three hours ahead of the United States) would electronically forward to us in Boston their development for the day, as well as any issues and concerns. Because of the time difference, the project staff in Boston still had about three hours of working time before the end of the day, which allowed us to review the work

TABLE 2–1

MGCG's Approach to ePM versus Conventional Project Management

Main Deliverables	MGCG's ePM Approach	Competitor's Conventional Approach	Cost and Schedule Variance: ePM versus PM
Total project duration	5 weeks	16 weeks	11 weeks earlier
Total cost of project (estimated cost with RFP as baseline)	30% less	10% more	40% less
Website framework	Up to 50 HTML pages, 10 categories	Up to 10 HTML pages, 5 categories	40 extra HTML pages, 5 extra categories
Back-end database and search engine	SQL, full site search	None	SQL, full site search
Logo, brand development	Yes	Yes	NA
Full calendaring capabilities	Yes	No	Calendaring
Administrator's control panel	Yes	No	Control panel
Multiple file-uploading system	Yes	No	MFAS

done, review code, respond to concerns and issues, and then hand it all over to our team in Hong Kong, which in few hours would be waking up while the team in Argentina was resting and sleeping. By the end of their day, the team in Hong Kong would then forward its work to Argentina and send us a copy in the United States. The cycle would restart the next day. As Figure 2–2 illustrates, Microsoft Enterprise Project Management (EPM) has enabled us to manage many projects virtually by providing us with portfolio, project, resource, communications, and collaboration management while promoting participation among all virtual teams.

FIGURE 2-2

Microsoft EPM provides portfolio, project, resource, and communication and collaboration management while promoting participation among virtual teams.

One of the main responsibilities of the project manager was to help our project teams stop dreading high velocity and rediscover the thrill of deciding, acting, and staying fast. How we did it and continue to do it day after day is the subject of this book. In the last eight years I have used ePM techniques to accomplish several dozen projects, small and large, always working with small SWAT-like teams, with no more than 15 people in each team. We would like to believe that we are the Navy Seals of project management. Throughout these chapters we will discuss in detail how to use ePM to your competitive advantage and mitigate the risks in conventional project approaches. For now, let's get back to basics and review how conventional project management differs from ePM.

AN EVOLUTIONARY APPROACH TO PROJECT MANAGEMENT

ePM can be loosely characterized as a collaborative effort toward a specific goal or accomplishment that is based on *collective yet remote* performance. ePM enables teams to work together yet remain apart. This mode of work requires management tools that enable communication and coordination at a distance. According to Margo Visitacion, of Giga Research, more than 60 percent of projects fail as a result of lack of monitoring and performance tracking information (Figure 2–3); this proves the importance of collaboration and effective tools for tracking a project.

Most projects require the concerted effort of several individuals who share a set of tools. For instance, a product development team might use a computer-aided design (CAD) program to develop and compare design alternatives without holding a physical meeting. The types of project management activities associated with this process are many:

FIGURE 2–3

According to Giga Research, more than 60 percent of all projects are canceled before conclusion.

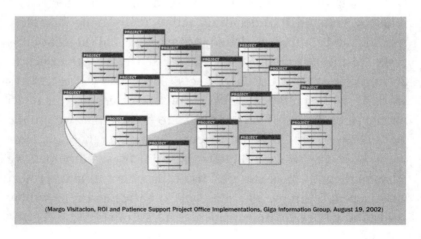

(Margo Visitacion, ROI and Patience Support Project Office Implementations, Giga Information Group, August 19, 2002)

- A task must be defined to develop alternative designs based on project requirements.
- Resources—people, time, and expenses—must be allocated to the task.
- The team members must communicate before and during the task both with each other (design issues) and with the project manager (administrative status reporting).
- The project manager needs to track the task and, based on performance relative to allocated resources, administer course corrections.

For these activities to be tracked, communicated, and shared, there is a need for several layers of information system support, including but not limited to the following:

- Communications, which implies e-mail, instant messaging (IM), phone calls and phone conferences, webcasting, memoranda (preferably as e-mail attachments but possibly as paper), and other media.
- Collaboration, which goes beyond basic communicating to sharing design information, which for all but the simplest projects will reside in specialized repositories such as CAD programs, CASE (computer and software engineer) tools, simulation software, ePM applications, and so on.
- Tracking and leveling resources, which are functions performed by traditional project management (PM) products, many of which are customized for ePM.

Again, for MGCG, Microsoft EPM has proved very effective in enabling virtual teams anywhere in the world to view tasks, update them, and even have them reassigned on the fly, as shown in Figure 2–4.

FIGURE 2-4

Microsoft EPM enables virtual teams anywhere in the world to view
their tasks, update them, and even have them reassigned on the fly.

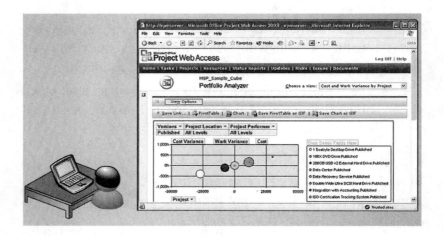

Another challenge with ePM is that some organizations
are required by regulation or commitment to use a specific
methodology (e.g., ISO 9000) to maintain complete configuration control over project artifacts. An auto company, for
instance, may need to store not only the final specifications for
the design and production of a new car but all alternatives and
iterations leading up to them. In such cases, all the nuances of
process management can consume more resources than the
projects themselves do.

Then there are those who say that we should not try to fix
what is not broken. Examples such as the one above from
MGCG may not compel them to adopt ePM. Car manufacturers and bridge builders were not on hold waiting for the advent
of distributed computing and ePM. All these PM activities have
been handled for years—since the start of the industrial revolution, as mentioned in chapter 1—with pencil and paper and

human ingenuity and then spreadsheets, which many companies are still using to track projects. How do electronic information systems and electronic project management change this, and how do Web-based applications add value? This is the million-dollar question.

Ubiquitous Project Communication

I work in Hopkinton, Massachusetts, but the people who report to me don't. They work in Fort Lauderdale, Florida; Vitoria, ES, Brazil; Buenos Aries, Argentina; Istanbul, Turkey; and Stuttgart, Germany. They are all over the world, and sometimes their offices become the client's site. To be able to manage people from a distance, you must rely on what I categorize as *ubiquitous communication*, not to be confused with UbiCom programs, which are multidisciplinary research programs aimed at carrying out the research needed for specifying and developing wearable systems for mobile multimedia communications.

By ubiquitous communication for ePM I mean technologies such as e-mail, which allows ideas to flow asynchronously (i.e., without parties online at both ends), enabling work to flow across holidays and time zones. E-mail also creates, with no incremental labor, a searchable audit trail, which is the key to many formal processes.

Taking this idea a step further, consider how products such as Microsoft Outlook support and extend project communication. Outlook integrates a multiprotocol e-mail client with directory, scheduling, and journaling functions. Through journaling, the process of keeping a record of work performed, Outlook extends the concept of an automatic audit trail to include phone calls, faxes, and other nonintegrated communications.

Collaboration: A Brief Overview of Software Applications

The ability to use ePM for competitive advantage and project execution would not be possible without shared storage and concurrent control. Integrated messaging tools such as Lotus Notes and design collaboration tools such as TeamFusion do a good job in their respective domains. When a project manager needs to lay out tasks, assign resources, and track performance, however, these tools do a terrible job, if they do it at all. Project management software adds value by facilitating the administrative chores associated with teamwork, from schedule production and cost estimation to critical path analysis.

Project management software's agenda is to answer this question, and as anyone familiar with tools such as Microsoft Project 2003 (Figure 2–5), Primavera Systems SureTrak Project Manager, KickStart, and PS6 can attest, they do little else. These products are intended for use by professional managers, not by the members of a project team. They add no value as task collaboration tools because they don't deal with the vertical knowledge of specific problem domains.

Even if we consider Microsoft Project Management 2002 and EPM versions, which provide great collaboration tools, the product still leaves much to be desired, as the vertical knowledge of specific domains is not present. There are products, such as KENROB's Symphony, that attempt to mitigate the problem and do a fairly good job.

Nonetheless, this kind of tool is indispensable within a narrow administrative domain. Some products, such as Sure-Trak Project Manager from Primavera Systems Inc. and Microsoft Project 2003 and EPM, can publish current project data to a Web server, making status information and associated files available to all comers through a standard-issue browser. Web publishing is much more efficient from both a cost and a

FIGURE 2-5

Microsoft Project 2003 makes it possible to create a new project plan through the use of wizards and post it on the Web for collaboration purposes.

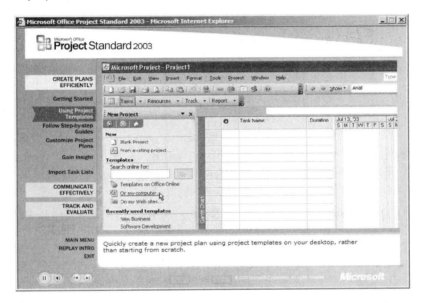

client configuration standpoint than the per-seat licensing model of older PM products, which required every user who might need access to install a full copy of the client software.

Both SureTrak and Project 2003 and EPM also feature extensive e-mail integration. In SureTrak's case, users can send messages about project data, screen captures, and selected activities through a gateway called Primavera Post Office to team members, who can then review, approve, and merge updates back into the project schedule. Microsoft Project 2003 and EPM go these work group capabilities one better by giving users a choice between e-mail and Web-based communications.

These features bring aspects of management by walking around to the ePM realm. It's important to remember, though, that collaboration in PM software remains strictly limited to PM functions. Even best-in-class products such as Project 2003 and EPM and SureTrak Project Manager can't reach out and touch vertical applications, for instance, a drafting tool such as AutoCAD for construction projects or Rational Rose, Rational Software Corp.'s system modeling tool, for software development projects.

As a result, teams have had to turn to a hodgepodge of non-integrated tools, much like KENROB's, each of which supports a facet of virtual work, such as project/process management, project communication, or collaboration on project tasks. Only recently have tools capable of providing a complete process management framework for virtual work begun to appear.

An Overview of the Minimum Software Requirements for ePM

At the heart of ePM there is the need for communication, collaboration, and project management. The current generation of software is intended to support work in each of these domains by leveraging client/server technologies such as shared data access, standards-based messaging, and browser economies.

But not until now, with the impending rise of Web application technologies such as Java, ActiveX, and XML, have project teams had access to integrated environments that bridge project domains. The goal of integrated process management through a suite of cooperating tools seems to be at hand. Popular high-end product offerings provide comprehensive process and project management through a rich mix of Java, JavaScript, and XML technologies. The recommended tools include the following:

- Projectplace.com (Figure 2–6), which provides full project management and collaboration tools over the Web (www.projectplace.com)

- Cardboard Checklist, which provides checklists to help you focus attention on the critical aspects of a project at the different stages of its life cycle (www.cardboard.nu/checklists.html)

- Methods123.com, a project management methodology that provides all the documents, processes, tools, templates, and methods required to succeed as a project manager (www.method123.com)

- Steelray, which provides a simple and easy way to view and communicate Microsoft Project information over the Web (www.steelray.com)

- SureTrak Project Management, from Primavera Systems, which is compatible with Microsoft Project but is more robust and is favored by the construction industry

FIGURE 2–6

Projectplace.com enables collaboration across the Web in virtually any language.

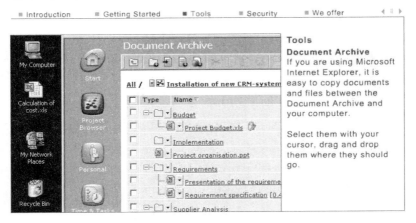

From Conventional Project Management to ePM

By definition, ePM is the system by which virtual teams collaborate for a finite period to achieve a specific goal. There are
several appealing definitions in the literature. Peterson & Stohr
identify virtual teams (geographically dispersed teams) as a
"group of individuals who work across time, space, and organizational boundaries with links strengthened by webs of communication technology. They have complementary skills and
are committed to a common purpose, have interdependent performance goals, and share an approach to work for which they
hold themselves mutually accountable."[1]

Recent technologies have greatly enhanced the possibility
of geographically dispersed project workers collaborating on
common projects. This thread of thought is woven into related
areas, such as a corporate structure with virtual companies and
virtual enterprises. Some concepts are taken from the older
topic of telecommuting. Still others come from CASE tools
that allow collaborative engineering.

Rather than being a mere curiosity, ePM offers many
advantages over the conventional approach to project management. A few of the drivers in favor of ePM that we have not yet
discussed are

- Attracting the best workers independent of location
- No need to relocate existing workers
- Flexibility
- Reduction in travel time and expense
- Environments requiring interorganizational coopera-
  tion
- Shift toward service work
- Global workdays (24 hours versus 8)
- Changes in workers' expectations

Whether from necessity or by design, companies are relying on new communicative technology with an impact on organizational structure. Betty Cooper,[2] for instance, takes a loose view of systems thinking and uses it as a framework in which to place teamwork. Her emphasis is on change, and the changes she considers relevant to contemporary organizations are

- Reengineering
- System integration
- Process redesign
- Total quality management
- Teamwork

These changes have been well promoted over the last decade and require a transition from traditional approaches to management that emphasize the analysis of individual problems and incremental change. Systems thinking is in a state of constant change. Teamwork is unique because it overlaps all these radical transformations. It is key to the success of these changes that all employees see their niche in the total environment.

Network organizations are a popular subject because of their novelty and interplay with new telecommunication technologies. Therefore, it is not uncommon to read about virtual teams in the context of virtual organizations. Obviously, by definition, any team in a virtual organization is a virtual team. Typically, virtual organizations are discussed in terms of a network, and the network model is imposed on the team structure as well. The appealing aspect of the network model is that it focuses on links and nodes. Since links are the distinguishing factor that sets virtual teams apart from traditional teams, examining links and nodes on a more microcosmic level may bring forth some enlightenment on the interaction between the individual members (nodes) and the types of links developed by successful virtual teams.

Gabriele Sandhoff[3] emphasizes real interactive structures in her analysis of organizations. She says, "From the perspective of those involved in it, a network presents itself as a loose, indirect and confusing structure of relations which is nevertheless able to influence social events."

This initial analysis yields the conclusion that successful network organizations are built on trusting relationships. The social network reduces uncertainty and increases performance by providing a sense of predictability and allowing the exchange of resources.

In *The Knowledge Tornado* I discuss the topic of virtual teams through the portal of network systems. I believe that twenty-first-century organizations will be network organizations with virtual team components, with each team networked with others. The key change will be the elimination of one-way paths within teams and organizations since teams function best through two-way communication structures. But does ePM work for everyone?

ePM IS NOT FOR EVERYONE OR EVERYTHING

Imposing ePM on semivirtual teams may be limiting since few companies actually subscribe to network structures over traditional structures, ePM over conventional project management. Therefore, seven basic types of virtual teams must be understood so that you can decide when ePM works for your project/organization and when it does not:

1. Networked teams, which consist of individuals who collaborate to achieve a common goal; membership is diffuse and fluid.
2. Parallel teams, which equates to work in the short term

to develop recommendations for an improvement in a process; have a distinct membership.

3. Project teams, which conduct projects for users for a defined period; tasks are nonroutine, and results are measurable; teams have decision-making authority (ideal scenario for ePM).

4. Production teams, which perform regular work, usually in one function; clearly defined membership.

5. Service teams to support customers in a typical service support role around the clock.

6. Management teams; work collaboratively on a daily basis within a functional division.

7. Action teams, which offer immediate responsiveness; activated in emergencies.

The challenge here is to determine not only if and when ePM is the right approach for a project but also how to implement it. Technology has become a commodity; thus, most of the issues you will face in developing an ePM are process- and human resources–oriented. In that context, ePM is

- A methodology for managing projects over the Web
- An evolutionary approach to conventional project management
- Used to address issues with a conventional approach
- Not for everyone of everything

ePM is not new. In fact, organizations in which project managers lead only people who work together regularly at the same time and location are becoming rare. Donald Eastlake, chief engineer at Motorola Laboratory, once told me, "In our part of the company, if you have more than 12 people reporting to you, you should expect to have remote people and a virtual team with people who live in several different locations."

Any ePM leader has special challenges associated with managing from afar. The scenario I depicted from MGCG's approach to ePM at the beginning of this chapter brings up some of the main issues, such as the following:

- **How can you ensure top performance from people you do not see too often, if at all?** At the early stages of our ePM practices this was a major issue. Four years later we are still trying to improve the level of communication and performance monitoring we have with our developers in Argentina and Brazil. Fortunately, we have been able to instill in them a sense of ownership, self-management, and eagerness to excel. When working with virtual teams, the key is to lead them to success, not manage their everyday tasks.

- **How do you help people and virtual teams work cohesively when they are not colocated?** As if managing a group of nine developers in Buenos Aires were not enough, we had to make sure the group was in sync with the virtual team of four people in Brazil, that they were passing the baton at the right time, with the amount of need-to-know information that would enable the Brazilian team to continue its work.

  Promoting teamwork between two Latin groups was not the most challenging task, as culturally these groups are very similar and are in the same time zone. Language is an issue, as Brazil is the only Portuguese-speaking country in South America. Thus, the e-project manager in this case not only had to speak fluent Portuguese and Spanish but also had to be aware of the multiculturalism permeating the two virtual teams and make sure to motivate them to work as one cohesive team.

The greater challenge was to help the South American team (Brazil and Argentina) work cohesively with the team of three professionals in Hong Kong, in a different time zone. This did not enable them to speak easily with each other on the phone, as on average (discounting energy-saving time adjustments) they were 12 hours apart (13 hours in the United States). Not only that, their cultures and language are very different.

- **How do you communicate effectively with people who work all over the world?** Language and cultural issues are a major barrier, but the vehicle of communication also is. In United States alone you are deceived if you think you can have a webcasting session with any team member across the country. To begin with, only about 40 percent of the country has access to broadband technologies (DSL, cable modem, etc.); the remaining parts are still relaying on dial-up connections that transmit at 56 to 90K at best, making it nearly impossible to benefit from multicasting communication over the Internet.

When you expand overseas, the situation can get bleak. Not only do you have bandwidth limitations, you tend to have systems limitations as well. For instance, in the United States it is very common for us to have our computer screen resolution set to 1024×768, at a minimum. But in South America it is still very common to find screen resolutions set at 800×600 owing to hardware limitations, as monitors and technology products in general are heavily taxed and overall are too expensive. To have a beta demo session of a product you are working on over the Internet can be a tricky proposition, as what you see may not be what you get (the non-WYSIWYG syndrome).

In addition, how can you address an urgent issue that just came up at your staff meeting at 4 o'clock in the afternoon when half the team is sound asleep on the other side of the world and the other half just left for the day? Of course, these are only some of the issues.

- **How do you lead teams composed of people both inside and outside your organization?** Dealing with these issues is challenging, but when you bring in an outsider, whether an outsourcing company, a stakeholder, a sponsor, or a partner organization, not familiar with your ePM organization, it can be a huge task. I have found myself in conference calls between our Argentinean and Brazilian teams with customers on the West Coast while I was in the East Coast, and orchestrating the three different time zones was the least of my concerns. Issues varying from one or both of the parties not understanding what the other was saying because of a heavy accent, bad choice of words, or misconceptions about a technical term or local/cultural slang; to telecommunication glitches; to different perceptions or understanding of the proposed or agreed SOW are only a few of the things you have to deal with during project execution.

- **How do you deal with motivation and coaching from afar?** Needless to say, when issues such as these creep in, your ability to motivate the team becomes paramount. When people can't understand what you are trying to say, when technology can't fulfill its promise, when you can't communicate urgent issues in a timely fashion because of time zone differences, when your sponsor is pressuring you for results, and when you begin to have the feeling of "where did everybody go?"

pressing the Escape button is very tempting. The temptation is to drop the whole project, to blame-shift, to lose your temper, to discredit and mistrust the virtual team. At this point it is very easy to discourage when in fact you need to encourage everyone, to motivate everyone to push harder, to set his or her mind on the finish line. To me that's the hardest part in project and particularly in e-project management. Coaching is a process that takes time, and time is almost invariably the greatest constraint on every project.

From personal experience I can tell you that in many ways managing with ePM is like trying to manage and lead with your hands tied behind your back while wearing a paper bag over your head. You can't see, hear, or speak face to face with those you are supposed to manage and lead, and you are not close enough to lend them a hand. This is difficult work. Although ePM practices can have unparalleled benefits that come from coordinating richly diverse experience and abilities, they also pose a tremendous managerial challenge.

With ePM, what once were dilemmas faced only by those at the top of large corporations are now common concerns. No longer is there an elite minority composed primarily of senior corporate executives, e-project managers, and e-leaders at every level of both private and public organizations. They may not like it, but there they are, handling some or all of the issues outlined in this chapter. I believe this trend will continue as the global economy expands. The only alternative for conventional project managers is to evolve and accept the role imposed on them of becoming e-leaders.

As I discuss in *The Knowledge Tornado*,[4] if you are managing a project today and are not experiencing some of the issues outlined above, don't be naïve. You are not in control or on safe ground; you are right at the center of *the eye of the knowledge tornado*, where everything appears to be fine and dandy. It is just a matter of time until the tornado begins to shake you, bounce you, and rip you off the ground. At that point, who knows where you will end up? Certainly, you will be thrown far away from your original position, which can be manifested in the form of a layoff, discouragement, lack of confidence in your project management skills, or even a demotion in your career.

If you are a project manager, you can no longer avoid ePM; you can only choose to do it well or do it poorly. E-project managers who do it well offer a tremendous competitive advantage to the projects they lead. Those who do not may watch the unraveling of both their projects and their careers.

A METHODOLOGY FOR DEVELOPING ePM

Effective e-project managers and e-leaders are competent in leading from afar. To be successful with ePM you must develop a methodology that encompasses the creation of a communication network that provides a virtual presence with those you manage and helps them find both the means and the motivation to connect with each other. Project managers who decide to adopt the ePM approach should still use their valuable face-to-face time with project staff, but only for the highest-leverage activities. Your goal is to teach others how to manage themselves when the manager is not around. For ePM to be successful, you must help people learn to manage themselves.

Approaching ePM One Step at a Time

You can approach project management in several ways. Thus, instead of discussing in detail which approach is best, let's stick with the Project Management Institute's (PMI) PMBOK approach and see how ePM and conventional project management differ from yet complement each other; this will be discussed in more detail in Chapter 3. In a traditional model of collaboration there are five steps:

1. Partner selection
2. Project manager team building
3. Stakeholder team building
4. Project implementation
5. Project completion and celebration of success

The first step is picking the right people. But you must be thinking that before you do that, you need to identify the project needs, promote/propose the project, and get the approval of the sponsors. Although this is true, with ePM this is not generally addressed since it is often not a distinguishing factor of ePM or the development of virtual teams. Rather, choosing personnel is the first place where traditional PM and ePM diverge.

Keep in mind that unlike the conventional PM approach, where you can walk around, check on people, and have face-to-face staff meetings with them, with ePM none of this exists. How can you manage or watch over a staff you can't see? Therefore, with ePM you leave the supervisory hat of project management aside and put on the leader's hat. Managing someone you can't see is considerably different from walking around the cubicle wall to see if he or she is there at eight in the morning. Instead, your approach should be to set the goals, hand out the work breakdown structure (WBS) and organization breakdown structure (OBS) as precisely as possible, implement software management tools that enable you to track the progress and performance of the project, and step out of the way.

What else can you do when someone is more than 2000 miles away? If the virtual team leader is telling you the team members are working hard when in reality they are drinking beer on the beach, how can you control that? How do you know? All you can do is trust and hold them accountable for meeting the deadlines set at the project kick-off. Paraphrasing Jack Welch, former CEO of General Electric, if you don't trust your people, do not hire them. If you do, trust that they will do the job and empower them.

Make sure they are reporting results and milestones when they said they were going to and when you asked them to. Make sure you are providing them with all the resources necessary for them to succeed. After all, if you don't know how a project can get one year late, very simply, it is one day at a time, and with ePM those days go by very fast.

Therefore, evaluation and control are crucial in ePM. To be effective, project evaluation and control require a single information system that measures project progress and performance against a project plan that supports delivery of the project on time, on budget, and in the form requested by the client and sponsors. The fact that you are managing the project virtually should never be an excuse for a failed project. On the contrary, you should have adopted ePM as a competitive approach to managing the project.

The caveat is that except for accounting controls, project control is typically not well performed in most organizations. Control is one of the most neglected areas of project management. Otherwise, how could we live with the high figures of budget overruns (168 percent on average) and low rates of project success (22 percent at best) we have these days? Keeping track of projects and people virtually is a lot more challenging. That's why with ePM you must start the project by identifying the people you will be working with.

As in a war, you don't pick the battle until you know who's on your team and know that you can trust them with your life, even though it would be easier to pick the battle first, find out what is at stake, and then decide on the types of resources you need. On a large scale you may want to do that, but on critical situations and projects you don't; you call the Navy Seals. An ePM virtual team is the equivalent of the Navy Seals in conventional projects. By now you probably have realized why most of the virtual projects outsourced overseas fail, but here is a list of the main reasons and how ePM can help:

- *Failure to set expectations properly.* ePm can help keep the strategic responsibilities close to the top (upper management) by facilitating intercommunication among these groups. The use of integrated and collaborative tools can also ensure that expectations are well set and understood.

- *Communication gaps.* ePM enables the creation of a multilevel organizational links by using technologies such as e-mail, IM, discussion boards, and project weblogs

- *Measurement and reporting along the way.* ePM enables the realization of informal on-demand meetings with all members of the project team, both colocated and virtual teams, as well as integrated measuring and performance indicator tools via Web-enabled technologies and the Internet.

ENHANCING ePM WITH THE CMMI MODEL

Implementing ePM in an organization almost always occurs in small, incremental phases. Different models are used to capture this evolution. Both the Software Engineering Institute and the

Project Management Institute at Carnegie Mellon University have developed maturity models that trace the evolution of PM practices in an organization. The Capability Maturity Model Integration (CMMI) model can be used to track your organization's ePM maturity as well.

Figure 2–7 shows a typical schematic of a maturity model used at MGCG to measure our level of ePM maturity, which of course evolves from our level of maturity in conventional project management. The model characterizes the maturity of an organization's ePM—or conventional PM, for that matter—development processes. The *I* stands for *Integration* and indicates that the CMMI does not apply only to software. Rather, it is an integrated model that embraces all development, including software engineering, systems engineering, supplier sourcing, and integrated product and process development.

Figure 2–7 also shows that there are two representations of the CMMI: staged and continuous. The staged representation of the CMMI identifies five process maturity levels, from level 1 (Initial) to level 5 (Optimizing). At each maturity level, a number of process areas represent the critical issues that must be under control for the organization to achieve that level.

The staged representation of the CMMI acknowledges that you can't do it all at once. There are simply too many issues to address, and many of them rely on others; therefore, the staged representation identifies a path of increasing maturity. For example:

- Until your basic "commitment process" is under control, you can't do much else, and so requirements management, project planning, and project monitoring and control are among the first topics to be addressed in pursuing maturity level 2.

FIGURE 2–7

The Capability Maturity Model Integration (CMMI) model.

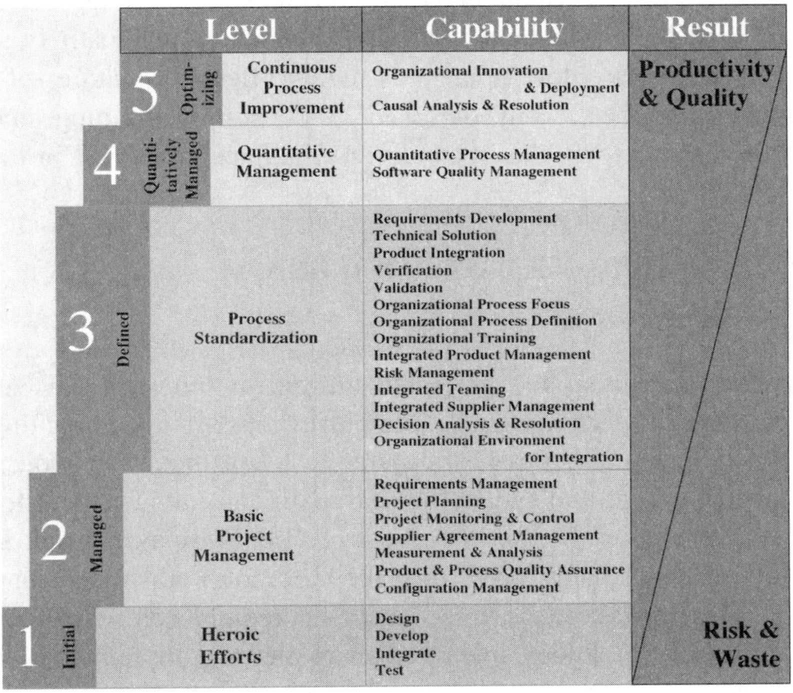

Level			Capability	Result
5	Optimizing	Continuous Process Improvement	Organizational Innovation & Deployment / Causal Analysis & Resolution	Productivity & Quality
4	Quantitatively Managed	Quantitative Management	Quantitative Process Management / Software Quality Management	
3	Defined	Process Standardization	Requirements Development / Technical Solution / Product Integration / Verification / Validation / Organizational Process Focus / Organizational Process Definition / Organizational Training / Integrated Product Management / Risk Management / Integrated Teaming / Integrated Supplier Management / Decision Analysis & Resolution / Organizational Environment for Integration	
2	Managed	Basic Project Management	Requirements Management / Project Planning / Project Monitoring & Control / Supplier Agreement Management / Measurement & Analysis / Product & Process Quality Assurance / Configuration Management	
1	Initial	Heroic Efforts	Design / Develop / Integrate / Test	Risk & Waste

- Trying to do process standardization (level 3) without the support of basic project management (level 2) is frustrating for everyone involved.
- Working on quantitative management (level 4) is not possible until the basic engineering practices of level 3 are stable.

The continuous representation of the CMMI quantifies the capability level of each process area. It allows an organization to address the process areas in whatever order makes sense. In the continuous representation, an organization might have a high capability level for some process areas and a much lower capability level for others.

The CMMI is not a process you can simply implement. It is a guidebook to help you navigate the difficult path from adhoc software development to highly effective, mature software processes. Many of MGCG's consulting, training, and other services revolve around the principles embodied in the CMMI.

CASE STUDY: THE IMPACT OF IT ON ePM

Marcus Goncalves

What is it about the project management industry that can cause smart people to make dumb decisions? In my consulting practices I see companies investing a lot of money in project initiatives that don't meet the minimum daily requirement for common sense. It's not that the project definitions are bad; in fact, most of them aren't. But they are not well thought out. They are simple needs assessments that require a clear scope of work, a methodology, and often a well-defined implementation strategy. It sounds simplistic, but if you, as a project manager, can get the senior staff of your organization, the sponsors of the project, to commit to delivering specific results on an information technology (IT) project, you will have done most of the heavy lifting necessary to ensure success.

A few years ago I reviewed a strategic plan for a company in the United States that provided thermic fatigue testing in which an investment of $100 million in tools and labs was recommended over a three-year period. This plan was generated by a very large, very well-known IT consulting company at the request of the CIO. Nowhere in the document was there any discussion of the business payback for this investment.

Another instance occurred at a large machine design company in Costa Rica. At my client's request, I intervened in a strategy project in which the approach was not going to result in specific value commitments. When I raised my concerns with the consultant (from another very large, very well-known IT consulting company), I was informed that there was no way to calculate return on investment for IT investments. Since he was missing the point, we spent the next two hours on "Business 101" and revised the approach accordingly. The sponsoring project manager specified value commitments, and the project received $10 million in funding.

Both projects got funded, but only the second was fully implemented. The real difference in the two examples, however, lies in the quality of the up-front planning. With the first, unsuccessful project, a significant amount of work had to be spent redoing the financials. By the time this foundation work was complete, the senior executives were suffering from hangovers caused by a series of bad projects (usually the result of lots of expenses and no discernible business benefit). In the end, they decided not to fund the rest of the project.

In the successful example, the work focused on supporting front-line operations, with clear benefits to the machine design company. The sponsoring project manager made sure the organization stuck to the plan so that it could implement the business change and realize the benefits.

Why is it so important to quantify the payback of ePM projects? Because project managers will focus only on the things that will make them money. No reasonable project manager is going to champion an ePM project—especially if he or she does not fully understand that environment—that is poorly defined or not worth doing, especially if it runs into trouble. When times get tough—and there are always tough times on

major projects—it's easy for executives to ax the initiatives
when the project rationale is not broadly understood, as with
the thermic fatigue testing example.

It's a mystery why seasoned project managers executives
follow the "build it and they will come" philosophy of technology investing. Many people believe that the rapid pace of business dictates this fire-ready-aim behavior. After one of my talks
at a PMI regional chapter in Massachusetts on this subject,
another consultant from another major IT consultancy let me
know that IT investment justification disciplines don't have any
relevance in the mechanical engineering world. Tell this to the
investors and project sponsors in a failed project.

Our current faith in the devil we don't know has given us
permission to hold technology above the long-established business codes of conduct that require investment justification and
accountability for results, especially in the mechanical engineering industry. Many CIOs and CTOs give lip service to
these disciplines. Although most prepare formal project justifications, very few of the justifications include commitments by
project managers to explicit results within a specified time
frame. In fact, in most organizations the IT department prepares the justification, which leads to the project being considered complete when the software has been implemented rather
than when the benefits have been realized.

As a result, the justification process becomes form over
substance, simply a box to check off on the way to obtaining
funding. This can be very dangerous for mechanical engineers
because the results of projects at times will be evident only several months down the road. In letting project managers get
away with not committing to projects, CIOs are putting their
projects and careers at risk and ensuring that IT is kept in the
back office, not fully integrated with mechanical engineering
projects.

If you want a seat at the boardroom and want to ensure success for your project, here are some rule for success to adopt:

- *Define the rules.* Make it clear that e-project definition and planning must demonstrate some type of business result for the IT investments. Make sure everybody knows that a big somebody will be watching. A CFO of a major petroleum company in Brazil not only reviews the business justifications when project plans are being drawn up but also remembers those commitments when budgets are reviewed.

- *Use operational measures.* It's admittedly difficult to draw a straight line between most investments and the financial impact. Fortunately, every business has operational measures such as customer service, cycle time, and product quality that over time will result in financial impact. These measures can be identified by examining the underlying drivers of the financial results. For example, for a manufacturer of turbines in South Carolina, a speedier production line affects peak time throughput and will increase sales (provided that there is excess demand for the product and customers are turned off by a long backorder waiting period). IT improvements that increase the speed of production are easier to commit to and measure than is the resulting increase in sales.

- *Be unreasonable.* Effective leaders ask their organizations to deliver what is believed to be impossible. When I was a practicing CTO, I once asked my network administrator to prove that his request for a new file server could pay for itself within six months. I thought I had killed the request. Imagine my surprise when he came back with a justification based on system payload reduction and less traffic on the network created by the system's more sophisticated data processing and network traffic capabilities. Even boring replacement projects can be made exciting if the team is challenged appropriately.

- *Stage the funding.* Most investments are a guess about the future. By staggering the funding in multiple stages, you motivate people to prove the concept continuously to gain more funding. Conducting pilot and proof-of-concept projects is the best way to do technology projects, because those projects allow us to refine our knowledge and understand the risks and the true scope.

- *Invest in the front line.* This is where your company or department interacts with its customers and its supply chain and channel partners and where small changes can lead to big dollars because you can influence thousands of transactions, decisions, and behaviors. For example, again in the turbine business, investing in IT at the manufacturing level is the only game in town. If you can save labor hours, millions fall to the bottom line. When you define assembly processes correctly, the average throughput of the assembly line increases, which has a huge effect on thousands of transactions.

- *Evaluate the portfolio.* Create specific measures for IT on ePM projects but allow some room for research and development infrastructure, and risky investments. Annually or more often, examine the impact over the entire capital budget. As with your personal financial portfolio, select a mix of sure things and fliers and base your decision process on the overall result.

If you are still wondering whether all this applies to you, ask yourself which part of return on investment your organization manages most closely: the numerator (benefit) or the denominator (costs, mostly IT). If your company spends most of its time discussing the cost side of the equation, you don't have good investment management processes in place and IT probably is viewed as an expense to be minimized rather than an investment to be optimized. Without measurable results, IT will be considered a necessary evil rather than a strategic management lever and will be subjected to the tyranny of subjective performance assessments.

In contrast, the road to specific business commitments for e-projects leads to a hundred valuable discussions about the concept, the work required, the skills necessary, the barriers, the accountabilities, and the measurements. If you haven't traveled down that path, as a first step, pick two projects—a dog and a star—and work with the sponsoring business executives to define and commit to a measurable business impact. My guess is that the dog will be redefined, reduced, or eliminated, while the star will be recognized for the jewel that it is and be better funded and championed.

Discussion Questions

1. Why is the development of a business case important in e-project planning?
2. Do you think every e-project must have a payback of investment? Why?
3. Why is it important to quantify the payback of IT on e-projects?

4. How can you identify the operational measures to be used in an e-project
5. Applying the rules of success described in this case study, envision a project you are involved in or an imaginary one and describe the outcomes. What results would change or have changed?

3

CHAPTER

ePM Versus Conventional Project Management

One of the motivations for implementing ePM is that location is no longer a barrier to choosing potential project workers. However, one must consider the requirements of virtual team membership, the technical skills the project requires, and the team members' ability to work virtually, on their own, never or seldom seeing their peers or meeting face to face with the project manager.

HUMAN RESOURCE ALLOCATION: A DIFFERENTIATING FACTOR

I have found ePM to be an evolutionary advance from the conventional project management approach, where selection of the project workers and the virtual team members falls into a series of varied criteria. The first and most important criterion is that participation in ePM must be voluntary, as virtual teams most likely will fail if they are not supported by their members. I have gone through situations where I insisted that a particular member of our conventional team, a project leader, enroll on a virtual team so that the virtual team could take advantage of his strong scheduling and leveling expertise. To my surprise, after we set up a state-of-the-art remote office for him at his home, it took only three weeks before he showed up in the office to say that ePM was not for him. He could not adapt to the new *on-his-own* environment, felt he was missing out on all the action in the office, and feared that eventually he would be forgotten and not needed in the company. All the investments in time, technology, training, and procedures were wasted, and we brought him back to the office.

Therefore, not only do the members of a remote team need to volunteer for the job, they also must have demonstrated satisfactory remote work responsibilities and habits. Being a telecommuter is only one of the requirements; it tells you only that the person can deal with and feel comfortable with remote access technologies. The social-cultural aspects of the job are a very important component, as the work the team members do will very likely be performed alone. Thus, ideal ePM team members must be able to

- Perform the work requirements with limited supervision and feedback
- Handle reduced social interaction
- Have good organizational and time management skills
- Be self-motivated
- Demonstrate good performance
- Be able to concentrate on the task at hand despite being away from a worksite and the rest of the team

When you are allocating human resources to a project that has some of its tasks managed through ePM or deciding if a project is a good candidate for an ePM approach, keep in mind that tasks involving the delivery of clearly defined pieces of information are most suitable for virtual and independent workers. This is a hard approach to abide by when allocating resources to your project plan, as typically project management, ePM or not, is oriented toward problem solving. To deal with this challenge, you will need to have efficient collaboration tools—software and hardware—to enable and motivate collaborating workers to engage in intense forms of communication that vary from constant e-mail exchanges to the creation of a virtual forum, have scheduled chat sessions using instant messaging (IM) tools, and have periodic teleconferences and, if the task requires it, interactive two-way webcasting meetings using products such as Webex.

To illustrate, take the project mentioned in Chapter 1: the development of a wireless and Web-enabled enterprise application product, that was awarded the Best Enterprise Product at Comdex Fall 2000. The project was not managed entirely through an ePM approach; it adopted about 60 percent of a conventional project management approach and used ePM for the remaining 40 percent. We had a team of 65 project workers based in our headquarters in Lawrence, MA, and three other members working remotely from Michigan and New Jersey. I was the project manager and was also based in Lawrence, but the chief architect was based in Michigan. If given the option, I would have brought everyone under the same roof, but this was a very risky project sponsored by a start-up company. A lot of the technology was being developed and patented on the fly, and we had no guarantee that the project would be successful, as it was a combination of research and development. Thus, I decided to keep those three key staff members remote until we delivered the project at Comdex. If we were successful, we would bring them all in for the second phase.

But having the chief architect remote was not easy, as the whole team depended on him to provide all the architectural information about the product; that required constant and continuous interaction between him and several members of the team in Massachusetts. Therefore, to mitigate the risk of lack of vital communication and misunderstanding of the information being exchanged and to enable newcomers to get up to speed on the background of the project, we implemented a knowledge management system that in addition to its knowledge base repository provided IM features (regardless of the platform members were in, such as Yahoo, MSN, Hotmail, and AOL) and a distribution list that captured all information exchanged via e-mail and IM and converted it on a threaded discussion board, which allowed us to read through the exchanges, keep abreast of project development, and address issues when necessary. This knowledge management system and the discussion board repository of *informal* (read: tacit) knowledge came in handy when the time came to document the whole project at delivery, when we finished it and handed it to the sponsors.

Figure 3–1 depicts the architecture of MGCG's knowledge management system. That system tracked information from various groups, including human resources (HR), finance, inventory, payroll, customer relationship management (CRM), and sales force automation (SFA). It also tracked personal information management (PIM), which was used to synchronize and integrate information coming from and going to personal digital assistants (PDAs) and other smart devices.

Technology Component: An Overview of a Knowledge Management System for ePM

As we began to adopt the ePM approach in our projects, we realized that most of our internal groups, partners, and clients

FIGURE 3–1

MGCG's knowledge management system as a backbone information system for ePM practices.

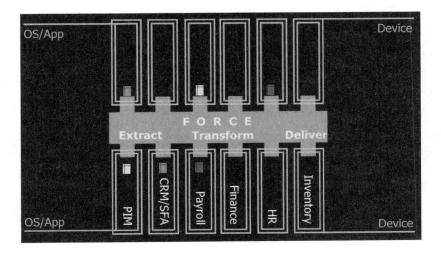

were loosely connected. Therefore, information technology (IT) organizations were being challenged, as they still are, to provide ever greater levels of data access and interoperability between local and roaming project workers, increase virtual teams' productivity and effectiveness, and reduce burdensome costs. Additionally, we realized that the corporate business processes were being challenged by ePM adoption to integrate supply chains with distribution channels, requiring the establishment of new business models.

These challenges required an increased focus on project management applications that would help project managers and project leaders establish and maintain relationships with project workers, sponsors, and customers rather than on technologies that simply automate complex business processes. We therefore began to assess how best to design and deploy these ePM solutions to increase the number of virtual teams and mobile project workers.

Today most of our ePM teams are equipped with one or more technologies such as the ones depicted in Figure 3–2, which provide the following benefits:

- The ability to initiate or receive phone calls from almost anywhere in the world. We chose Nokia 6800 cell phones for their GSM/GRPS capabilities and handy full keyboards for urgent IM sessions.
- The capability of synchronizing e-project applications and information on the fly via wireless or cellular by using the Nokia 6800 to give PDAs access to the Web.
- Technology that enables remote offices to take advantage of PANs (personal area networks) for synchronization of personal devices and printing through Bluetooth-enabled printers, LANs (local area networks) for virtual team workgroups, and WANs (wide area networks) for access to the knowledge base and best practices repository, e-learning, and webcasting.

When it comes to communication technologies for remote teams, make sure, as shown in Figure 3–2, that these technologies

- Are communication-centric, not productivity- or multimedia-centric. For instance, it is better to invest in a GSM phone with Bluetooth capabilities than in one with a camera and better to invest in a phone that is triband-capable and has extended connectivity capabilities than in one that comes with games and FM radio.
- Give users access to project information anywhere by formatting project information in a Web-enabled format that allows information to be retrieved from any device

FIGURE 3-2

Wireless and cellular-enabled technologies allow virtual teams to be more efficient and effective.

equipped with a Web browser and access to the Internet, including cell phones, laptops, PCs, and Internet kiosks.

- Support information agent technologies for the issuing of alerts, notification, and customization, enabling the development of automated alerts and threshold systems embedded in the project management tool of choice and linked to communication devices.

- Allow dynamic Web communications through links, annotation, views, and so on, by using some of the technologies listed above.

- Provide natural and intuitive interfaces, that are easy to use and do not require extensive training for effective use.

- Enable handwriting capabilities for quick notations by using systems already in place, such as Palm's Graphite language, the Windows cursive system, or even the free style used on Tablet PCs.
- Provide speech capabilities for quick recordings.
- Allow for decent visibility of screen and keys.

Be careful when implementing information mobility for ePM, as making the wrong architecture choice can drive up costs. Inefficient applications for mobile users can eliminate return on investment (ROI) and send total cost of ownership (TCO) out of control.

The Information Technology Challenge

As IT organizations embrace the challenge of providing employees, customers, and partners with untethered access to business-critical content, the need for reliable virtual access technology solutions increases. Whether involving packaged applications or custom-built solutions, this new breed of information mobility systems for ePM is becoming a necessity.

Traditionally, the default application architecture to support virtual teams has been a remote access connection (RAS) to the central database and application servers as an extension of standard client/server applications running on corporate networks. Some organizations add a wireless communications connection. Although this standard approach may seem logical and practical, it fails because most remote communications infrastructures are slow and unreliable. Recently, a wave of proprietary application vendors have attempted to provide organizations with information mobility solutions for not only ePM but also for field sales and service forces and remote offices; however, their success has been hampered by their inability to universalize disparate application data. It is not easy to exchange project data between a Primavera system, an MS Project system, and Excel and Lotus spreadsheets, let alone project data residing informally in project workers' heads, notepads, and sticky notes.

Applications used by mobile users must be written to function at a connection speed between 36.6 and 56/90 Kbps, especially when there are overseas infrastructures. The challenge of transferring data over remote connections is even more severe, as wireless connections are slower (typically 20 Kbps), less available (most estimates say wireless services will cover only 85 percent of the United States by 2005), and less reliable than wired connections. This scenario will continue to be true through the 2.5G wireless platform and the early stages of the 3G.

The challenge lies in delivering project information in a timely fashion regardless of network bandwidth, but the performance of most client/server applications across analog or wireless modems has been lagging. As a result, e-project managers must choose between functionality and response time. This compromise, though feasible in the past, is unacceptable to today's project workers, who expect broadband-quality content and flexibility over wireless connections. Simply put, the RAS approach lacks the requisite combination of speed and functionality required by an ePM decentralized workforce with information-hungry project needs. The proliferation of legacy paradigms presents yet another hurdle for IT organizations that seek to deliver data mobility solutions for ePM, ultimately requiring enterprises to explore an entirely new architectural approach.

With that challenge in mind, MGCG built a flexible XML-based data extraction, normalization, redirection, and delivery platform, which we dubbed FORCE (Framework for Open Redirection of Content Exchange). We suggest that you build a similar platform if you really want your virtual teams to be effective. There are many similar solutions available on the market, mainly via IBM, WebMethods, HP, and Microsoft. In our case, similar to other third-party vendors, the solution enables information mobility on both wired and wireless devices such as Internet kiosks we can place at the client's site, PDAs, SHDs (smart handheld devices), and WIDs (wireless Internet devices), as well as WAP and i-Mode phones. The technology provides those devices with virtual access to project information stored in our corporate repositories, including access to

- CRM data
- Address books and contact lists from popular applications such as
  - MS Project 2003
  - MS Excel
  - MS Word
  - Lotus Notes
  - Goldmine
  - Act!2000
  - Eudora
  - Netscape Messenger
  - Microsoft Outlook
  - Outlook Express
  - LOAP Data Interchange Format (LDIF)-based applications

The technology, which we call iCloud, gives remote project workers access to any of these applications simultaneously without sacrificing application performance, data integrity, or platform interoperability. By virtually accessing data, remote project workers avoid the slow and insecure data synchronization and download traditionally associated with wireless connections. Further, iCloud preserves the data integrity in the corporate repository while facilitating access to a host of proprietary information types from a variety of devices.

MGCG's dynamic transcoding proxy (DTP) technology enables transformed data to be dynamically transcoded into a variety of formats to suit a multitude of devices without the need for users to interact with the server to specify the type of device used.

The Architecture

MGCG's iCloud technology (Figure 3–3), is focused on integrating data from disparate silos—"information islands"—and making the data available to mobile project workers. The process involves extracting data, converting the data into a neutral XML format, and then transforming the data into a format that a wide range applications and devices can access. Further, to ensure that the accessed data remain current, the data must be synchronized with the original repository at periodic intervals.

In the iCloud framework, a virtual access server (VAS) initiates, monitors, and performs the process of extraction, normalization, transformation, and delivery of project data. The VAS provides an array of value-added services, including the Adaptor Management Service (AMS), the View Service (VS), and the Portal Customization Service (PCS).

The AMS intelligently controls the deployment of a software component (agent) with intelligent data adaptors to the source machines (i.e., clients) and handles any subsequent configuration and communication. Once deployed on the source machine, the adaptors conduct configuration and initialization

FIGURE 3–3

Architecture of MGCG's iCloud technology for virtual access to project data.

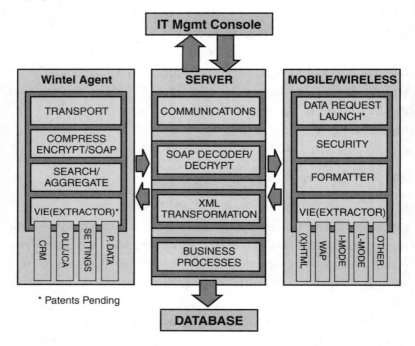

checks and communicate the status back to the server, which then reengineers the instructions. These instructions serve as directives to the adaptors for data import-export functions from the data stores. Based on the server's instructions, the data are transported by the agents using the Simple Object Access Protocol (SOAP) to a specified location over HTTP. The timing and the process of import-export and transport processes are easily configurable.

Project data from diverse repositories are pushed to the server, as described in Figure 3–4, by the transport agents and appropriately indexed for easy retrieval. Upon a request from any wireless or wired device, the data are processed, tagged, and made available to the device in a format consistent with the requirements of the accessing device. For example, the presentation capabilities of a palm device are vastly different from those of an iPaq or a PC browser. Thus, the transformation service automatically detects the requesting device and transforms the content appropriately.

Because the data needs of virtual project teams vary with the job function and usage context, the iCloud server enables administrators to specify access privileges and requirements for individual users or classes of users, such as sponsors, stakeholders, project managers, project leaders, and project workers. As illustrated in Figure 3–5, the VS handles all the tasks associated with integrating, organizing, and delivering real-time views of information based on users' requests and queries.

Although handheld devices are constrained in terms of display size, resolution quality, connection speeds, and overall reliability, iCloud's architecture maximizes the capabilities of each scant resource. For example, the PCS enables virtual team users to customize their portal interface, easily accessing data that are presented in a format consistent with their preferences and the device's configuration. This feature allows users and administrators to specify parameters, including content priority, presentation format, and frequency of update. The

---

What Is SOAP?

SOAP is the standard for Web services messages. Based on XML, SOAP defines an envelope format and various rules for describing its contents. Seen (with WSDL and UDDI) as one of the three foundation standards of Web services, it is the preferred protocol for exchanging Web services but by no means the only one; proponents of REST say that it adds unnecessary complexity.

FIGURE 3-4

Smart agent technology enables intelligent handling of ePM data among virtual project users.

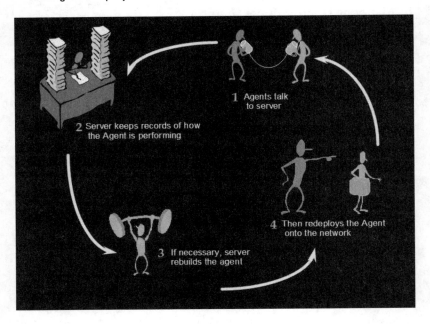

server automatically tracks user sessions and, based on the preestablished parameters, automatically pushes information to the user's device.

The number of participants on such infrastructure is theoretically unlimited, but for the sake of performance it should be limited to a few. My recommendation would be for no more than 25 to 30 people per project. I find that number reasonable considering the network structure previously discussed, as each member added to the team increases the number of links. Even with the best technology, communications along those links are slow, making collaboration more difficult than it is in face-to-face teams.

FIGURE 3-5

iCloud's VS handles all the tasks associated with integrating, organizing, and delivering real-time views of information based on users' requests and queries.

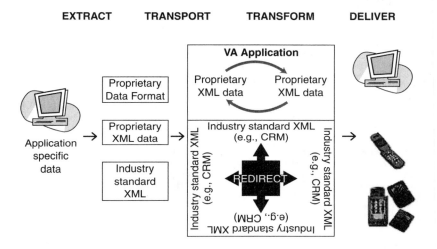

THE CONVENTIONAL WAY: OPTIMIZATION VERSUS ADAPTATION

Figure 3-6 depicts a conventional project's life cycle stages. As the figure illustrates, any project goes through these four distinct stages throughout its life cycle. In each stage a series of tasks are implemented, and the level of effort invariably tends to increase. A well-managed project life cycle will always display a bell curve (Figure 3-6); it will always strive for optimizing that bell curve as much as possible.

Of course, this happens only in an ideal world, but the closer you can get your project life cycle to a bell curve, the more smooth and well balanced your project execution will be. It is here that the Capability Maturity Model Integration (CMMI) model will work well as organizations and project

FIGURE 3–6

Characteristics of conventional project management.

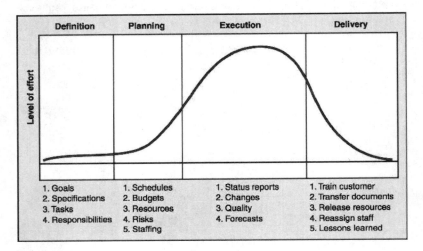

managers strive to climb up the five levels of the model all the way to level 5: continuous improvement of process through optimization.

Figure 3–7 provides a summary of the main characteristics of conventional project management:

- Project life cycles consist of seven phases.
- They are built for known functionality. Eventually there is a time for "ready."
- The process focus is more on optimization than on adaptation.
- Change is more of an exception than the norm.
- There is a tendency for a predictable future (lifetime).
- Matured technologies are used.

Let's review each of these characteristics before we take a look at ePM.

FIGURE 3–7

Characteristics of the conventional project management approach.

Conventional PM
• Made of "seven" phases. Requirements, Design, Operations • Build for known functionality. There is time for "ready" • Process focus is more on optimization than adaptation • Change is more of an exception than the norm • Predictable future (lifetime) • Matured technologies

The Project Life Cycle Consists of Seven Phases

Although I acknowledge the technical correctness of the PMI's PMBOK in defining the project life cycle as having four major stages (definition, planning, execution, and delivery), I expand that to seven: the four authentic and tangible stages defined by PMI and three more "pseudophases."

To clarify, let's do an overview of PMBOK's four phases and see where I introduce the other three:

1. **Definition** is where all the specifications of the project are defined, project objectives are established, teams are formed, and major responsibilities are assigned.
2. **Knowledge management (KM)**—to me the second best practice phase—is where we build the necessary KM systems, as discussed in the previous section, establish mentorship relationships, and apply our Knowledge Tornado methodology to turn every ePM member's knowledge into action, trying to capture not only explicit knowledge but tacit knowledge as well.
3. **Planning**, the official second phase (my third), is the

stage where plans are beginning to be developed, the level of effort (LOE) increases, and the goal is to determine what the project entails, what its schedule looks like, who the stakeholders are and whom it benefits, and what quality level will be maintained and what budget will be determined.

4. **Change management** is to me the fourth stage (not explicitly defined in PMBOK four phases but loosely embedded throughout the phases), where project staff, environment, stakeholders, sponsors, and the project itself are assessed to determine the degree of change that will be promoted through the execution and successful delivery of the project and what proactive actions must be taken to increase the level of success of the project as a whole and prevent resistance to change and/or the new benefits introduced by the project.

   For instance, I was once retained on a huge user-application migration that did not take into consideration change management. Technically, the project was a success, but as far as the bottom line was concerned, the project was a major failure and required a new project to mitigate all the problems—mostly resistance to change—created by the original project. It all happened when one major national bank acquired another in Boston and set out to migrate all its users from MultiMate (word processor) onto WordPerfect. Technically the project was well thought out, and in a single weekend we migrated all the users to the new WordPerfect platform, converted their files, and installed new templates to ease their initial adaptation to the new system. Half-day training was provided on the use of WordPerfect.

The problem was that no one took into account users' likely reactions when they were asked to change the way they worked and use a new system they knew nothing about. There were also several different groups, some clearly needing more than a half day of training and others barely needing any training. In addition, the users could not understand why the changes needed to take place. Some felt they were being pushed out of the organization; others felt their performance would suffer tremendously, causing them to miss their deadlines; and still others were lukewarm about the whole transition as they felt the changes were being imposed on them. As the popular saying goes, "Whatever is imposed is also opposed." As a result, very few users were functionally using the system, many were wasting unbelievable amounts of time trying to re-create the familiar environment they knew in MultiMate, and some refused to work on the new system, choosing to continue to work on the old system underground and submit converted files to peers when necessary. To correct the situation, Fleet Bank implemented change management techniques that varied from listening to frustrated users and pledging full support during their transition to extending training in three different categories and in some cases allowing the coexistence of both systems.

5. **Execution** is PMBOK's third level of the project life cycle. This is where the major portion of the project work takes place. Time, cost, and specification measures are used for project control and performance assessments.

6. **Risk management** is my sixth stage (an embedded process in PMBOK's model). Although risk manage-

ment is a necessary step during project definition and planning, there are several risks that are nearly impossible to detect, never mind have a mitigation plan for, prior to the actual start of project execution. Therefore, I always recommend keeping a close eye on risk management throughout the project and having the well-known risk matrix converted into a dynamic system much like the U.S. Department of Defense's DefCon system. There will be days when the whole project is operating under green alert, other times under orange, and, one hopes, never under red alert.

7. **Delivery** is my seventh and last stage (the fourth under PMBOK). It typically includes two main activities: the delivery of the project and the redeployment of project resources. In our practice, knowledge and change management play a major role in the process of transferring knowledge and making sure customers and stakeholders can benefit from the project and the changes it introduces.

In practice, the project life cycle not only can be broken down into four to seven stages but also can be used by many project groups to depict the timing of major tasks over the life of the project.

Built for Known Functionality

Typically, conventional project management is built and developed with a known functionality, which is usually the result of a vision and the establishment of very tangible objectives. Objectives translate the organization's mission into specific, concrete, measurable terms. Thus, project definition works around the understanding of the vision and the ability to translate it into an attainable objective. This objective becomes the goal, the focus of the project, setting targets for all levels of the organization. These objectives also pinpoint the direction in which project managers believe the project should move.

To be successful, the project manager needs to make sure those objectives are achieved in a timely fashion and within the budget set during the definition stage. To achieve a project objective means to enable certain functionalities—the benefits of the project—to be obtained. A project will be successful if it meets the goals—the list of functionalities—set during the definition stage.

In summary, in a conventional project the functionalities are known from the start through the objectives, which determine *where* the project is heading and *when* it is going to get there; a baseline is established. Any variation from that baseline causes a series of reactive and corrective actions so that the objective can still be achieved. Thus, when setting objectives, make sure their characteristics are SMART:

- **Specific.** Be specific in setting your objectives.
- **Measurable.** Establish a measurable indicator(s) of success.
- **Assignable.** Make sure the objective is assignable to a person for completion.
- **Realistic.** State what can realistically be done with available resources.
- **Time-related.** State when the objective can be achieved: its duration.

Process Focus on Optimization Rather Than Adaptation

A conventional project management approach focuses on optimization rather than adaptation. Strategies are formulated to include well-determined and evaluated alternatives that support the project's objectives and ensure that the best alternatives are selected.

Cause-and-effect worksheet diagrams, as shown in Figure 3–8, are often used to develop a priority system that helps optimize project execution and troubleshoot problems along the way. The fishbone diagram is also an excellent tool for analyzing and isolating symptoms and causes of problems.

Change Is More of an Exception Than the Norm

In conventional project management change is more of an exception than the norm. Thus, a myriad of evaluation and control mechanisms play an active role on any project. This

FIGURE 3–8

A cause-and-effect diagram can help develop a priority system to optimize project execution.

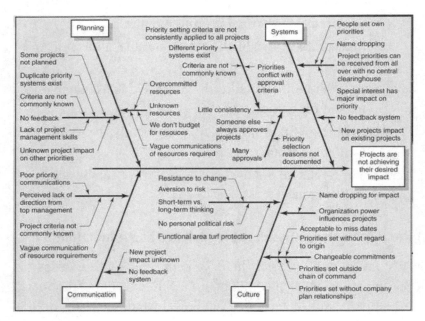

requires a single information system that measures project progress and performance against a project plan that supports the delivery of the project on time, on budget, and in the form requested by the client.

Project schedule control charts, such as the one in Figure 3–9 are one of many tools used to monitor project schedule performance and current performance and estimate future schedule trends.

In an attempt to prevent changes in the expected project tasks and deliverables, systems for monitoring project performance attempt to provide project managers and stakeholders periodically with

- The current status of the project in terms of cost and schedule

FIGURE 3–9

Project schedule control charts are used to plot differences between the scheduled times on the critical path at the report date and the actual point on the critical path.

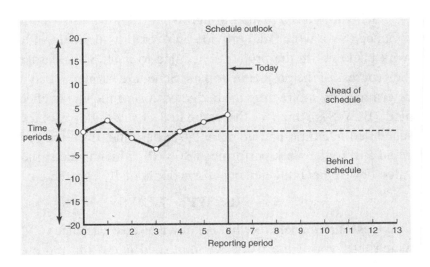

- The forecast cost of the project at completion
- The estimated date of project completion
- The exposure and highlighting of any potential problems that need to be addressed immediately
- The reasons and locations of any potential cost and/or schedule overruns
- The ROI for every dollar spent on the project
- Identification of potential problems before they strike or it becomes too late to correct them

There are several simulation software programs available on the market that allow conventional project managers to establish "what if" scenarios. SimProject[1] is one of them.

Tendency for a Predictable Future (Lifetime)

In conventional project management, managers are always comparing the actual cost and schedule with a baseline and attempting to forecast or predict the estimated lifetime of the project: when the project will end and be delivered.

Schedules are tracked through what is known as schedule variance (SV), which can provide an overall assessment of all work packages in the project scheduled to date. SV measures the progress of the project in dollars. Schedule variances can be determined by subtracting the budgeted cost of the work scheduled (BCWS), which is the estimated cost of the resources scheduled in a time-phased cumulative baseline, from the budgeted cost of the work performed (BCWP), which is the earned value or original budgeted cost for work actually completed:

$$SV = (BCWP - BCWS)$$

Costs are tracked to what is known as cost variance (CV), which tells you if the work accomplished is costing more or less than what was planned at any point over the lifetime of the project. Cost variance can be found by subtracting the actual cost of the work performed (ACWP), which is the sum of the costs incurred in accomplished work, from the budgeted cost of the work performed (BCWP):

$$\mathbf{CV = (BCWP - BCWS)}$$

Figure 3–10 shows a sample cost-schedule graph with variances identified for a project at the current status report date. The graph also focuses on the predictability of the expected lifetime of the project by showing two projected variables: the EAC (estimated cost at completion), which includes costs to date plus revised estimated costs for the work still to be done on the project, and the BAC (budgeted cost at completion), which shows the total budgeted cost of the baseline (project cost accounts) of the project.

Matured Technologies

Finally, conventional project management normally adopts matured technologies that have been proved to work with stable results. Since the whole management approach relies on predictability and stability of project execution, the least desirable scenario is one where a technology may not work or provide the expected results.

For that reason, it is very unusual to find cutting-edge technologies and approaches to conventional project management, as it would be too costly to have to deal with unexpected data losses resulting from patchy wireless coverage, data corruption generated by virtual servers during transcontinental synchronizations, or data corruption caused by data transmission via a satellite-based car phone.

Many large organizations, in particular in the construction

FIGURE 3-10

A cost-schedule graph provides variances identified for a project at the current status report date.

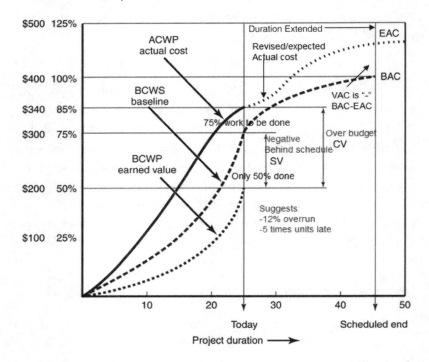

industry, are still using faxes to report project data to a project assistant who later will enter all the information on an Excel spreadsheet or MS Project. Not that these companies don't believe in technology or don't have the ability to implement it, but they would rather work with a proven system than take the many risks associated with early adoption of new technologies.

THE ePM WAY: ADAPTATION VERSUS OPTIMIZATION

The adoption of ePM should be an attempt to address the problem of managing large projects to improve the economics of their planning and execution. This is a critical problem that can benefit from an ePM approach tied to the rapid emergence of the Internet and other global networks and their role as a global disintermediated service marketplace.

Current project planning is plagued by logistical problems such as identifying and assembling skilled teams of people, timely procurement of products and services, and optimal decomposition of a project into biddable pieces. Project execution almost invariably suffers from scope, schedule, and cost creep. Tracking the progress of a project and recovering from schedule disruptions are ad hoc activities at best, level 1 of the CMMI model.

The ePM approach is aimed at radically changing the way teams are constructed and projects are conducted. It aims to alter the economics of providing large-scale services and significantly improve the efficiency of implementing large projects. In ePM, several of the conventional approaches to project management either do not exist or have a different role.

The technical management issues of ePM provide a new paradigm for building complex projects faster and cheaper by employing the power of distributed computing and operations. As was discussed earlier, ePM is not new and does not replace conventional project management. It can be adopted as a way to manage critical projects with heavy resource or technical constraints, and to institute improvements to conventional project management that has drifted off course.

As the demand for integrated project solutions constructed from a combination of existing and newly developed projects increases, many project managers find themselves with shortages of the critical skills necessary to compete in many of these newly created global markets. Virtual collaborative project development provides a dramatic increase in a project manager's opportunities to complete a project on time and under budget; it also increases the organization's ability to compete in the marketplace by delivering efficient products and services quickly.

ePM provides a broader skill and project knowledge base coupled with a deeper pool of personnel. It removes two of the major barriers to the success of any project: company affiliation and physical location. ePM focuses on critical characteristics that underlie the way projects actually get done in traditional collocated environments and attempts to adapt its process to a distributed operations framework. The following is a list of the main characteristics of ePM:

- Web-based project management
- No time for "ready"; always on "fire"
- Projects that are "research-like" yet "mission-critical"
- Not sure of lifetime
- Risk-driven
- Breakthrough and evolving technologies
- Need for integration of speed, change, and radical innovation

To understand ePM, let's take a look at each one of these characteristics in more detail.

Web-Based Project Management

In recent years, the potential of the Web as a viable networking medium for distributed or wide area software applications is becoming increasingly attractive. This is the case because the Internet can now be perceived as a

- Ubiquitous client/server platform for software applications

- Global programming infrastructure for software applications that can run on any machine connected to the Internet
- Global execution environment for software applications that may involve
  - WAN
  - Structured or unstructured collaboration among scattered people, often across organizational boundaries.
  - Access to human or computer resources on a global scale

The Web has the potential to become an attractive infrastructure for large project management in the future. In place of a traditional project management team, a virtual team now can be assembled from a global resource pool, as in MGCG's example discussed in Chapter 2.

Once a team is assembled, a project management process can be initiated on a Web server by project managers and their teams. Team members can receive their work packages directly from the Web server and interact with the server from their respective clients (a desktop, a laptop, a PDA, or even a smart phone) over the Internet. The workflow and project network loaded onto Web-enabled project management applications such as Microsoft EPM guide the project execution process through its various stages until it is completed.

Of course, the process is not as easy as it sounds, and various challenging technical issues can be anticipated in this context. Project management is a complex process even when the development efforts are concentrated in one location. Is it worthwhile to investigate the feasibility of ePM? I believe it is, and the reasons are primarily economic. The emerging project management era is beginning to show certain interesting characteristics:

- The project management pool is now global. According to the Project Management Institute (PMI), there are at the time of this writing about 70,000 project manager professionals (PMPs) all over the world. Project management and contract development companies are available in different parts of the world. Figure 3–11 shows the PMI website, listing all the PMI chapters outside the United States.

- The quality of project management infrastructure (professionals, technology, PMI resources, etc.) in different parts of the world is comparable. Operating systems are ubiquitous, as are relational database systems. Project managers are using the same project management tools, such as MS Project 2002/03 or EPM, Primavera, Kickstart, and Projectplace.com.

- Complex projects often involve unique, one-time processes that require participants with specialized talents and skills for the duration of the project. Contracting the best people for a project is a viable option; hiring them is not.

- A truly global communication infrastructure for electronic mail, file transfer, remote log-in, and the Web is emerging as more countries join the Internet.

In view of these factors, ePM can offer unique advantages:

- Access to a global resource pool for project management talents.

- Effective resource and skill utilization. This is true of unique projects as well as large projects operating out of multiple sites.

- Reduced costs in the absence of travel and related overhead.

FIGURE 3–11

The PMI website, listing all the PMI chapters outside the United States.

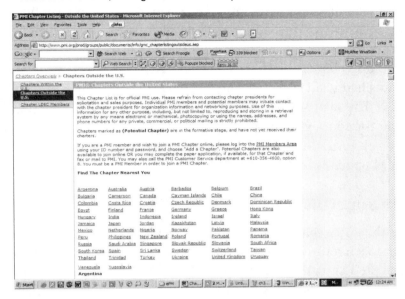

No Time for "Ready": It Is Always on "Fire"

The ePM environment does not allow time for "ready," as the project is dynamic and tends to change on the fly. For that reason, the project execution is always on "fire." The best way to characterize it is when a major problem emerges during the execution of a conventional project and a project leader or even the project manager paraphrases the astronauts of Apollo 13 and says, "Houston, we have a problem!" From that point on it's ePM. You have no idea when ready means ready, but you are on fire to produce results.

Projects Are "Research-Like" Yet "Mission-Critical"

Since ePM does not seek predictability, the nature of the work is much more like a research task, yet it is still mission-critical.

Again, in the example of the Apollo 13 "project," there came a point, after the astronauts communicated to mission control in Houston that they were in trouble, when all the conventional approaches for managing that project failed. NASA had to bring experts into a room and tell them to innovate, to research a solution based solely on the materials and resources the astronauts had inside their capsule in space.

The team of experts had a very limited and precise timeline for coming up with a solution. That portion of the project was on fire, and the project became a very mission-critical one. ePM operates in this mode most of the time.

Not Sure of Lifetime

Without the basic data a conventional project management approach relies on, such as time, resources, and cost, no project can predict its lifetime. With ePM, the fact that it is always in a research-like mode could cause its sponsors to pull the plug on the project at any time and deprive it of its funds. By the same token, even if financial resources are not an issue, the lack of an acceptable solution for a particular problem can derail the whole project.

Since virtual project managers have very little supervisory control over their staff, their role has shifted to become more of a boundary manager than a supervisory one. Crossing a boundary may mean a project is dead. Having excellent parallel execution of several tasks may mean that the project will finish ahead of time. In other words, the lifetime of an ePM project is very difficult to predict.

Risk-Driven

The challenges of completing projects within the expected time frame have increased over the last 10 years. Many projects managers have relied on more effective application tools, better forecasting, and the accumulation of best practices resources, leading to continuous decreases in personnel. In the "do more with less" project management world, project managers have also experienced decreases in skilled staffing and in budgets. Consequently, it is very common to find projects being driven by unrealistic time constraints and typically being delivered late. ePM attempts to find a balance in planning and executing projects. Risk management is the key to finding the acceptable balance within the project management methodology.

Realistic project planning and execution requires project teams to develop and practice proactive risk management. The vast majority of tools and applications for various project management processes stressed by PMBOK (work breakdown structure, network logic, estimating, resource allocation, earned value, lessons learned, and risk analysis) are all directed at reducing or removing risk impacts on a project or capitalizing or opportunity within a project.

For all the characteristics of ePM discussed earlier in this chapter, the virtual project manager has a more significant project role as a "risk manager" than he or she does in other project roles. However, paraphrasing Professor Vijay Kanabar[2] from Boston University, the top reasons for project failures love remained virtually unchanged for the last several decades. The development of and operation in a proactive risk management environment within projects and project teams is the basic philosophy behind risk-driven project management.

Breakthrough and Evolving Technologies

Virtual project managers must embrace breakthrough and evolving technologies to mange their projects cost-effectively and on a timely basis. Fueled by technological advances, cross-functional collaborative teams, and a competitive job market, alternative work practices (including virtual project teams, telecommuting, and remote management of geographically dispersed employees) can improve the quality of project deliverables (e.g., to transmit an Excel attachment via e-mail or IM instead of faxing the sheet), saving costs and boosting productivity.

The growth we are seeing in the adoption of ePM is being enabled by digital technology—e-mail, Web conferencing, high-speed Internet connections—but businesses wouldn't encourage ePM if it didn't have bottom-line benefits. Although it may not be feasible for all projects at all times, in today's global economy proactively adopting and encouraging ePM is essential. Services such as WorldCom Conferencing enable project managers to manage their e-projects without having to pack up and take meetings on the road.

Experts agree, however, that far-flung project workers need both effective technology and effective communications skills to sustain a successful virtual work environment. No longer are face-to-face meetings the only way to build trust and teamwork. Armed with new technology and new best practices, ePM offers new ways to connect on a human level with people anywhere, anytime. Studies such as Meetings in America III[3] show that having the technologies is the ante needed to get into the ePM game. Mastering how to use them is what will distinguish the winners from the losers.

Table 3–1 provides a comparison between the main characteristics of conventional project management and those of ePM.

TABLE 3–1

Main Characteristics of Conventional Project Management versus ePM

Conventional Project Management	ePM
Project life cycles consists of seven phases	Project life cycles loosely coupled
Process focus is more on *optimization* than on *adaptation*	Process focus is more on *adaptation* than on *optimization*
Client/server-based	Web-based (distributed computing)
Built for known functionality; eventually there is a time for "ready"	Unsure functionality. No time for *ready*; it is always on "fire"
Change is more of an exception than the norm	Projects are research-like yet mission-critical
Tendency for a predictable future (lifetime)	Not sure of lifetime
Risk-avert, conservative	Risk-driven
Matured technologies	Breakthrough and evolving technologies
Need for integration of predictable processes, standards, and best practices	Need for integration of speed, change, andradical innovation

4

C H A P T E R

The E-Project Management Process

As corporations migrate to a project-centric approach, planning, leadership, and board and executive management support become crucial. However, project management (PM) is not easily plugged into a return on investment (ROI) equation if it is not being well monitored; this is one of the reasons the majority of projects fail. In addition, the early years of the twenty-first century have been characterized by the first economic downturn since the information-driven economy emerged in the early 1990s. As a result, project managers' performances should no longer be measured only by actual results but also should be compared with their goals.

A project may be delivered in time and under budget, but if it didn't meet its objectives or if the defined goals did not solve the problem the project was intended to solve, is this project really a success? At the end of this chapter there is a case study titled "Defining a Project: The Compressor Tester

System" that illustrates this scenario. You might want to stop here and read the case study unless, of course, you have been through similar situation and already understand my point.

The theory that a project management system is only as good as its information technology has been nearly unquestioned, but the thinking behind the theory is murky. Just as the first generation of management information systems (MIS) professionals came from accounting and financial departments as those professionals attempted to enhance their accounting and financial practices, the first breed of project managers came from the construction industry, information technology, information systems, and management. Thus, the first generation of project management professionals and practices has been heavily focused on the construction industry, information systems, and technology. That is precisely why most project management problems occur.

As companies have started to focus on building project management database repositories and data mining techniques, the majority of them have ignored their people and their cultural issues. In addition, the massive investments in project management in the last decade were thought to underlie the historical globalization and merger and acquisition (M&A) activities around the globe that characterized the 1990s. Technology became one of the most active M&A sectors in the late 1990s, as Figure 4–1 shows. Consequently, the need for information sharing among disparate systems and project-based ones was too great, although the objective evidence for that claim is controversial at best; nevertheless, project management has had a free ride for at least the last three or four years.

Thanks to the Project Management Institute (PMI), this scenario is changing fast. Project managers are now encouraged to become certified professionals, and that is helping the

FIGURE 4-1

Technology became the most active M&A sector in the late 1990s.

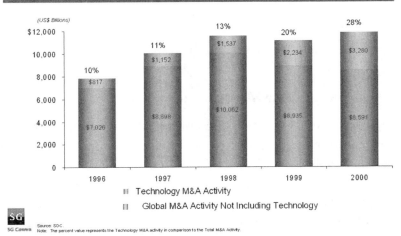

Technology Became the Most Active M&A Sector During the Late 1990s

(US$ Billions)

Legend:
- ▮ Technology M&A Activity
- ▯ Global M&A Activity Not Including Technology

SG Cowen

Source: SDC.
Note: The percent value represents the Technology M&A activity in comparison to the Total M&A Activity.

community of professionals fill in the gaps in their formal PM education while embodying the PMI's body of knowledge.

THE ERA OF PROJECT MANAGEMENT ACCOUNTABILITY

The free ride is over. The era of project management accountability has come, and corporate PM practices will be judged on the basis of their ability to deliver quantifiable competitive advantage that will make business smarter, faster, and more profitable. In the process, the need to sell the PM concept and process to employees shouldn't be underestimated. After all, the great majority of companies are not project-oriented, and becoming that kind of company is not easy.

The major challenge here is that in a fast-paced global

economy, ePM managers not only should be proficient in the conventional project management body of knowledge but also should strive to promote an environment where virtual project workers do not feel isolated but feel that their knowledge is valued and rewarded, establishing a culture that recognizes tacit knowledge and encourages everyone to share it despite the fact that people may never see each other face to face. How e-project managers go about doing that is the challenge.

Applying Knowledge Management to ePM

The conventional practice of employees being asked to surrender their knowledge and experience—the very traits that make them valuable as project workers—must change. That's why we at MGCG, began to apply knowledge management (KM) to the project management process three years ago. We understand that if knowledge cannot be captured, it dies. Thus, we make sure to motivate project workers to contribute to KM activities, but not through the implementation of incentive programs, which are frequently ineffective, especially with ePM. In reality, workers tend to participate in such programs solely to earn incentives, without regard to the quality or relevance of the information they contribute. The only way this can work is if you are able to inspire your virtual team members and, despite the distance, they feel they are really part of the team.

The main challenge in applying KM to project management (PM) is that KM is overwhelmingly a cultural undertaking. Before implementing KM into PM and deciding on KM technologies, you have to know what kinds of knowledge your ePM project workers need to share and what techniques and practices should be implemented to get them to share. This is not an easy task if you have the whole team under the same roof. It is much harder when they are scattered all over the world, speaking different languages and having different culture and belief systems. Also, your foreign teams already have developed an attitude against the American culture and way of life the last few years with all the political conflicts around the world.

You can't dissociate the political environment from the business one. You need a knowledge management strategy that should reflect and serve as the business goals and attributes for your ePM project. Therefore, a dispersed ePM global organization, for example, is probably not well served by a highly centralized knowledge strategy.

To be successful, e-project managers, and project managers in general, must be able to implement a very transparent KM activity into projects, one that is focused on simplicity and common sense and is never imposed. Whatever is imposed will always be opposed, and that immediately compromises the value and integrity of the knowledge being gathered or shared throughout the project and the virtual teams. Ideally, participation in KM efforts should be desired by every project worker, it should come from within, and participation should be its own reward. After all, the goal of such initiatives should be to make project execution easier for virtual teams, thus positively affecting the bottom line. Otherwise, such efforts will fail.

Unfortunately, the majority of KM implementations in PM have not achieved the level of success expected. The lack of transparent integration between information technology (IT) KM tools and PM workers often makes those workers think KM professionals don't know what they are doing and don't understand PM, in particular ePM, challenges. Thus, KM implementations must be able to leverage the promise of KM, its peril, and in many instances its eye-popping costs in infrastructure, deployment, implementation, and use of the system in a PM context. At MGCG I developed a methodology, *Knowledge Tornado*, that seamlessly integrates knowledge with project, risk, and change management. Figure 4–2 illustrates the disciplines in any project environment and shows how they are integrated.

KM can revolutionize a corporation's capital knowledge and its sharing, but it won't be easy and is not likely to be cheap. The challenges are many, and breaking down users' resistance is one of the major challenges project managers and KM professionals face. You don't get moving just by buying and installing one of the many KM applications available on the market. My advice is to spend quality time planning your

---

FIGURE 4–2

The Knowledge Tornado methodology enables a seamless integration of knowledge management (KM), project management (PM), risk management (RM), and change management (CM) during project execution.

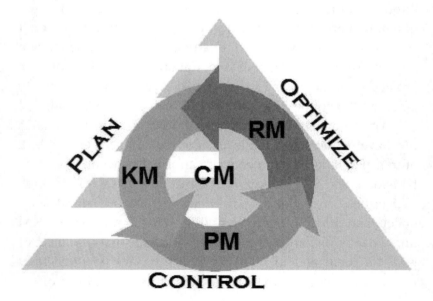

KM strategy, making sure to align it with your project goals, and be forewarned that the initiative may be expensive not only in terms of capital investments but also in terms of human, resource, and organizational investments. With that in mind, you will be able to plan for it. You should begin with the challenges discussed here. Then you should focus on the many strategies you probably have outlined for your project, which should affect not only IT support but also cultural and business issues and ultimately the role of KM as a catalyst and the flagship of the whole project management process.

Defining Success in KM Implementations: Vision in Action

The ultimate goal of a KM professional working with PM implementations is to bridge the gap between the project staff members' *know-how* and their *how-to*. Even if KM implementation is successful from the point of view of technology, usability, knowledge aggregation, and retrieval, empowering the organization to transform its know-how into how-to is virtually a utopian goal. But the definition of success is vision in action. Seeking PM success, several companies undertake tremendous reengineering cycles and hire expensive consultants to tell them what they often already know and have known for years from reports generated by a number of management and business consulting firms.

You may have a clear vision of your project management KM goals, but if you don't have a clear action plan that can be measured using reliable metrics, you won't succeed. By the same token, you may have a clear action plan that has been outlined, developed, and recommended in-house or by outside consultants, but if you don't have a clear vision of where you are heading—the results you want to achieve—you won't get there.

Don't underestimate the complexity of KM implementations in projects. If you look at enterprise resource planning (ERP) and customer relationship management (CRM) solutions, you will have some idea. Very few ERP implementations have been fully successful; most of them are still in the implementation phase, clogged up with CRM solutions or already undergoing some level of business process rethinking.

Surveys are underlining increasing skepticism about intelligent systems. Project managers must be able to avoid, if not eliminate, them. To get 100 percent satisfaction in KM implementations in project management is not only very expensive but nearly impossible. It's not enough to install a KM system. You need to persuade your people to use it, starting with upper management.

In addition, immediate results are nearly nonexistent, especially in an ePM environment, until users are able to feed the system with all their best practices, explicit knowledge, and whatever knowledge they believe can earn them the announced motivational perk. Of course, you can always mention the success of the KM system used by British Prime Minister Tony Blair in his massive electoral victory.[1] But that system had a very specific and narrow goal of attack and rapid rebuttal of the opposition party, which made it unique. Today's KM challenges are much broader in scope as well as influential. The following are the most important ones.

The Challenge of Managing Information Overflow in ePM

According to the Meta Group, in 2002 the average company was managing 1200 gigabytes (GB) of information, with volume forecast to increase to 4500 GB in 2005. Such data show an exponential growth that is not expected to slow over the coming decades. At MGCG, a small firm, we already manage 250 GB of information among no more than 120 contributors, of which about 100 are or were contractors. Just imagine how much more large corporations are managing. Do you know how much your organization is managing? Figure 4–3 provides a sample of the repositories of corporate knowledge, according to the Delphi Group.

According to Maureen Grey, a Gartner Group analyst, through 2005 enterprise mailbox volume is expected to increase 55 percent per year. E-mail users at enterprises are spending an average of 2.5 hours a day on mailbox management tasks, and by 2006 they will be spending an average of 4.5 hours per day maintaining their mailboxes; this will prompt about 60 percent of enterprises to augment their messaging applications with a mechanism to manage must-keep e-mail. Have you stopped to figure out how this affects productivity for ePM implementations? Since virtual teams must rely on electronic forms of communication, how much of their time should be allocated to checking e-mails and voice mails and spending time on instant messaging (IM)?

As an ePM manager, you will have to work very closely with CIOs and CTOs to devise a strategy to manage the overflow of data flooding their virtual teams. You will have to find innovative ways to manage the huge volumes of information being automated and delivered by publish/subscribe technologies to your virtual teams across the building, the country, and the world. By investing now in information and knowledge management technologies, you will be able to stay ahead of the curve. This situation is so challenging that delaying such information and knowledge management initiatives a year or two may cause your organization to lose its ability to amass these data, much less provide intelligent, convenient access to it.

FIGURE 4-3

Repositories of corporate knowledge.

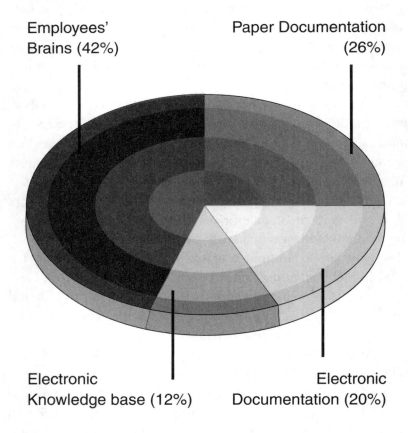

Employees' Brains (42%)

Paper Documentation (26%)

Electronic Knowledge base (12%)

Electronic Documentation (20%)

Source: Copyright ® The Delphi Group

According to the Seybold Group,[2] those wanting to manage and control the huge amounts of information contained in their unstructured text documents need content management solutions "with an explicit focus on security, access control and an expansive taxonomy of terms that are oriented around a problem-solving focus."

Cleaning Up the Act

Of course, e-mail control and message management are not typically the responsibility of project managers, and neither are the tasks of cleaning up and maintaining the current archive of documents. However, managing unneeded documents, even though it doesn't increase the value of the documents or the efficiency of the organization, is a vital part of managing an ePM knowledge base. That is where e-project managers play a major role in interactively working with information systems and technology professionals.

As a project manager, you should implement at least three record management practices through the life cycle of the project, making sure your KM professionals understand them and developing and implementing the process with the support of information systems and technology (IS&T) groups. These record management practices should consist of the following:

- Defining policies, criteria, and time frames for retention of project information online, based on regulatory requirements, mission-critical status or operational nature of the information, and/or any other relevant criteria.
- Establishing ownership for business data records: whose responsibility it is to define the policies for retention and use of online data?

- Implementing these policies across the organization for both paper and digital files so that in partnership with CTO/CIOs you can consider the technology alternatives for managing unstructured online text documents.
- Managing documented and undocumented intellectual assets, which includes identifying unique technology and processes and securing patents and copyrights when appropriate.

Defining Broader Content Management

According to Cyveillance, in midyear 2003 the total number of pages on the Internet topped 4.1 billion. By the end of 2005, the company predicts, there will be more than 7 billion pages. If you consider that the average Web page is 10 KB in size and contains 23 internal links, 5.6 external links, and 14.4 images and that if you add in the terabytes of unstructured documents in project file systems and databases, you can understand why ePM environments need text mining technologies so badly; this has ratcheted up automated analysis and classification of natural language communications.

One of the ePM manager's challenge here is that project workers will search for what they know is in a document collection but generally won't or can't specify a query for what they don't know is in a document collection. The art of effective text mining is to use computation power to suggest relationships that may lead to new knowledge discovery on the part of the user.

According to Gartner Research director Alexander Linden, there are four kinds of text mining applications that have been proved to enhance ePM implementations:

- **Fact extraction**, also known as information tagging, seeks to derive certain facts from text to improve categorization, retrieval, and clustering. IBM's DB2 Intelligent Miner for text does fact extraction.

By using DB2 Intelligent Miner Modeling, you can discover hidden relationships in project data without exporting data to a special data mining computer or resorting to small samples of data. DB2 Intelligent Miner Modeling enables virtual teams to do the following modeling operations:

- **Association discovery**. For instance, you could attempt to discover project task associations in a critical path analysis virtually.
- **Demographic clustering**. Application examples include project task segmentation, project worker profiling, and resource allocation patterns.
- **Tree classification**. Application examples include profiling partners and outsourcing groups based on a desired outcome such as level of knowledge in a particular field or familiarity with ePM approaches.

- **Semantic nets** are link analyses, that measure the occurrence of key phrases in a document to aid navigation.

- **Text categorization** uses statistical correlations to construct rules for placing documents into predefined categories.

- **Topic-based applications** or a clustering of documents via linguistic and mathematical measures of content similarity can be done without using predefined categories. The result is a general taxonomy or a visual map that delivers a quick overview of large amounts of project data. Figure 4–4 provides an example of statistical analysis of a similar system on MGCG servers and the types of data being accessed and researched.

FIGURE 4-4

Topic-based reporting system used at MGCG for KM in PM.

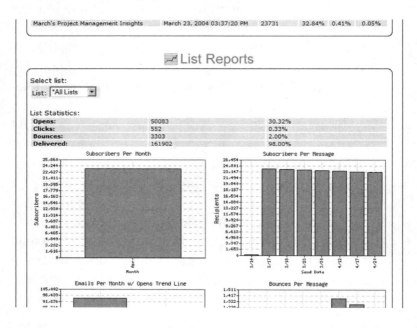

As an ePM manager, you can only gain by introducing text mining capabilities into your KM system and putting them to work in ePM applications, from virtual project worker skills profiling to automatically pushing and/or pulling information based on interest profiles and generating overviews of project documents for research and reviews. These tools, as well as those which analyze data and information to help people acquire knowledge, are now much more accessible to a larger swath of project workers thanks to graphical user interfaces (GUIs), Web-enabled applications, and simplified languages that enable data analysis from desktop computers.

In addition, you should take advantage of powerful analytic capabilities when business intelligence (BI) systems, which include query and reporting tools, data mining, and online analytical processing (OLAP), are linked to projects, virtual teams, and trading partner information sources. These tools enable KM to automate analytic processes to spot patterns on which to base predictions and suggestions that aid sales and efficiency initiatives.

Companies such PeopleSoft and SAP are capitalizing on this challenge. PeopleSoft's Business Analytics offers a variety of domain-specific business analytics, including workforce, customer relationship management, financial, and supply chain analytics. Its Profitability Management for Financial Services combines a number of industry-specific engines to create an integrated suite of analytics for banks and other lending institutions. Analytic applications within SAP Business Intelligence also integrate business processes. Its business area-based applications include customer relationship analytics, enterprise analytics, supply chain analytics, and marketplace analytics.

When digital content is tagged with common descriptive mechanisms for data representation and exchange, the activities and transactions of multiple processing technologies— workflow, integration software and middleware, business applications—can be unified and coordinated.

THE CHALLENGE OF TECHNOLOGY-DRIVEN ePM

A mistake several organizations are making with ePM initiatives it to think of ePM as a technology-based concept. There are no all-inclusive ePM solutions, and any software or system vendor touting such a concept is deceived or grossly misinformed. To implement solely technology-based systems such as electronic messaging, Web portals, centralized databases, or any other collaborative tool to manage projects and think you have implemented an ePM program is not only naive but also a waste of time and money.

Of course, technology is a major ePM enabler, but it is not the end or even the starting point of ePM implementations. A sound ePM program should always start with two indispensable and cheap tools: pencil and paper. The ePM manager's challenge here is to plan, plan, and plan. ePM implementation decisions must be based on strategies defined by the acronym W3H (who, what, why, and how), or the people, the knowledge, the project objectives, and the technology, respectively. The technology should come later.

Another challenge that tends to be technology-driven is the online/virtual knowledge flow, which is often a stumbling block in ePM programs. The big mistake ePM managers make is to look at technology as the main way to support the flow of knowledge among virtual teams. Project knowledge flow is a much more complex issue that involves the process of the creation and dissemination of new knowledge, as well as human motivation, personal and social construction of knowledge, and virtualization of organizations and communities. I believe knowledge flow in general is sustained only by the human desire to make sense—common sense, that is—of issues that transcend the everyday business scope but is very much present in every moment of a professional's life.

Every day we work on a project, as we assimilate, store, and disseminate knowledge about the project being executed—organized or not—we are trying to make sense of issues that relate to our interests, passions, lives, work, and families. No technology system can capture such unstructured and tacit knowledge, and trying to do so, instead of supporting its flow, stops the process. The situation becomes even more complex when we consider the cultural aspects in multinational project organizations.

Common sense should also apply to project business processes. Most of our PM reasoning and purposes are built around a process of justifications for what we would like to do to satisfy a project or business requirement (or is it to satisfy ourselves?). In this process, project managers should be aware of tacit knowledge that is present by virtue of previous experiences in all project workers, as well as their studies, thinking, and cultural background, while they attempt to verbalize it in the form of their responses. Technology alone won't help you in this process.

The Challenge of Defining Specific ePM Goals

Since the late 1990s PM has been emerging as a preeminent articulation of postmodern, postindustrial innovational management theory, increasingly adopted by corporations and governments, thanks in great part to PMI's ambassadorial and technical work. However, defining specific PM goals has never been harder.

Although proponents of structured PM see it as the ultimate New Age management construction, so vital that yesterday is too late to start a program and so intangible that no one can agree with what the BoKs should consist of (see the discussion on BoKs in Chapter 1), major challenges are still being dealt with, including the difficulty of classifying project phases and data, the behavior modification required of project workers in complying with PM standards and a code of ethics, and the buy-in of corporate management.

Nonetheless, in a survey MGCG conducted in summer 2003 with 9000 organizations across the United States and a few international ones, 94 percent of the surveyed executives endorsed the strategic importance of PM. If these results are accurate, why are there still so many unsuccessful PM implementations? Why are only about 22 percent of PM implementations successful?

First, there has always been confusion about the term *project management*, which has been used in information systems, strategy meetings, and many other business disciplines without any consistency. Often you find the term used in trade magazines and by technologists, financial analysts, and even sociologists, all in their own contexts. Unfortunately, there is no clear agreement about what PM is unless you have gone through PMI's PMBOK and become a certified project management professional (PMP). And even then, when we acknowledge that the PMBOK is only one of many BoKs, as was discussed in Chapter 1, the definition of specific PM goals becomes even more difficult.

Second, companies need to be on the lookout for information overload, as quantity rarely equals quality. Thus, another challenge faced by project managers, in particular ePM managers, is to identify and disseminate knowledge pearls from an ocean of information. For instance, an online graduate class I taught at Boston University during spring 2004 may illustrate what I mean. The "project" had an objective: to enable 140 graduate students in a master's in insurance program to undertake an online e-commerce class within six weeks and fulfill all the course requirements, which included exercises, quick quizzes, and exams, all conducted online, and then post the outcomes of those activities on discussion boards, IM chatting, and videoconferencing.

The amount of information generated by 140 students was such that I found myself spending five or six hours every day, for five weeks, sorting an average of 230 e-mails a day, 780 lines of discussions, and at least 130 paper analyses, not counting the course information and short videos I uploaded. I quickly learned that the activities I generated induced class participation but also generated so much information that it was impossible for the students and me to assimilate it. I did have 10 facilitators helping to handle interaction with the students, review of papers, and the like. The course ended, and it took almost two weeks to make sense of the avalanche of information exchange it generated. As I gear up for the next course, one lesson that I learned is very clear: Quantity rarely equals quality!

Therefore, an ePM program should always be in tune with business goals, and no matter what the project goals are, there must be an underlying business reason; otherwise, ePM is a futile venture. In addition, to gauge the degree of alignment of your KM program with the project and business goals, the following are some good questions:

- Does your KM program address the strategic notion of organizational survival and competence in a fundamentally changing and unpredictable organizational environment?
- Does your KM go beyond the traditional information management needs?
- Does KM take into consideration the human-centric notion of knowledge in relation to the professional activity context of the organization, as well as a lack of it, which will define levels of performance?
- Does it provide for incorporation of the creative capabilities of people needed for innovative breakthroughs with the optimization-based, efficiency enhancement capabilities of advanced information technology?

When defining specific KM goals, project managers must keep in mind that such programs are not static, as the value of knowledge can decrease over time. To prevent knowledge from getting stale too fast, KM program contents should be periodically updated, amended, and even discarded when necessary.

Innovation will address the nature of knowledge as prone to changes at any given time, often as a result or catalyst of changes in employee skills sets. Therefore, there is no end point to a KM program. Like product development, marketing, and R&D, KM is a constantly evolving business practice.

IDENTIFYING THE RIGHT PEOPLE

The ePM manager plays a key role in assembling the virtual team. Although there are a variety of ways to identify the right people for the team, here is our recommendation. Note that since the nature of this team is to work virtually, most of our approach in recruiting is also virtual, but we do conduct occasional face-to-face interviews:

- The ePM manager announces a project (project description) and notifies "interested parties" via focused e-mail, newsgroups, or mailing list broadcasts;, directing them to an Internet site for the project.
- Interested parties visit the project site and gather information.
- Interested parties choose to bid on biddable project parts. A bid involves
  - Filling personal and professional information forms as well as any other pertinent forms
  - Estimating and budgeting time and costs via tools provided by project sponsors or the e-project manager (these tools may be downloaded from the project site)
  - Other miscellaneous information

- The ePM manger evaluates bids and notifies bidders of acceptance or rejection.
- Winners are invited to join the virtual team.

Although this procedure works very well most of the time (and allows us to feed our knowledge-base database), sometimes there are challenges, especially if recruiting is done overseas and is not hosted on our own servers in the United States for reasons that include language localizations not supported by Microsoft's ASP.NET platform, bandwidth limitations, and project-specific reasons. Most of the technical challenges we face are listed below, and you should be aware of them:

- Need for reliable, comprehensive locator services (Yellow Pages–like) on the Internet
- Designing a set of bidding protocols for the electronic marketplace
- Managing and evaluating a potentially very large set of bids
- Verifying the identity of responders and bidders as well as their credentials
- Managing the project using workflows

Once the virtual team is assembled, the next step is to structure the project team by designing and instantiating a workflow that models the integrated, multiorganizational project.

STRUCTURING PROJECT TEAMS

Think for a moment about the environment John H. Foster, chairman of NovaCare, deals with:

We have 17,000 people dispersed in 2000 locations—none of which we own—in 43 states, serving 35,000 patients a day.

And the question is, what are they all doing? Especially since each one could put me in jail each day … We've found that after developing the technology to connect and communicate to dispersed personnel, the challenge is to develop the operating culture that allows for its utilization. Our culture is the only thing—except for our name—that connects all of these people in all of these units.[3]

Foster's statement should show you how important it is to structure virtual teams, particularly as they cross time, space, and organizational boundaries. Understanding these three variables is important in determining what kind of virtual teams you are leading and helping you decide on appropriate actions to improve them. In this process you will very likely do the following:

- Define and/or refine the software development workflow. This involves specifying
  - The project tasks and their sequences, which should include but not be limited to
    - Designing
    - Prototyping
    - Implementation
    - Unit testing
    - Building
    - Integration testing
  - Virtual team members' roles (see the case studies at the end of this chapter for some of the main roles in a project), including
    - Organizational executive committee
    - Project sponsor (PS)
    - End user (user)
    - Business area project manager (BPM)

- Project leader (PL)
- Project manager (PM)
- Project team member (PTM)
- Quality assurance (QA)
- Configuration management (CM)
- Independent validation test (IVT) team
- Contract authority (CA)
- Subcontractors
- Designers
- Programmers
- Testers
- Maintainers (collectively called participants)
  - Tools associated with tasks and roles, such as
    - Project management tools
    - ePM configuration tools
    - Configuration management tools
    - Programming environments
    - Testing environments
  - A project development workflow that will be instantiated on an Internet-enabled workflow server. The workflow ensures the logical progression of work across the multiple participants and can be monitored and visualized by both the owner and the participants.

Key technical issues you should be aware of when structuring the ePM environment include the following:

- The Internet will serve as the networking backbone for the transfer of project tasks, project forms, and measurement of results and performance, as well as the virtual team and its members.
- The workflow model used must be rich and flexible

enough to support the concept of multiple participant organizations and teams in which each organization selectively exposes its resources and internals to its project partners. This introduces the concept of privacy.

- When a part of the project (a subworkflow) is assigned to a participant virtual organization or virtual team member, it is up to that organization or person to assign its own resources to the project. The project manager does not have any control over specific assignments as long as they conform to the project constraints. As was discussed earlier, in ePM projects managers do not have a supervisory role; they manage boundaries.

- It may not be feasible to expect multiple virtual teams to use the same set of tools and environments. Therefore, the participants may utilize local tools and environments, especially if they are located overseas.

- The workflow management system will be distributed in nature, with each virtual team leader running its own workflow server that can execute the workflows downloaded to it. The owner's server can coordinate with participants' servers. Heterogeneous workflow servers will necessitate interoperability among servers.

When developing workflow protocols, make sure to pay special attention to the design characteristics:

- Virtual project workers should have a view of the project development process and their role in it; MS Project EPM is excellent for this purpose. This view is updated by a push from the workflow server. Work is assigned to a virtual project worker as a part of this view, and that worker in turn can explicitly request a view refresh (a pull). MS Project EPM refreshes automatically.

- The workflow server administrator, very likely the project manager or an assistant, should be able to initiate, suspend, abort, resume, and execute other exceptions that are transmitted to the virtual project worker's workflow server for appropriate action.

PM Tool Kits, Environments, and Protocols

Each ePM worker user interface should include a virtual environment online that contains a tool kit or workbench that allows that worker to perform his or her assigned tasks. These environments should be role-specific. For instance, the project manager's environment should consist of tools suitable for e-project management, estimation, planning, budgeting, and so on. Software developers' environment should consist of tools needed for software development and access to the tasks assigned to them. Some examples include the following:

- ePM manager's environment
  - Project site management tools
  - Workflow design
  - Coordination and monitoring tools
  - Project management tools

- Virtual team leader's environment:
  - Workflow coordination and monitoring tools
  - Project management tools

- Software developer's environment:
  - Editor
  - Workflow client
  - Libraries
  - Compilers
  - Debuggers

- ○ Analysis tools
- ○ Visualization tools
- ○ Configuration management system
- • Software tester's environment:
  - ○ Editor
  - ○ Workflow client
  - ○ Test case generators
  - ○ Configuration management system
- • Software designer's environment:
  - ○ Editor
  - ○ Workflow client
  - ○ Design tools
  - ○ Visualization tools

Although many tools may be local to the virtual project worker, it may be advantageous in the context of the Internet to centralize certain tools and environments. For example, shared software artifacts can be maintained in a server-side repository that is accessible over the Internet through the project site Web server and CGI (common gateway interface) gateway. This can work for shared resources such as a configuration management system, search tools, and code query processors. The shared artifacts may include specs, design documents, code, versions, documents, test cases, bug reports, and any other relevant information.

Although building the structure of the ePM environment is very important, keep in mind that culture is even more important than the project organization and structure in determining what kind of virtual team you want to work with. Thus, your goal will be to build a cohesive team across project and organizational boundaries. The way you handle space, time, and culture can increase or decrease distance, making your team more or less cohesive.

BUILDING TEAM COHESIVENESS

As we saw in the previous section, workflow systems handle the structured aspects of the project's business processes. Equally critical to the success of team projects is unstructured and semistructured communication. Thus, a well-established infrastructure for team communication is essential for a virtual team.

When a team must function around the clock, space, time, and culture can increase or decrease the distance among the team members. For instance, how do you ensure that information from one shift gets to the other ones? How can you ensure continuity, fairness, and appropriate standardization? How do best practices get coordinated? How do organizationwide problems get solved? How do you get real-time input and buy-in from across an operation when important team members from other shifts or time zones are home asleep?

What seems simple in a conventional project management synchronous environment can become a nightmare in an asynchronous one. I have had team members in Hong Kong ask why important conference calls "always" happen when they are asleep. Of course, none of them want to get up in the middle of the night to participate in a conference call. Figure 4–5 shows a 24-hour global clock that specifies windows of time in which one could actually schedule a conference call without much sacrifice from project members all over the world.

To make matters worse, space and time are not the only challenge ePM managers face. Aside from bridging those gaps, you have to deal with cultural differences. How to work together—the culture of the project—includes several issues, from organization to language and ethnic norms. Gaps in this area can make you feel that your virtual teams are very far away.

FIGURE 4-5

A 24-hour global clock.

24-Hour Global Clock

United States (East Coast)	Australia	Scotland	Comments
12 midnight	2 PM	5 AM	
1 AM	3 PM	6 AM	
2 AM	4 PM	7 AM	
3 AM	5 PM	8 AM	
4 AM	6 PM	9 AM	Australia handoff for off-shift review
5 AM	7 PM	10 AM	
6 AM	8 PM	11 AM	3-way conferencing window (Primary)
7 AM	9 PM	12 noon	3-way conferencing window (Primary)
8 AM	10 PM	1 PM	3-way conferencing window (Primary)
9 AM	11 PM	2 PM	
10 AM	12 midnight	3 PM	
11AM	1 AM	4 PM	
12 noon	2 AM	5 PM	Scotland handoff for off-shift review
1 PM	3 AM	6 PM	
2 PM	4 AM	7 PM	
3 PM	5 AM	8 PM	
4 PM	6 AM	9 PM	3-way conferencing window (Secondary)
5 PM	7 AM	10 PM	3-way conferencing window (Secondary)
6 PM	8 AM	11 PM	U.S. handoff for off-shift review
7 PM	9 AM	12 midnight	
8 PM	10 AM	1 AM	
9 PM	11 AM	2 AM	
10 PM	12 noon	3 AM	
11 PM	1 PM	4 AM	
12 midnight	2PM	5 AM	

☐ Prime time   ▨ Secondary time   ☐ Down time

During a consulting project I delivered for ABB in
Argentina I noticed that the marketing group, which was much
more in tune with ABB in the United States, had a culture very
different from that of the people at manufacturing, on the fac-

tory floor, where I found subcultures. Groups such as manufacturing were predominantly staffed with nationals, while marketing had few professionals from the United States and some Argentineans who spoke fluent English and interacted very well with their American peers.

My approaches when having a local meeting overseas vary with where the meeting is held. Not wanting to stereotype anyone, when I meet with professionals in Brazil and Argentina, timeliness is viewed as approximate and varies according to the time of the day. With that in mind, I never try to schedule a meeting in Brazil for 3 in the afternoon, especially if it's summer and very sunny outside. It may never happen, as people tend to leave early or meet you and invite you to have a beer with them by the sidewalk or at the beach. But if I am in Berlin or Boston, a meeting at 5 P.M. on a Friday, if scheduled, will happen, and it better be on time, especially in Germany. Can you imagine the repercussions of such a simple view of timeliness if you are working with several different cultures?

Therefore, the sociocultural challenges of enabling virtual teams may outnumber the technical challenges. Existing technologies that can be used for such communication in virtual project management include

- E-mail
- Mailing lists
- Newsgroups
- Discussion forums
- Videoconferencing

In the future, it may be desirable to include collaborative activities as integral components of workflow systems. Workflow systems that offer native support for synchronous and asynchronous collaboration among groups of people may be indispensable. Groupware tools such as Lotus Notes may aid asynchronous collaboration. Another product I recommend is TeamIntel (www.virtualglobal.com), which encapsulates the five core team functions into a single system:

1. Meetings (in our virtual workshop)
2. Collaboration
3. Management (assign, coordinate)
4. Information generator
5. Tracking and reporting

In addition, to build team cohesiveness your team first needs to be developed and prepared for the task at hand. One method I tend to use is the nine-step Xerox model:

1. Form the team
2. Communicate the vision
3. Develop a mission statement
4. Define goals
5. Develop norms
6. Develop roles
7. Develop meeting processes
8. Develop communication processes
9. Develop work processes.

This is a sound model, but it does not distinguish virtual teams from traditional ones in enumerating steps. This is not incorrect, but the implementation of the steps will require different practices and areas of emphasis for virtual teams to achieve the level of cohesiveness desired.

Therefore, organizational, job, and team designs are important early elements. This is the case because within organizational design, business goals are defined in the context in which their members operate. Virtual members need to recognize the team values of others, and the team needs to develop an infrastructure for involvement and design the configuration of the team while setting boundaries. Virtual members also need to be clearly aware of the team's expectations of how each person will participate. Therefore, up front, job design should consist of

- Defining realistic job previews
- Designing accountability
- Giving decision-making power to the team
- Discussing compensation
- Providing feedback for team member development and recognition

Finally the team needs to be clearly defined. The team should have a clear identity, create a statement of purpose, name goals, and make connections with those outside the team who can provide resources and support. More than ever before, project managers need to be smarter, faster, more innovative, and more adaptable. They must be able to lead teams with unprecedented vision and execution to keep pace with evolving technology and customer needs.

As Evan I. Schwartz writes in *Digital Darwinism*,

> The world's biggest companies are gazing toward a future in which much if not most of their purchasing, invoicing, document exchange, and logistics will be transferred from stand-alone computer networks connected by people, paper, and phone calls to a seamless Web that spans the globe and connects more than a billion computing devices.[4]

Therefore, e-project managers must be able to surf the waves of ePM at Internet speed. To do that and get loyalty and buy-in from their virtual teams, ePM managers must become *enchanters*, or *wizards of odds*. They must be able to understand and take advantage of quasi-magic events such as sending a wireless fax from the beach; reading, if not producing, a customized multimedia newspaper on a portable electronic tablet; and conducting due diligence on a proposed project auditing result from a plane 35,000 feet in the air and then beaming the report to the project sponsor in advance of his or her arrival.

Any ePM manager should be aware of how important leadership is. Leadership is the main reason why some projects, teams, and business ventures succeed when others fail. The credit or blame for any endeavor most often goes to the project manager, the coach, or the principal of the organization. Thus, the factor that empowers the project workforce and ultimately determines which projects succeed is the leadership of the project.

However, one must not confuse management with leadership. Management can be defined as a mental and physical effort to direct diverse activities with the objective of achieving a desired result. This managing process may include planning, staffing, directing, and controlling. Leadership, however, is a natural and learned ability, skill, and personal ability to conduct interpersonal relations that influence people to take desired actions. In other words, you lead people and manage things.

The Art of Enchanting

In the twenty-first-century economy customers are much more educated and aware of products and goods than ever before. They can go to the Internet and compare prices and specifications, develop a competitive report about the vendors who supply the product they want, and even discuss the technology and features of those products.

Therefore, e-project managers today must do more than lead. There was a time when the hard-line style of leadership exemplified by Lee Iacocca was necessary and would pay off, as it did for some time at Chrysler. But then, as the third wave of knowledge began hitting the shores of business, hard-line traits had to be replaced with traits of persuasion, cohesiveness, nonbickering, and non-self-aggrandizement. Instead of commanding, project managers today must be able to coach, counsel, manage conflict, inspire loyalty, and enchant subordinates with a desire to remain on the team, beginning with the project staff. In the words of former President Harry Truman, the "definition of a leader in a free country is a man who can persuade people to do what they don't want to do, or do what they're too lazy to do, and like it." That takes enchantment.

Not convinced yet? According to *Roget's Super Thesaurus*, to lead is to direct, show the way, conduct, usher, head, spearhead, and escort. To enchant is to mesmerize, captivate, hypnotize, and sweep off the feet. Which traits do you think make a successful project manager? Competence alone is no longer sufficient for a project manager's success. Managers must be able to enchant their followers to accept their leadership by gaining, through ethical means, the followers' consent to be led. Thus, leadership becomes an activity, an influence process, in which the project manager gains the trust and commitment of his or her staff and every project worker on the team, all without recourse to formal position or authority, to induce the organization to accomplish one or more tasks.

To be successful in the twenty-first-century, project managers must become enchanters. They must be able to get people excited; otherwise, they will lose them, especially when they don't see the manager often or at all because they are located overseas. People willingly sign up to serve under enchanters. Ask Steve Ballmer of Microsoft and Bill Gates's first generation of executive staff and consequently the whole company. At Microsoft people work long hours, under pressure, in a very challenging and competitive environment. Yet their loyalty and commitment to the company are unprecedented.

Another well-known example is Jack Welch, former CEO of General Electric (GE). Addressing GE's corporate officer, back in 1987, Welch commented that "the world of the 1990s and beyond will not belong to 'managers' or those who can make the numbers dance. The world will belong to passionate, driven leaders—people who not only have an enormous amount of energy but who can energize [enchant] those whom they lead."

The Reality Factor: Assessing Good Leadership

Successful changes in any project, ones that can really bring cohesiveness, depend on leadership excellence, not project management tools. Leadership is a vital catalyst for individual, team, and organizational success. With ePM, coleadership partners have a unique opportunity and an enormous responsibility to shape the future of their projects in a direction they want rather than be slaves to it.

One of the major traits of successful project leaders is the ability to create a climate of trust among their peers and the people reporting to them. Trusting relationships are vital in virtual teams because project leaders cannot be sure about anything more than a few months ahead. Thus, when these leaders ask the team to move ahead, they are actually saying that they

believe this is the right action to be taken but are not yet certain
how it will work out.

Consequently, those being led will be able to buy into it,
especially in a virtual environment, only if they trust their leaders. The following is a list of key behaviors and attributes successful project leaders display:

- **Putting the project staff's interests first**. Before you
  can win the trust of your followers, you must give them
  a reason to trust you. Thus, you must give before you
  can ask or receive. When followers can see that their
  leaders are aware of their needs and care for them, they
  commit. At this point, instead of hired hands, leaders
  have willing followers. If you are this kind of project
  leader you will get tremendous satisfaction from the
  success of your team, not from your success alone. In
  addition, as you care for your virtual team members and
  inspire them, they will tend to be more successful and
  have a stronger commitment to you, enhancing feelings
  of support and group cohesiveness. There is nothing
  more powerful than team players who volunteer their
  work and see the financial remuneration as a consequence of it. As a leader, if you are not an enchanter and
  do not lead by example, you are using people to further
  your own ends and will quickly be exposed.

  I once worked for a project manager who over a
  period of two years built a very effective team of IT
  education consultants. With the crash of the stock market in 1987 and the eventual closing of the company, he
  helped all the members of his team find new jobs even
  though his own future was uncertain.

- **Doing the talk and walking the walk.** It takes time for a virtual team to trust the leader. Although team members can act in the spirit of trusting the leader, only their behaviors and actions over time really attest to their character. Thus, it is very important that leaders keep their commitments and hold the team accountable as well. There will be times, however, when leaders or team players find themselves in situations were they feel that they have not kept their commitments. In this case, project leaders should be candid as early as possible about the reasons. As for judging their team members, coleadership is very beneficial, as project leaders may be in the best position to address, admonish, and counsel the team members, while the project manager (the leader with a capital L) works on helping the individual to recommit, to regain the vision, to re-engage … to be enchanted.

Acting as project manager at Virtual Access Networks, I was able to persuade a key member of our project team who already had a resignation letter in his hand to reconsider and stay. He not only decided to stay but became a key player in the group, with renewed vision and commitment. He willingly agreed to become one of the "samurais" (the identity we created for ourselves to distinguish us from the rest of the organization) in the R&D group in the development of a project called Unagi.

Therefore, project managers who embrace the role of leadership can continuously enchant only if they consistently live the message they preach and consider it a gift when someone points out inconsistencies in their role as leaders. Followers watch what you do or don't do, not what you say.

- **Being aware of people's feelings.** As was pointed out earlier, real motivation and commitment come from the heart, not from the head. That's why volunteers are powerful players. To reach your project workers' hearts you must care about their feelings. In bridging the knowledge gap within organizations you must be able to bridge the gap between the head and the heart of everyone in the project. Otherwise they may fail by about 13 inches: roughly the distance between the heart and the head.

  Don't underestimate the power of reaching for people's hearts, for being interested in what they do outside work, their families, their likes and dislikes, their fears, and their personal goals. This is definitely a win-win situation. Just as in the stock market, you must make consistent deposits into the hearts of everyone in your organization. This way, in times of green pastures and emotional commitment (emotional heart = profit) you will have fully committed professionals. But in times of hardship, whether caused by your mistakes as a leader, economic downturns, or scope creep and business realignment, their trust level will sustain disappointments, hardships, and even project failure.

  While I was the CEO of TechnoLogic, a systems integration (SI) company, in the late 1980s, we all were traversing hard times in the U.S. economy, in particular with the savings and loan scandals. I eventually had to realign the business and close down the SI activity of the company, but, my team remained more committed than I would have expected. A couple of them—my right arm, a Brazilian woman named Beatriz Salles and another Brazilian, Victor Murad—stood behind me all the way. They forfeited their salaries for more than a couple of months and at the end were willing to lend their own money to the organization.

At Virtual Access Networks, a start-up company, cash flow was precious, and at times we didn't have enough funds to cover all the trips associated with the project as we were finalizing it for launch at Comdex Fall 2000. Fortunately, friendship and concern for people paid off again as the project's chief architect, Vijay Gummadi, volunteered to take a salary cut to help the project organization finish the product and get it to Comdex. Not only that, but during business trips (he was based in Michigan and often came to Lawrence for project meetings) he stayed with friends to cut down on the cost of lodging and even shopped for cheaper gasoline for a rental car. There is no amount of money or other corporate perk that can buy this level of commitment. Because of project team members like Vijay we were able to finish the project on time, on budget, and successfully. The product worked and was awarded the Best Enterprise Product at Comdex, and six months later the company was acquired by Symantec.

- **Handling pressure and crises calmly.** Enthusiasm is an emotion every project staff should have, in particular the project manager. However, while fear and panic generally are understood in the project organization, its leaders should never convey it even if they are feeling it. Instead of running around like chickens without heads, leaders and coleaders should use their energy for thinking the situation through.

  When leaders must make quick and major decisions in a crisis, there is no time for enchantment, no time for thinking the situation through and preparing the organization. It is very hard to remain calm in situations like that. In those situations we should worry about crossing a bridge when we come to it, not before. Thus, in a crisis project leaders should support project managers by focusing on the action needed to relieve the situation and continue to move forward. One of the main challenges in bridging the knowledge gap in any project organization is worrying about tomorrow, trying to anticipate the outcomes of innovation (read: project). If one could anticipate the end result of an innovation, it would not be innovation but a reinvention.

- **Being honest and truthful.** Leaders must have integrity, which should be based on clear knowledge of their own values. They should be genuine in their discussions with their teams, especially in hard times and uncomfortable situations.

  Project organizations often are derailed by a betrayal of trust. The lack of honesty among senior project staff, deceit, and dissension are the cardinal sins of leadership and management. When reality does not match expectations, leadership is faced with a number of disappointments and disillusionment.

- **Not taking personal credit for other people's work.** If leaders want to lose the trust of team members and the organization, they should take credit they do not deserve. Credit must go where credit is due. Nonetheless, in virtual project organizations, collaboration and teamwork are more than ever a necessity. Effective leaders will work as a team and be level with the team. They should have a hands-off approach, leading from within or behind as much as from the front. Recognition should come from the success of the team and the growth of the individuals in it.

Acting as the CTO at Virtual Access Networks, I was responsible for the research group and innovations in the area of virtual access technologies and wireless. However, as a group, we were pretty flat. We used to call ourselves musketeers and use the motto "One for all and all for one." But since that group was hooked on sushi, we decided to call ourselves samurais. As a group, we all worked together, trying to build on our strengths and overcome our weaknesses.

- **Always being fair.** To be effective enchanters, project managers must always be fair, not exhibiting personal favoritism or inconsistent behavior or relying on status or perks. Leaders must also make sure to stick with the code of ethics and best practices of the company.

Watch for your own biased opinions. In Wonderland it is very easy to believe in whatever we want to (the sacred cow concept). Thus, look for feedback. In my case, once a month or so I take my project staff for sushi, and we go around the table asking each other how can we better serve each other both at the professional level with the project's Gantt chart on hand and on the personal level so that we can continue to grow in our friendship. It has paid off, and we have been able to under-promise and overdeliver in our projects, often coming in two weeks ahead of schedule and always delivering more than was expected.

I am proud of that group of samurais because we have managed to earn such high accolades despite the fact that each one of us is from a different nation and culture. Vijay Gummadi is from India, Thavoring Heng is French and Japanese, Rick Castello is American, and I am Brazilian. As individuals and professionals we are many, but in project execution under a chief enchanter we were one.

DEVELOPING A REALISTIC PROJECT PLAN

Every hour invested in developing a realistic project plan will result in several hours avoided in reworking the deliverable. Hence, an experienced project manager with an in-depth knowledge of the technology and the ability to listen, communicate, and guide the project team is invaluable.

A project leader should ask, What makes up a good project plan? Appropriate answers would be qualified individuals, commitment from team members, and communication among players. These are the foundation of any group activity.

Narrowing the focus a little further, what makes a successful project given a good team? Appropriate answers would be clearly defined goals, access to resources, and a supportive environment.

Finally, let's factor in the virtual qualifier. How does this change what is required of the team and the project? The answer here is that it changes none of the requirements. It does, however, make the requirements more difficult to arrive at because of reduced communication channels. The technologies made available in the last five years merely add broadband to narrow channels. This broadband not only increases the amount of data that can be transferred but improves the richness of communication.

You should be aware, however, that virtual behaviors are influenced by

1. The nature of the work
2. Management of critical supporting work processes
3. Organizational context
4. Geographic context

5. Communications support

6. Other environmental contextual factors

7. Individual characteristics.

In the end, you will find that the best colocated teams use principles incorporated by the most successful virtual teams: a clear purpose, a focus on people, and concentration on the links that connect them.

A realistic and successful virtual project team is successful because it emphasizes the necessary components of project teams. The introduction of the virtual world may be beneficial because it demands that the e-project manager, throughout this chapter characterized as the leader, and the project workers take a step back and ask themselves, With this new twist on project teams, what is required of my group and me? It requires an absolute commitment to project management methodologies. Virtual project teams are successful because the leaders and members put forth the extra effort to overcome communication barriers.

CASE STUDY 1: DEFINING A PROJECT— THE COMPRESSOR TESTER SYSTEM

Marcus Goncalves

At an air-conditioning company a research engineer developed specialized automated test equipment for the company's internal use. One strategic objective of the company was to reduce the number of incorrect warranty returns of compressors. That objective evolved as the company realized that the number of compressors returned under the warranty was growing every day.

Furthermore, when the compressors were cut apart for inspection, many were found to be in good working order.

What had caused the air conditioners to require service had been incorrectly diagnosed as the compressor. A good compressor was replaced and returned for warranty credit while the fault that had initiated the problem remained unsolved. The company had no easy way to check out the compressor upon its receipt from the field and routinely cut apart each returned compressor for failure analysis. After a compressor was cut apart, it became apparent after inspection that it was in good working order.

To address this strategic objective, a project was initiated to develop a computerized compressor tester system. The system specifications called for the completion of tests on returned compressors in five minutes. With this tester in place, returned compressors could be verified quickly and warranty credit could be denied without having to cut the compressor apart.

An aggressive $200,000 was defined to develop and manufacture four of the testers, locating one at each of the company's independently owned and operated remanufacturing centers. The project was long and difficult but technically a success. A compressor tester system was developed that would evaluate the compressors in under five minutes, and four of them were assembled, delivered, and installed at the remanufacturers' locations.

Unfortunately, the remanufacturers had not been included in the project discussions and were not happy about their installation and use. They felt that the level of warranty returns was not their problem and were unwilling to invest time, effort, and space in resolving this issue. Each remanufacturer demanded additional money for storage, use, and maintenance of the compressor tester system. The amount of money requested by the remanufacturers was excessive and was greater than the amount of loss the company felt it was incurring from the invalid warranty returns. Unfortunately, the compressor tester systems were never used by the remanufacturers and were eventually shipped back to the main plant and placed in a warehouse.

Discussion Questions

1. In this case the strategic objectives were not attained. Why?
2. What could have been done differently so that the strategic objectives could have been attained?
3. In determining strategic objectives, three general types of information must be gathered before starting to define a problem: (a) technical, (b) market and application, and (c) financial data. Which area(s) did the management team fail to gather data from? Explain.

❧ CASE STUDY 2: ePM GUIDE—GENERAL ROLES AND RESPONSIBILITIES

Marcus Goncalves

The project organization structure supports the completion of project activities and provides an adequate level of oversight, review, and contribution from the necessary parties. Clearly defining the project organization structure up front is a critical success factor for projects.

Your project may not require a separate individual to fulfill each of these roles, but it is important that the tasks and responsibilities associated with each role be clearly assigned to specific project team members, especially in the ePM scenario, where you may never see that project worker. For example, in a smaller project the project manager may also fulfill some of the project team member activities. With ePM, it is critical that a dedicated project manager with no other responsibilities be identified and assigned to the team.

The roles and responsibilities outlined below provide a baseline from which your organization can develop specific and tailored definitions. Your ePM plan documents the roles and responsibilities specific to your project.

Role	Description and Responsibilities
Organizational executive committee	Oversee all project activities from the organizational point of view. The committee establishes priorities for project funding and resource allocation; it allocates the available budget to defined projects.
Project sponsor (PS)	Responsible for ensuring that the organization understands the value and importance of the project and ultimately for realizing the benefits predicted for the project. The project sponsor is typically a senior officer in the organization responsible for the business function that the project will support. The project sponsor should have a major say in the release of funds after a review.
End user (user)	Business clients represent the final end user or beneficiary of the project deliverables and/or objectives. They play an important role in defining project requirements and ensuring that delivered features meet their business requirements.
Business area project manager (BPM)	When a project is sufficiently large, a business area project manager may be appointed to manage the day-to-day operations of the project activities within the business area.
Project leader (PL)	Has overall responsibility for the project and is accountable for all external and internal aspects of it. The project leader is typically a senior officer of the organization or company.
Project manager (PM)	Has specific accountability for achieving all the defined project objectives within the time and resources allocated. The project manager performs the day-to-day management of the project. One or more assistant project managers with the same responsibilities for specific portions of the project may support the overall project manager without diluting his or her responsibility. Project managers should have demonstrated knowledge, skills, and experience commensurate with the size, complexity, and risk of the project. Since different levels of competency are required for different levels of project management and project size, the project manager's role is divided into three proficiency levels. Depending on the size, complexity, and risk of the project, more than one level of project manager may share the responsibility for managing the project. *(Continued)*

Role	Description and Responsibilities *(Continued)*
Project team member (PTM)	Core team project team members include architect; software, hardware, and mechanical engineers; and tester or writer assigned to a project. Responsible for completing project tasks, providing input to plans, and providing status.
Quality assurance (QA)	Responsible for quality assurance activities.
Configuration management (CM)	Responsible for configuration management activities.
Independent validation test (IVT) team	Plans and performs independent validation testing and approves the system or software product before acceptance testing can begin.
Contract authority (CA)	Provides project-specific procurement services, supports the project in accordance with any existing legislation or general arrangements, ensures the legal soundness of contracts, and maintains the industry and government standards of prudence, probity, and equity when dealing with the private or public sector.

Discussion Questions

1. What is the main difference between the project sponsor and the project leader? Explain.

2. The General Electric Company was shocked to learn in 1984 that almost two dozen employees were implicated in the theft of turbine trade secrets. Based on the organizational structure outlined above, what actions or defense programs might a firm institute to reduce the likelihood of this happening?

◼ CASE STUDY 3: THE PROJECT-BASED ORGANIZATION— ORGANIZATIONAL CHANGE AND CUSTOMER FOCUS

Marcus Goncalves

We hear these words all the time, particularly among professional organizations facing increasingly competitive environments. Yet when you get beyond the talk and the meetings, the organization often is not focusing on its customers and their needs.

The focus is still on the management hierarchy, bureaucratic procedures, and interdepartmental politics. In my book *The Knowledge Tornado*, I dedicate almost half a chapter to discussing how PowerPoint presentations can become "powerless" in these environments. They talk the talk and fill out new forms to track cycle time and quality levels. However, the talk and the paperwork do not change the organization's focus or increase the attention paid to delivering what the customer wants.

Becoming a project-based organization is not only a matter of becoming more organized and effective but above all an engineering economy matter. Any engineering project must be not only physically realizable but also economically affordable. For example, a child's tricycle can be built with an aluminum frame or a composite frame. Some engineers may argue that because the composite frame will be stronger and lighter, it is a better choice. However there is not much of a market for a thousand dollar tricycle. Thus, developing a stronger emphasis on customer focus not only requires a change in the organization's culture but can save a lot of money and prevent project failures. But how do you measure a project success, by finishing it on time or by achieving the desired ROI?

The example above should convince you that it is not enough to become a project-based organization. Several changes also must take place in the organization. To say the least, we need to change the reward systems, the rituals for bestowing them, and the criteria used to identify heroes and heroines.

An organizationwide approach to project management

can drive this change effort through cross-functional projects aimed at better meeting customers' needs. An emphasis on cross-functional projects diminishes the orientation toward hierarchy and procedure and strengthens cross-functional orientation. It aims project teams at delivering measured results to the customer. The project-based management (PbM) approach changes the way the organization uses projects; it makes project management a tool both for getting things done and for changing the organization. However, aligning projects with organizations and leaders can be a challenge.

Aligning Projects with Organizations

Often a project is defined in an organization and then handed out to another organization where the PM does not have to transfer people from their "real" jobs. Instead, the PM selects the people he needs and "owns" the time for which he has contracted. The PM evaluates the people on the project team, and that evaluation affects their compensation and promotions. The project team is an organizational entity with its own budget, staff, and performance criteria. This entity cuts across departmental lines. People commit to the project success measure because it is worthy of commitment and because their pay will be affected by the project's success.

Aligning Projects with Different Kinds of Managers

The project manager assigned to a project may not be a technical expert in mechanical engineering, training, or customer service. The PM should be an expert at running cross-functional projects. She takes her assigned measure of success and breaks it down into smaller achievements, which she then assigns to teams or individuals.

For instance, a training department should not only conduct classes. Its assignment should be to teach the customer service reps to diagnose a customer's problem in the first 15 seconds of a conversation. The PM might assess the training department's performance by testing the reps after the course. The information systems department of a power plant does not just write software for accessing customer history. Its assignment is to give the reps access to the relevant portion of a customer's history in 20 seconds.

The PM controls the scope, budget, and duration by evaluating each change request from the perspective of whether the change contributes to reaching the assigned achievement.

The Project-Based Organization Is Different

Over time, this approach changes an organization. The hierarchy and bureaucracy become weaker. Career success depends on the results of the projects on which one work, not just time in a position or politics. The organization develops executives who manage projects. They are not necessarily technical experts; they are experts in running many different kinds of projects. Finally, the organization becomes more agile, able to respond to changing customer needs.

Discussion Questions

1. Explain the difference between a project-based organization and a non-project-based organization.
2. Describe two projects in your organization or elsewhere that could benefit from a structured project management approach. Explain why.
3. Identify a project that is risk-free. Explain why this project is not subject to risk.

4. Why do different kinds of managers affect the management of a project?

5. Identify a project with which you are familiar and describe its life cycle phases and 5 to 10 of the most important activities.

5

C H A P T E R

Techniques for Keeping
an E-Project on Course

To be successful in today's competitive business world, ePM managers must deliver results on time and within budget. If you apply the process, tools, and techniques outlined in the Project Management Institute's (PMI's) PMBOK while using common sense, wit, and a bit of enchanting in your communication area, you should be very successful in this task. However, you take those skills sets and couple them with the ePM techniques discussed throughout this book, you will maximize performance and ensure optimum results every time.

This chapter equips you with the know-how to lead and keep an e-project large or small, on course to a successful conclusion. From starting a project effectively to motivating your virtual teams and overcoming problems despite distance and often time zone chasms, every aspect of ePM is clearly explained.

REVIEWING THE PLAN AND HANDLING UNCERTAINTY

Keeping a project on schedule and within budget is neither rocket science nor black magic. It does require a good project management team, good designs, good market conditions, good labor relations, low inflation rates, the ability to control changes, the appropriate use of management tools, and of course keeping the virtual teams connected, engaged, motivated, and efficient.

Obviously, we have more control over some of those factors than we do over others, especially when managing virtual projects. We can't do much about the high price of wireless services in the United States, the lack of widespread broadband infrastructure throughout the world, or the rate of inflation. But by far the most critical factors in managing virtual projects are good rapport and cohesive virtual teamwork among all the workers and organizations involved in the project and the technology that enables such interaction and collaboration.

At MGCG, much of our success in keeping virtual projects on course and within budget has come from the working relationship between the company, the contractors, the partners, and all the virtual team members regardless of their location, level of involvement with a project, and cultural background. This relationship has allowed us, as a cohesive group, to carry out our project obligations cost-effectively and cost-efficiently. Together, these virtual workers have formed a very effective and dedicated team that is determined to adhere to the schedule and budget commitments.

For instance, as I write these pages, I am managing a virtual project in Brazil, overseeing a virtual team of 15 people in three different states in that country. I just received an e-mail from the project leader there, letting me know they decided to change the location of one of our offices to another area in town so that they could realize a savings of 30 percent on operation expenses. The e-mail said I'd receive another e-mail later with the new address and phone numbers.

I had no idea the team members were looking for ways to save the project money or that one location was better suited than another. I also was not consulted to help them decide when the transition should happen. After all, we'll have to change the contact information on our website for that team in Brazil. What amazes me the most is that looking after operation expenses is not in the job description of any of them. They don't get paid to worry about that and don't even get a bonus for realizing such savings. But clearly, they care for the project and the team and would rather have that 30 percent savings as a contingency fund, as an overall performance indicator. Best of all, the team members are very independent out there, know they have the latitude to spend our money and submit their reimbursement forms at the end of the month, and know we trust them. That shows as we allow them to make this level of decision.

Setting Project Milestones and Anticipating Risk

One of the best strategies for keeping ePM on course is to make sure you clearly define your baselines for scope, cost, and schedule. Also, make sure to present those baselines to your virtual teams, along with the management plan, a matrix structured organization breakdown structure (OBS). As part of the kick-off virtual meeting (I find that you don't have to fly everyone to an island in the Caribbean to have this initial meeting; that can be done after the project), make sure to present the project budget and schedule baselines with clear stipulations as to when the project must be completed and at what estimated cost.

You don't have to go into too much detail on the cost structure, but I recommend presenting a costing structure, such as the apportioned method, per major deliverable (Figure 5–1), so that the whole virtual team has a chance to comment on it. Even if their comments do not in the end, affect the cost structure, this will show that you value their opinions and trust them. An alternative for delivering these types of presentations is technologies such as Webex (www.webex.com), where everyone can dial a toll-free phone number and be part of a conference call while going to Webex's website and watching a PowerPoint presentation. The technology allows conference participants to ask questions, comment on the presentation, make notations to it, and even run a demo of a particular application if necessary.

Figure 5–2 shows that the Webex technology provides a working area for your presentations, allowing you to create tabs such as information, annual report, and sales forecast. It

FIGURE 5–1

The apportioned method of allocating project costs.

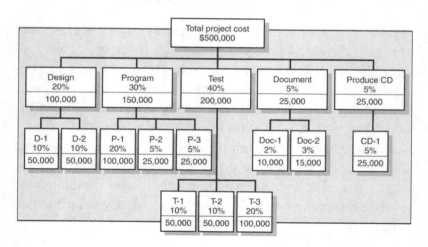

FIGURE   5 – 2

Webex technology provides a working area for presentations and
allows you to create tabs such as information, annual report, and sales
forecast.

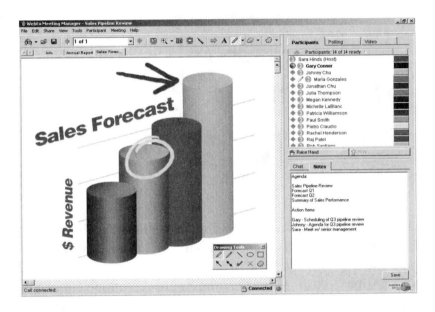

also has an area where you, as moderator, can view everyone
participating in the meeting. You have the option to "raise your
hand" to have an opportunity to speak and can also mute the
system so that you can have side conversations without everyone listening in. There are other products similar to Webex. I
suggest you evaluate them and consider adopting one of them
for your meetings.

You can also use Microsoft NetMeeting, (Figure 5–3).
This solution provides Windows real-time collaboration and
conferencing, which comes equipped with a Web phone, as
well as a tool for corporate productivity. NetMeeting delivers a
complete Internet conferencing solution for all Windows users

FIGURE 5-3

Microsoft NetMeeting provides real-time collaboration and conferencing, which comes equipped with a Web phone as well as a tool for corporate productivity.

with multipoint data conferencing, text chat, whiteboard, and file transfer as well as point-to-point audio and video. Companies such as Boeing, Dow Chemical, Ford Motor Company, and Northrup Grumman are adopting this solution. This alternative makes a lot of sense if you area a running Microsoft Office suite and operating system at your organization. The application comes bundled with Windows 2000 and above.

No matter how you choose to deliver this initial presentation, make sure to convey to the group that these baselines constitute the project commitment to sponsors and customers. Also make sure the team is committed to achieving them.

Throughout the life of the project you must be able to track those commitments by means of periodic (and even automated) reviews. I also recommend that you have informal meetings with your project leaders over the phone or even by instant messaging (IM). I typically discourage mandatory weekly meetings, typical with the conventional project management (PM) approach, for the same reasons I give virtual workers the latitude to make decisions and have their own initiatives: I trust that they are doing their work, and so I don't need to check on them, and I trust that if there is an issue, they will bring it to my attention.

As I write these lines, Fabian, my chief architect in Argentina, just popped up in my IM (make sure you have an unique ID for your project and another for the rest of the world: wife, kids, etc.) to let me know we have a problem and need to talk on the phone. This is a great way to avoid unnecessary international calling expenses. We always IM each other, via the computer or the cellular phone, trying to find out when we can talk and what the issues are so that when we actually talk, we are prepared for it, with all the necessary documents in front of us, and have had a chance to think about the issue at hand. We have not talked for about 10 days, and the project we're working on is ahead of schedule, but it seems we have a little problem.

I believe that treating the whole virtual group as an army platoon, committed to each other and with the philosophy that "no one is left behind (or in the dark)," has enabled them to have a great commitment to the baseline, have the ability to make timely decisions, and be willing to take corrective actions when they are called for, which has always kept the project within budget and on schedule.

Another important factor in keeping our virtual projects on time is the culture we have of building only what is necessary and avoiding "gold-plated" solutions. The change in office locations in Brazil is a good example. Your virtual teams should be aware that the original project design tends to be very realistic but that design changes are almost always required to resolve unforeseen problems. Especially with virtual teams, you need to give people the latitude to look for ways to optimize their tasks and ultimately the project. Thus, providing the whole team with an online capability maturity model integration (CMMI) primer is a tremendous investment.

We begin training our teams on basic CMMI practices even before a kick-off meeting for a new project, as soon as we select the team. Not only do we prepare them to be critical participants in these kick-off meetings, we also use the event to deploy our team-forming practices. For example, another project in Brazil called for partnership with a major petroleum company to build an office facility as fast as possible so that the company could begin staffing the offices and have us train its workers on project management fundamentals. Our role in the construction phase was only in management consulting, but our project leader in Brazil made the effort to review the project plan, survey the land where the building was going to be constructed, forecast the weather conditions for the next few months, and anticipate some delays and extra expenses for that portion of the project.

He decided to contact a local real estate company there and find out if there were any industrial buildings available for sale as an alternative to constructing the building. What he found was a struggling four-star six-story hotel building only a few miles from the planned construction site. After some negotiation, we recommended that the company purchase the hotel, convert the first five stories of guest rooms into offices, and keep the upper two guest rooms for visitors. Making this change allowed the project to capture savings in construction and maintenance costs, energy consumption, and water use, but mainly it saved the client a lot of time. Experience counts, so hire few but hire the best.

Before we discuss risk management and ways to handle uncertainty, let me make a few remarks. Managing virtual projects can be exciting but also frustrating. Therefore, make sure to be flexible at all times and learn to accept the inevitability of change. Of course, you can and should always hope for the best, but you should always plan for the worst as well.

In a rapidly changing business environment the ability to think ahead and anticipate changes can make the difference between keeping a project on course and achieving project objectives and failing to do so. You must be prepared to change your plans in a flexible and responsive way. Despite the best planning, gaps always emerge between the model and the reality of most projects. Often, when unexpected problems arise during ePM operations, quick thinking and a pragmatic approach are the tools one needs to bridge the gap. Developing alternatives and being pragmatic will help you counteract the time zone limitations and inability to bring virtual teams together in a short period of time.

Best of all, keep it simple! The unknowns of project work often require immediate response, but high-performance results don't necessarily require high-tech solutions. Quick, simple, and inexpensive fixes are sometimes the way to keep a virtual project on schedule and within budget.

Assessing Constraints and Handling Uncertainty

In my opinion, all current project risk management processes induce a restricted focus on the management of project uncertainty, especially with regard to virtual project management, because the term *risk* encourages a threat perspective. That's why I chose to address the issue from the view of *uncertainty* rather than risk, as I believe this can enhance project risk management in terms of designing desirable outcomes and planning how to achieve them.

Current comprehensive project risk management processes are compatible with a focus on uncertainty, but I believe they require some adjustment to reflect a more helpful uncertainty management paradigm.

Every virtual project faces a lot more constraints and uncertainties than do conventional projects, which focus on predictability instead of adaptation. But uncertainty and the need to manage it are inherent in all projects.

One of the basic strategies to mitigate uncertainty is to begin the process from the earliest *conception* stage to the final *support* stage of the project life cycle, clarifying what is to be done and ensuring that it gets done. Sometimes the implications of uncertainty are threats in the sense of *potential adverse effects*; at other times uncertainty implies an *opportunity* in the sense of *potential welcome effects*, as in the case of the petroleum company's project in Brazil. Effective risk management aims to improve project performance by helping to manage both threats, (downside risks) and opportunities (upside risks) in line with the Project Management Institute's (PMI's) *PMBOK Guide*, which refers to uncertainty as an event or condition that, if it occurs, has a positive or negative effect on a project objective.[1]

You can't predict the future, but accurately gauging the degree of uncertainty inherent in a project can help you adapt to it quickly. As you already know, virtual project management tends to bring a lot more uncertainty and constraints owing to the fact that team members may be in locations within the country or overseas where you have no control over the environment.

For instance, one of my major uncertainties in executing projects in South America is the inflation rate. In the United States, if you forecast 6 percent inflation in your project budget, it should be plenty. However, there were times in Brazil when inflation was as high as 35 percent a month! In Argentina, multiple changes in the federal government often bring changes in the economy, and this affects our projects.

There is no way I can account for all the constraints on operating in those regions. I do account for some as a result of best practices and the fact that I pull in virtual teams in the region for assistance during the planning phase. But having a clear understanding that certain constraints may render a project infeasible allows me to make sure that virtual team members understand the constraints in advance and are able to work within them.

You can overcome most constraints by planning ways to get around them. Just make sure to face up to constraints in a logical fashion and find shortcuts to success. For the most part, I find that constraints are often related to resources. Here is a five-step approach I typically use:

1. Assess whether time is of the essence.
2. Analyze what resources you will need and whether you can afford them.
3. Look into using existing processes or resources.
4. Identify any external constraints, such as legal or environmental regulations. This can be very tricky when project operations are conducted overseas. In this case, don't try to mitigate them yourself; hire a local law firm to do any necessary research and represent you.
5. Decide whether to proceed within the given constraint.

With ePM, foreseen uncertainties become identifiable and understood influences that the virtual team cannot be sure will occur. Unlike variation, which comes from combined small influences, foreseen uncertainty is distinct and may require full-blown risk management with several alternative plans. In the pharmaceutical industry, for example, the development of a new drug is a perfect example of foreseen uncertainty. The whole development process is geared toward detecting and managing risks, primarily in the form of side effects. Scientists developing a new drug may be able to anticipate possible side effects that have appeared previously in related drugs. Based on that information, they may be able to outline contingency plans to change the prescribed dosage or restrict usage to certain indications or well-controlled circumstances. The side effect is the foreseen uncertainty. The contingency plan may never be used, but it is there if the side effect occurs.

E-PROJECT CONTROLS

Small projects have all the same problems as large ones, with two substantial differences. First, they have fewer resources available to resolve those problems. Second, there is less time to seek a solution. In many ways the need for an easy but effective control system is greater on a small project than on a large one and is much greater on projects that are managed virtually.

Without effective progress and performance measurement it is impossible to determine current and future project status accurately. Effective implementation of an e-project control program on any virtual project requires experienced, highly specialized professionals in the areas of planning, estimating, scheduling, cost control, and overall integration.

When performing e-project control processes you must develop a graded approach to the project, (Figure 5–4) to ensure that project control is commensurate with the project's cost, schedule, and technical risk.

FIGURE 5–4

A graded approach to project control processes is essential to e-project management.

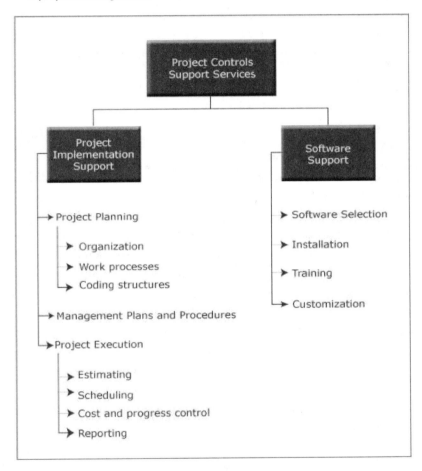

Tracking Progress

Keeping control of e-projects involves carefully managing the plan to keep it moving forward smoothly. Effective monitoring allows you to gather information so that you can measure and adjust progress toward the project's goal. It enables you to communicate project progress and changes to virtual team members, stakeholders, superiors, and customers and gives you the justification for making necessary adjustments to the plan. It also enables you to measure current progress against what was set out in the original plan. Throughout this process,

- Never relax control, even when all is going to plan.
- Ask the team for ideas on speeding up progress.
- Keep comparing current schedules and budgets with the original plan.

In addition, external suppliers can be a threat, especially when they are far away, since you do not have direct control over their resources; this is typical in virtual project management. Remember to monitor their progress, too. Make them feel part of the team by inviting them to meetings and informal gatherings. If these suppliers are based overseas, make sure to motivate your virtual teams to host the gatherings and get to know them. This will help you and your virtual team members track their progress throughout their involvement in the project rather than only when they are due to deliver.

The use of periodic reports is very important as well. In the next section we will discuss the technological aspects of keeping projects in check, but for now make sure that anyone responsible for an activity or milestone reports on his or her progress. Encourage the virtual team to take reports seriously and submit them on time. How good can a full-fledged deployment of Microsoft EPM be if not every member of the team who is supposed to use the system doesn't?

Reports should account for

- The current state of the project
- Achievements since the last report

- Potential problems
- Opportunities for milestones
- Threats to milestones

As an ePM manager, you should review the reports and summarize the current status of the project to the sponsor and stakeholders.

Once you gauge the importance of the issues reported, I recommend that you use a red, amber, and green status system to draw up a review meeting agenda so that the most urgent items, those with red status, take priority. Microsoft EPM (Figure 5–5) is excellent for that purpose. Note that the application allows you to gauge the project within the system, enabling you to print status reports or have them online when meeting through a webcasting session.

FIGURE 5–5

Microsoft EPM allows you to gauge the project within the system, enabling you to print the reports.

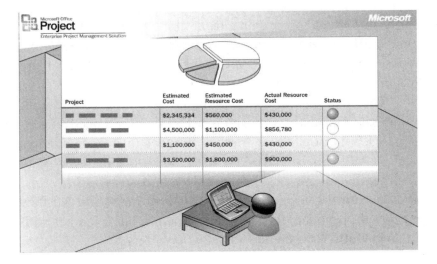

How Much Planning and Control Is Enough?

When thinking about how much planning and control is enough, think about how often you will need progress reports and review meetings. You may require weekly or even daily reports, depending on the harm a problem can do to the project if it is not detected and reported.

Regular online webcasting or teleconference review meetings provide an opportunity to resolve issues, discuss progress, and review performance. But as was pointed out earlier, with ePM you may want to meet only when there is a need to meet; after all, your virtual teams are on their own anyway. This is not to say that local project leaders should not have regular meetings with their teams; they should. Of course, only you will be able to decide how much control is enough. On very complex projects you may want to meet on a weekly or monthly basis.

In ePM, your major focus is to coach from afar, over the wires. Let the local project leaders be the supervisors. You should be more concerned about how you can create peak performance from a distance. Goals and measurements are especially important in coaching from afar. In ePM, metrics are almost like a virtual project manager that keeps everyone focused on the most important priorities. They are always there whether the coach is physically present or not.

The effort lies in determining, communicating, and reinforcing performance goals and metrics. You don't need a meeting to learn about those metrics. Project management tools such as MS Project EPM do a very good job (Figure 5–6), by centralizing all metrics in a single database repository and allowing virtual access to all virtual team members. All they need to do is update their task information. You even get notified via Outlook when new updates come in.

FIGURE 5-6

Microsoft Project EPM makes it easy to update and disseminate information about a virtual team's progress.

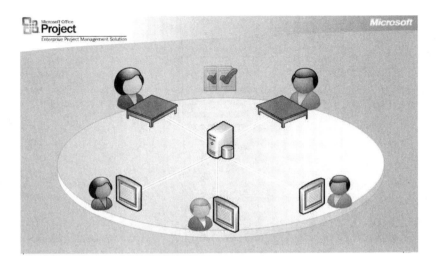

In addition, as illustrated in Figure 5–7, Microsoft Project EPM can send you alerts about any specific threshold that is broken, such as a particular task experiencing a cost overrun or schedule delay. By relying on technologies such as these you can concentrate on coaching your virtual teams, which consumes a significant amount of time. As virtual project members take on increasingly complex tasks and the decision making and problem solving associated with working remotely, this function becomes an even greater necessity.

I have found that Socratic coaching works very well with virtual teams. It is an excellent tool for checking the metrics of your teams while indirectly checking your team members' performance metrics. The key to the Socratic coaching method is to induce people to think about their tasks, their jobs, and consequently the results of their actions or nonactions. Typical

FIGURE 5-7

Microsoft Project EPM can alert project managers and virtual members to important data changes in a project.

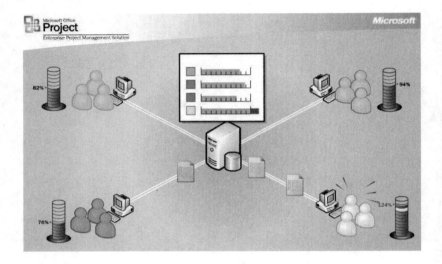

questions would include the following (avoid at all cost yes/no questions, which usually inhibit the thinking process; you want thinking and analysis to be exercised):

- How will you know if you are successful when you finish task A, or B, or C?
- How will you measure progress?
- What information will you need?
- What are the priorities?
- How will you work with other team members on this?
- What process and/or tool will you use?
- How will this affect quality?
- How can I help?
- What went well in this project or activity?

- How much will this cost?
- What will be the impact on the budget?

Finally, keep in mind that review meetings typically are held throughout the life of a project to discuss progress and achievements and mark milestones. You should run these meetings effectively to encourage teamwork and provide everyone involved with an accurate picture of how the project is faring. You can conduct these meetings via satellite (videoconferencing) or over the Internet, through webcasting. The important point is to have as much interaction with the virtual team as possible.

You should also take advantage of program evaluation review technique (PERT) and critical path methods (CPM) analysis in your effort to keep e-projects on course. These analyses are even more vital for ePM, as you don't have the flexibility of managing by walking around and directly questioning project leaders and key personnel that you have with conventional project management.

SETTING UP A VIRTUAL PROJECT MANAGEMENT OFFICE

At MGCG, we have been using ePM for years, and along the way, through trial and error, we have devised what we call *effective infotech for virtual teams.* Our main goal in the process, every time we plan to start a new virtual project, is to enable our virtual teams to accomplish five basic tasks. Everything else they can accomplish is considered high-ROI. These tasks are to

1. Develop effective virtual teams (workgroup)
2. Be able to get all the data they need (workflow)
3. Share their learnings and best practices, locally and remotely, with other virtual teams (collaboration)

4. Facilitate technology transfer (KM)

5. Reduce cycle time with repetitive and optimal processes (basic and informal CMMI)

Training is also very important but is not classified as a task for the virtual team. Getting the right technology is only 10 percent of the solution. You have to get people trained in using the technology.

Cutting-edge technology won't necessarily provide the best ROI. More important than the latest technology, success in establishing a virtual project management office (ePMO) resides in how these technologies are used.

Selecting and Evaluating Products and Services for ePM

For virtual team members to work effectively from their remote offices or homes they need to have the appropriate equipment. Although the specific type of hardware (desktop, laptop, table PC, etc.) and communication medium (dial-ups, DSL, cable modem, satellite, wireless, T1, ISDN, etc.) will vary from business to business, location to location and country to country, there are some basic recommendations that are appropriate for the vast majority of virtual offices.

Of course, providing you with a very specific configuration on hardware, communications, and software would be a waste of our time, as these technologies change so fast that by the time this book is published and you read it, my recommendations would be obsolete. Therefore, Table 5–1 provides a general overview of the technologies you should consider for the ePMO, the ePM manager, the remote users, and the remote branches of your firm or business.

Figure 5–8 provides some criteria you should keep in mind while evaluating products and services for a virtual team

TABLE 5-1

The Essential (Minimum Requirement) Technologies for a Virtual Project Management Operation

ePMO	ePM Manager	Remote User	Remote Branches
• LAN	PC with	Laptop/Tablet PC with	• Internet
• Printer(s)	• E-mail	• E-fax/fax	• Extranet
• Server(s)	• IM	• E-mail	• Intranet
• Fax/e-fax	• Software (productivity)	• Software (productivity)	
• Teleconference equipment	• Antivirus software/ personal firewall	• Antivirus software	
• Internet connection	• Internet access	• Personal firewall	
• Broadband connection	• Intranet access	• Internet access	
• Firewall	• Extranet access	• Extranet access	
• Antivirus software	• Webcam for videoconferencing	• Intranet access	
• Videoconferencing equipment		• Cell phone with voice mail, Web access, GSM/GPRS (for international)	
		• Portable printer	
		• PDA with Internet access (via cell phone or embedded)	

or a globally dispersed project. Note that the criteria for functionality and stability are indicated differently because they are common criteria for every software and system; the majority are oriented toward the needs of virtual teams and distributed projects. The branches with book symbols are the ones discussed below; the ones without it are self-explanatory. Keep in mind that these examples and branches are very dynamic and need constant updates.

FIGURE 5-8

Criteria for evaluating products and services for virtual teams or globally dispersed projects.

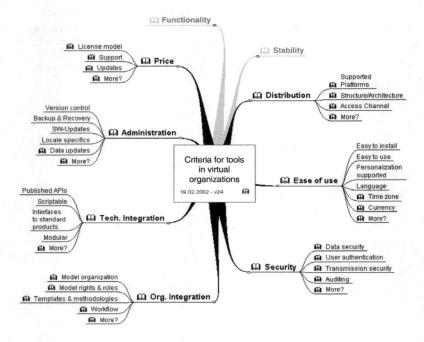

Price

Many virtual project managers make the mistake of miscalculating the cost of supporting virtual teams. The total cost of a product or service is determined not only by the monthly rent or the cost of the product. It also consists of other factors, such as yearly support fees and update fees. This may not seem different from normal price reflections, but virtual project teams (and their organizations) may change more often than conventional ones do. How does the cost model of the vendor help there? Is it flexible enough for you? Factors you should pay special attention to include the following:

- **License model.** The license model is important since certain types of virtual project organizations may have a high fluctuation rate. Therefore, the license model should offer you some flexibility. Today most software license models tend to be rigid: You order a set of licenses and have to pay for them whether they are used or not. In a conventional organization with not too much fluctuation this may be manageable. In virtual organizations it may be too inflexible. Here are some strategies to try:
  - Would your vendor allow you to add licenses for a peak period only, for instance, 150 licenses for three months?
  - Would your vendor accept back surplus licenses?
  - Is there a way to measure the real license usage and pay only that amount?
  - Can you have different license models per location (e.g., per country)?
  - Can licenses easily be moved and reassigned between locations in different countries, servers, and so on?

- **Support.** Some questions you need to answer include the following:
  - How is the support handled and priced?
  - Can the vendor support all your locations, or do you have to use third-party support with additional costs?
  - Does the vendor support cover the user's native languages (idioms) and different time zones?

- **Updates.** Does the update policy include all required versions (language, hardware, and operating system)? Virtual project organizations tend to have different equipment across locations, and the language needs may vary.

Administration

Administering a virtual system that is installed in different locations with different hardware and software configurations can be a difficult task. Here is more Socratic coaching for you:

- How does software help you with this issue?
- Are important mechanisms such as version control and backup and recovery provided, or do you have to find your own solution?
- How can software and data updates be executed?
- How can location- or culture-specific features be administered?

Factors you should pay special attention to include

- Version control
- Backup and recovery
- Software updates
- Locale specifics
- Data updates: Do you think it is easy to update data that change often? Examples could be exchange rates or cross-border cost calculations, tax rates, and contractor rates.

Technical Integration

In a networked world systems must be able to integrate with other systems, including your customers', your suppliers', and your own systems. What kind of integration is possible? Does your supplier have preconfigured interfaces to popular systems such as enterprise resource planning (ERP), customer relationship management (CRM), and product life cycle management

(PLM)? Are the supplier's application program interfaces (APIs) published so that you can write a custom solution if necessary?

Whatever system you adopt, make sure it has scripting (customized coding) features, as they may help your users to adapt the system to their specific needs. Thus, a few questions to ask are as follows:

- Is the system modular or monolithic?
- Do you have to deploy it at once, or is it possible to introduce the software module by module, as needed? The latter may help if you are replacing an existing system and your deadlines are near.

Other factors to watch for include

- **Published APIs.** Make sure you have access to the applications APIs.
- **Scriptable.** Make sure you can customize and/or modify the product if necessary.
- **Interfaces to standard products.** Make sure the product has common interfaces to standard products such as e-mails and productivity tools.
- **Modular.** If the system is not modular, you may have a major undertaking in implementing it up-front.

Virtual Organization Integration

One important question when you are focusing on virtual organization integration is whether the software fits your virtual organization. You should not need to reorganize the firm or your processes completely to use new software, as a few ERP systems attempted to do in the past. Most of the other factors, such as certain functionalities, technical specifications, and price, are not important if the project software does not fit your needs.

These are all important factors to consider, but in the end you have to integrate the acquired system into the daily life of your virtual teams. Unfortunately, the integration specifics too often tend to be ignored, causing an avalanche of processes that have to be changed later. Changing business processes can be a nightmare!

It is often difficult to change established workflows or introduce new ones, particularly with virtual organizations. There is where management consulting firms are brought in, but that is not the focus of this book. Thus, make sure to keep an eye on features that allow you to adapt a tool to existing workflows and structures rather than vice versa.

A common approach here is the introduction of new processes together with the tool, providing an opportunity to change the things you always wanted to change. The problem is that often the effort needed for organizational changes is underestimated. You paid a lot for the tool, and so there often isn't much left to plan and execute organizational changes properly.

Look at the possibilities the software provides to adapt it to your needs:

- What kind of organizational model underlies the product? For instance, some products require only one project manager. Can you change it and build custom roles?
- What templates are provided? Can you use your own? How much of an effort is it to change them?
- What about processes and workflows? Can you build new ones?

Here are some other factors to consider:

- **Model organization.** Is it possible to build a model of your virtual organization(s)? If it is not, it may be difficult to use the tool efficiently.

  Virtual organizations often already have directories with personnel and other organizational data. If that is the case, can they be integrated? Take the example of existing Lightweight Directory Access Protocol (LDAP) servers: They are often used for more than one system and/or purpose, in which case integration can save you a lot of work. This is also an area where technical and organizational integration meet.

  Another point is the legal conformance of the selected solution. In the modeling of a virtual organization a lot of personnel data are used. How does the software support compliance with existing standards or laws, such as data security and privacy laws? What about cross-country or international virtual organizations?

- **Model rights and roles.** Is it possible to model the virtual organization's hierarchy with the members' roles and rights, or do you have to specify processes on an individual or personal level? The latter could cause a lot of maintenance effort because of the normal fluctuation. A better solution would be to attach the person to a role with his or her responsibilities. Processes then could work with roles and organizational entities. This way, model changes would be necessary only when processes changed.

  New, more or less short-term forms of collaboration between virtual organizations and ePMO make it possible for enterprises to be in multiple relationships with each other at the same time for a wide variety of purposes, such as a joint venture, an alliance, and a supply chain. In these cases the hierarchies, processes, and other structures can overlay each other, allowing roles and individuals to participate in multiple processes and hierarchies. Can this be made visible? It could be important to detect overload, bottlenecks, or security problems in the organizational structure.

- **Templates and methodologies.** Templates are useful and can save a lot of work. This means not only document templates but also process templates and methodologies. Some products offer standard process libraries that you can use or adapt to your needs. This may be simpler than inventing your own templates, especially if the templates must adhere to standards such as ISO 9000 and government standards. It should be possible to integrate your own document templates in some way.

  The layout of the user interface should be considered as a template too. Special attention should be given to corporate identity, cobranding, and team identification, which are extremely important for geographically dispersed teams without a lot of physical contact.

  Methodologies also play an important role in virtual organizations, as the all-important mentoring relationships (learning by watching others and asking others) are not possible or more difficult in a virtual team. Thus, you should make it easy even for someone working alone in a satellite office to learn a new process or get the most recent template by looking it up in the methodology database or whatever mechanism there is. Again, the CMMI model plays a major role here

- **Workflow.** The integration of processes or workflows into the system provides the possibility of their full or partial automation. By being automated they can't be forgotten and can become much faster. Typical examples are approval and alert processes. Documents or events that reach a defined status (threshold) can be automatically—rule-based—sent to the responsible entities. The system could even balance the workload of the recipients and search for the shortest route according to predefined rules.

Without the functionality to model processes, the workflow has to be defined externally, probably with all the disadvantages of written procedures (old documentation, forgetting to read it, etc.).

Security

The security aspects of virtual teams stretch from the trust-building authentication and/or identification of the users to data security and privacy while using the software and include the possibility of reconstructing the deeds and misdeeds of the system's users.

In other words, how do I know I am exchanging an instant message or an e-mail with my chief architect in Argentina? How do I know that someone else is not sitting at his desk and asking me highly confidential questions? Security is more important in virtual projects than in conventional ones because you must compensate for the lack of direct personal contact (trust) and the increased exposure of project data to systems or networks you don't control (secrecy).

Therefore, when you are assessing security, here are important factors to consider:

- **Data security.** Specific issues include the following:
  - What are the vital components of the project management system?

- ○ Where are data stored, even temporarily?
- ○ What data security mechanisms are provided?
- ○ Does your data security strategy include privacy for virtual team members, sponsors, stakeholders, and customers?
- **User authentication.** This is a person-to-person concern:
  - ○ Do you know whom you are talking to?
  - ○ Can you prove who accessed your project documents?
- **Transmission security.** This is a data transport and connectivity concern:
  - ○ Through which channels are data being sent?
  - ○ How are the data sent? Are there encryption standards in place?
- **Auditing.** This deals with traceability issues:
  - ○ What data are being sent?
  - ○ What mechanisms are provided to audit the system?
  - ○ If you chose a service provider, can you control the access to your data and verify data integrity?

User-Friendliness

A system that will be used by different groups of people, perhaps in different locations and even across the globe, must be easy to understand and use. If there are too many culture-specific features that can't be changed, users in different countries and cultures may find the software annoying to use.

A typical example is the date format: In South America we use the format DD/MM/YY, as opposed to MM/DD/YY in the United States. Another is time format: In South America we use the military format of 24 hours, as opposed to the U.S. 12-hour format. Thus, not many people know what time they need to be at a meeting that starts at 14:15 (2:15 P.M.). It is therefore especially important that the software can be personalized so that the standards of the locations (language, currency, etc.) or the user's culture settings can be used.

Factors to consider include the following:

- **Easy to install.** Make sure the software has an executable file to automate installation and provides wizards for customizations.

- **Easy to use.** The system must be user-friendly, equipped with a graphic user interface (GUI) that is intuitive.

- **Personalization supported.** Users should be able to personalize the system to their own needs,

- **Language.** Make sure system is supported by multiple languages and that conversion is simple. Most of Microsoft's ASP.NET applications are acceptable.

- **Time zone.** How are time zones handled in the calendar? A common example is the arrangement of a worldwide telephone conference: Can you see easily the time zones (and the corrected time and date information) of the participants when you invite them?

  What about time information for due dates, alerts, and service license agreements (SLAs)? Is this information relative to a reference time (GMT/UCT) or to the local time zones of the concerned participants? Especially for defined service levels this may be important.

- **Currency.** Questions to consider include the following:
  ○ Can you run a double-currency system or does the

system allow for currency adjustments? I once was involved with two projects with US-AID missions in Costa Rica and Brazil that required such systems. Although we did find couple of vendors supporting the feature, neither of them had a good customization interface.

- Can multiple currencies for efforts and expenses be used?
- How are these currencies handled in reports (i.e., items are reported with original currency and project currency)?
- How can the exchange rates be kept current?
- Is it possible to evaluate the influence of exchange rates on total costs?

System Distribution

System distribution is a core requirement. Make sure to assess the following:

- If you have a project or a team that is widely dispersed, how does the software support this distribution?
- Does its architecture support it?
- What channels can you use to communicate and transfer data?
- Do you have to use the same equipment everywhere? If so, evaluate carefully the usage scenarios the vendors offer and compare them to your requirements.

Here are other factors to consider:

- **Supported platforms.** Will you support PCs/laptops only or will you consider other hardware too, such as tablet PCs, PDAs, mobile phones, and thin clients? Also, do all team members need to be on the same operating system? Depending on the application you are running, they may.

- **Architecture.** What type of systems architecture do you need?
  - Do you need support for multiple locations, connectivity, local languages, currencies, and so on?
  - Do you need a central architecture (client/server) or a distributed P2P (peer-to-peer) one?
- **Access channel.** Your concerns here should be the following:
  - What are the communication mechanisms?
  - Does every client need to have the same kind of access, or does the software allow for variations? Because of different responsibilities and requirements in different locations or groups, it may be more efficient or more economical to use different communication channels.
  - Will you need (can you benefit from) replication features, such as in Lotus Notes, or database synchronizations?
  - What type of online/network services will you need? Some of the services you might consider include the following:
    - LAN, PAN, MAN, WAN, broadband, wireless, and satellite networks
    - Intranet and Extranet (virtual private networks)
    - Direct connections
    - E-mail
    - File transfer
    - Videoconferencing

- **Stability.** Basically, is the system stable and usable?
- **Functionality.** Are you happy with the functionality of the system?

Finally, always keep in mind that virtual project management relies on communication. The entities these projects consist of, such as individuals, committees, work groups, geographically dispersed companies, and globally active enterprises, depend on the fact that distance and time zones do not hinder work. The advantages provided by the more flexible form of virtual project organizations should not be ruined by personal alienation, lack of necessary processes, or technical systems that are difficult to use.

◥ CASE STUDY: LODIR COMMUNICATIONS CORPORATION

Marcus Goncalves

Lodir Communications is a start-up firm that develops, manufactures, and markets a miniature wireless telephone. Last year's sales revenue was $5.6 million, resulting in the first profitable year in its first three years of business. The phone is unique because it is only two inches long and weighs two ounces, and a miniature receiver is worn in the ear. The phone speaker and microphone carry out all the normal functions of a phone (except dialing) without the use of a mouthpiece. The phone uses bone conduction technologies that detect minute vibrations in the skull when a person talks. The phone sells for $99. Lodir's market has grown quickly and has become worldwide; analysts believe the market will grow 50 percent per year for the next five years.

Most of the development of the miniature phone was done by the founder, Ms. Lourdes Amaral, an electrical engineer.

She is also the primary source for more than 20 new products already designed with accompanying engineering drawings. Lourdes believes that innovation in modes of telecommunications is the key to the future success of the company. She believes that quality is number one; profits and returns to stockholders will follow.

Only last month the company purchased a small circuit board company that specializes in bonding small silicon chips to printed circuit boards. Lodir Communications stock sells over the counter. Management is thinking it will be necessary to become listed on the New York Stock Exchange if expansion becomes desirable.

The company employs 120 people and is organized in a matrix form to facilitate the project environment. Every employee behaves as if quality were an obsession. Lourdes believes the management style should be collegial and the workplace environment should be one that employees enjoy. Marketing is responsible for original equipment manufacturer (OEM) sales. Engineering is responsible for the design and improvement of all products. Manufacturing controls production and product quality.

The Market Landscape

The market for telecommunication products is supposed to grow by 20 percent for the next seven years. Although Lodir Communications has no competitors today, many new entries in the market are expected in the near future. Time to market will become more important with each passing day. Keeping a flow of new products will be necessary for survival. Strategic alliances with computer and communication firms appear inevitable as the industry and product lines develop. The biggest threat comes from Asia.

Internal Developments

The most exciting new product prototype is the cordless miniature phone, which will allow people to walk around and use their hands while wearing the phone. The phone fits in the ear and requires the user to carry a pack abut the size of a chewing gum pack and weighing approximately one ounce. Marketing expects to sell the phone for $150. The next step is setting up for manufacturing large quantities as quickly as possible. Manufacturing is asking, "Do you want the new phone good, fast, or cheap? Pick any two."

Another product is a miniature phone that uses voice-activated technology for computers to dial customers and record and transmit data. This prototype has been demonstrated with the Apple line of computers. Because the phone uses bone conduction technology (not air), the background noise is virtually filtered out, and so sound is significantly improved over traditional phones. Marketing believes this phone can sell for about $200.

Other products designed but not developed as prototypes include

1. Voice imprint documentation
2. Miniature programmable phones to hold more than 100 telephone numbers
3. Reduction of printed circuit board size by 75 percent by the new acquisition.

Lodir Communications management feels now is the time to prepare for full-scale manufacturing and a marketing thrust into the communications and computer industries. The company currently has $2 million in cash reserves to start this effort. Additional funds for future expansion are available though stock issues.

Your Task

Lourdes has asked your team to develop a mission statement, three major goals, and objectives for Lodir Communications. She also wishes each functional area to develop four key objectives that support the corporate objectives. Be prepared to justify the document you submit to her.

6

CHAPTER

Virtual Project Management Controls

As a project manager or an executive manager of a virtual project, you know that the project's success is driven by the success of each task you schedule and execute. Especially with ePM, if you maintain tight control over project details, you will be rewarded with greater profitability and competitiveness; anything less and you are inviting trouble.

Therefore, one of the concerns of ePM managers is to manage their project control processes better and help their virtual team leaders do the same thing. In this process, ePM managers should make sure to provide virtual project staff with common tools for budgeting and scheduling virtual project labor, expenses, and subcontractors—often at a distance—across all their projects.

An e-project control system, however, should simply be a tool for the ePM manager. It should enable recognition of problems before they become impossible to solve. The essence of this system is that it integrates the actual work to be done with the cost of doing the work and the time needed to do it. How elaborate a system it is depends on the size and scope of the task to be managed as well as the size and distribution of the team working on it.

Large, lengthy, distributed virtual projects are more likely to require elaborate, disciplined systems to ensure that all the pieces remain coordinated. Smaller projects usually tailor the formal system into an informal systematic approach that may trade off a virtual project manager's skills against detailed, formal procedures.

Products such as Wind2 RSB (www.wind2.com) provide project leaders and managers with an intuitive interface that works the way they normally work in the conventional project management approach. It adds the necessary virtual structure and consistency to the budgeting and scheduling process and offers important features such as Gantt charts and project networks. The interface can also be integrated with the financial management system, enabling up-to-the minute data and reports to support resource management decisions, which often are time-constrained because of time zone differences and less than optimal synchronization of resources that are not colocated.

Nonetheless, unless you are familiar with the core techniques and tools for managing conventional projects, tools such as Wind2 RSB will not help you manage schedules and budgets on virtual projects. This chapter adds on to the techniques and management processes discussed in Chapter 5 to keep your e-project on course by expanding your ability to take advantage of program evaluation review technique (PERT) and critical path methods (CPM) in scheduling and budgeting virtual projects.

AN EFFECTIVE SYSTEMATIC APPROACH TO ePM CONTROLS

The merging of conventional project management functions with the ePM techniques discussed in this book can result in a more efficient operation, with ePM managers being able to control virtual project decisions directly, resulting in a better controlled project. The issue, of course, is that the conventional project management tasks adopted by many of us in the past may have been transparent, embedded, and unfamiliar to the virtual project management environment.

These tasks include the integration of e-project management, management of cost and schedule reserves at a distance with different currencies and economic indicators, virtual team building, e-procurement of goods and services, development of remote (and virtual) facilities, Web-enabled data archiving, shipping, distributed risk management, quality management, and performance reporting.

Therefore, in this context, a successful ePM control process is one that accomplishes the measurement objectives that are needed for the research and analysis activity, within the time and funds approved and/or available, regardless of the fact that the project is being managed virtually. No distinction should be made here between ePM and conventional project management (PM).

In other words, you are responsible not only for the success of the mission in achieving technically what you planned but also for virtually controlling and managing the costs and schedule of the project; its virtual nature should not be an excuse for mediocre results or a failed project. You need to be prepared to pull the plug if it appears that the project will not succeed—losses on ePM projects tend to be exacerbated in comparison to those in conventional project management—based on cost, instrument, or project performance.

Additional funds to bail out "I forgots" and problems with the e-project that should have been resolved through appropriate management are not available. It is therefore in your best interest to do the following:

- Make sure that you understand what needs to be done and what risks are associated with your ePM objectives.
- Make sure to control costs so that costs are not incurred for which funds do not exist, since virtual teams may not be aware of policies and procedures guiding budgeting, contingency funds, and management reserves.

Therefore, an effective systematic approach to ePM cost controls has three elements:

1. Define the baseline to set the milestones along the way to the final goal.
2. Track progress against the milestones so that you know where you stand.
3. Decide when corrective action is needed to achieve the final goal.

Defining the e-Project Baseline

Any kind of performance reporting requires a standard against which performance is to be measured for both conventional or ePM project implementations. In project management that standard is the project baseline. In conventional PM, to create the project baseline, the overall project is explicitly defined into its contributing components, into lower and lower levels, until each component can be specified, priced, and scheduled. The same is true for ePM, where the components are then summarized and reintegrated into a baseline plan that represents the overall standard against which the ePM manager will track the virtual project team's progress.

In practice, the baseline plan is normally a description of the project components (a work breakdown structure is a standard method), accompanied by a time-phased spending plan and schedule with discrete milestones representing substantive work.

Progress Reporting

As an ePM manager, you will need to keep track of the work being accomplished by your team remotely, as well as the costs. You should plan for a reporting system that will collect the information (over the Internet, remotely) you need to know what is happening on the e-project. The information needs to be comprehensive, addressing all components of the project, and should directly correspond to the information in the baseline plan.

For example, if you planned the budget, schedule, and implementation by blocks of tasks and one of the virtual team members is responsible for more than one group of tasks, you will need to track the multiple activities by that team member separately. That will seem intuitively obvious for technical performance of the tasks being executed and progress along the schedule timeline, but you will also need to know the costs separately, meaning that that team member will have to note separately the work hours and materials spent on each task.

There are different ways to collect progress data: written reports, monthly cost reports, periodic visits by the manager to the virtual project sites, and weekly or monthly staff Web conferencing meetings where individuals report on tasks accomplished and possibly labor hours spent, invoices, and shipments received, and so on. The key is that information is collected the way the project was planned, scheduled, and budgeted, and the status information then is compared with the baseline plan.

The result is a periodic assessment of whether the project is on track regarding time, cost, and technical performance.

Corrective Action

It's inevitable that the project won't happen exactly the way it was planned. The utility of a project control system is that the ePM manager not only knows when the virtual teams diverge from the plan but knows it sooner because he or she is consciously staying aware of the project's progress through whatever method was chosen to collect status data. The ePM manager also has trend data that can be used to assess whether the different path that's developing will get the team to the final goal.

It is here that a risk management plan and a quality management plan can make a difference. These processes encourage ePM managers to think ahead and consider more precisely what performance is necessary for success and what to do to ensure the right performance (quality management plan) as well as to consider what could go wrong and what might be done instead (risk management plan). When the project manager has planned for contingencies, decisions to descope or implement alternatives can be made more quickly with fewer arguments and less time to set up alternative work plans. For example, if you've thought about whether a particular component will meet the performance specification, you will have decided already whether you can live with reduced performance or will need an alternative component already have selected along with a vendor and possibly even the backup components, either ordered or in stock.

The key is that these decision points are considered ahead of time so that when decisions to adjust or replan have to be made, you are not paying your full manufacturing-test-integration team while you stop and think about how to replan the e-project. Thus, effective management of e-project resources is paramount.

MANAGING E-PROJECT RESOURCES

There always will be more project tasks than there are available resources. This is especially true in ePM, as virtual project workers often multitask and split their daily activities among a few projects. Thus, you need to make sure there is a priority system in place that will select the best project based on the strategic goals of the organization or those of the client. If all projects and their respective resources are computer-scheduled, the feasibility and impact of adding a new project to those in process can be quickly assessed.

However, even after you decide which projects it makes sense to pursue, resource allocation questions may be floating in your mind:

- Is the assigned labor or equipment adequate for the task?
- Will the assigned labor and equipment be available to be fully dedicated to the project?
- Will you have to use outside contractors?
- How much flexibility do you have in using resources?

The list goes on. Thus, a successful ePM manager must effectively manage the resources assigned to the project whether those resources are colocated or distantly located or based overseas. This includes the labor hours of the designers, the builders, the testers, and the inspectors on the project team. It also includes managing labor subcontracts.

However, managing ePM resources frequently involves more than people management. An ePM manager must also

manage the telecommunication equipment used for the project
and the material needed by the people and equipment assigned
to the project, which may include the following:

- **People:** project workers, both local and virtual, vendor
  staff, subcontract labor, and so on
- **Equipment:** cranes, trucks, backhoes, other heavy
  equipment or development, tests, staging servers, CD
  burners or a recording studio, tape decks, mixers,
  microphones, and speakers
- **Telecommunication gear:** Internetworking equipment
  such as routers, switches, multiplexers, very small aper-
  ture terminals (VSATs), and modems, both in-house
  and at remote sites
- **Application software:** project management tools, collaboration tools, workflow, telecommunication tools,
  and so on
- **Material:** concrete, pipe, rebar, insulation or CD
  blanks, computers, jewel cases, and instruction manuals

Managing the people resources means having the right
people, with the right skills and the proper tools, in the right
quantity at the right time. It also means ensuring that they know
what needs to be done, when, and how. Finally, it means motivating them to take ownership of the project.

Managing direct project workers normally means managing the senior person in each group and virtual team assigned to
the project. Remember that these project workers also have a
line manager to whom they report and from whom they usually
take technical direction. Some of them are based at remote sites
and may not have some of the in-house resources available to
local staff; that may increase the level of complexity in
responding to or following a process or procedure.

In a matrix management situation such as a project team, your job is to provide project direction to the workers. Managing labor subcontracts usually means managing the team leader for the subcontracted workers, who in turn manages the workers.

The equipment you have to manage depends on the nature of the project. A project to construct a frozen food warehouse would need earthmoving equipment, cranes, and cement trucks. For a project to release a new version of a computer game, the equipment would include computers, test equipment, and duplication and packaging machinery. The key for managing equipment is much like that for managing people resources. You have to make sure that you have the right equipment in the right place at the right time and that it has the supplies it needs to operate properly. In any event, when part of the project team, if not the entire team, is virtual, the right selection of technologies (hardware and software) is imperative. Make sure to allow for backup hardware and disk images in case remote offices run into problems with their gear.

All your skill in managing resources won't help, however, unless you can stick to the schedule. Time management is critical in successful project management.

MEASURING ePM RESULTS

Part of the life cycle of any e-project includes the measurement of gains and efficiencies achieved. In many cases, a project will be approved on the basis of anticipated gains in business efficiency, and those gains provide the return on investment (ROI) that pays for the system costs. If the project began by analyzing the potential benefits of reengineering a business process, for instance, at some point after installation those gains should be measurable.

If the project is based on a positive cost justification analysis, the groundwork for the postimplementation study already has been laid and the tools for measuring results are available. If the project is not based on a cost justification analysis, it may be difficult to measure gains since there is no benchmark against which to measure.

For example, the easy way to review a document imaging project against the original cost justification would be to ask quantifiable questions such as the following:

- Was the 35,000 square feet of floor space recovered?
- Were 20 FTEs (full-time equivalents) released or reassigned as predicted?
- Is paper usage down from 500,000 sheets per month to 10,000?
- Are business processes completed faster, such as resolving a claim in 3 working days instead of 15?

In other words, you must build baselines. The answers to these questions are relatively easy to determine and will provide part of the answer or at least an indication that the newly installed system is working as expected. However, what if your system purchase is not based on retrieving floor space, cutting printing costs, or eliminating FTEs? What if it is based on intangible benefits such as improving customer service or providing work processes that were not previously used? What if the new system is not based on previous processes?

Intangible benefits are difficult to prove or disprove and even harder to measure. How do you know that employee morale has improved as a result of the new system and is responsible for an 8 percent decrease in absenteeism? How do you measure customer satisfaction in dollars, and how do you attribute the increase (or decrease) to the new processes and systems?

Measuring the benefits of a system must be planned for as part of the overall cost justification process. In reviewing that basic process, the following areas are typically considered:

- **Current operations.** This is an analysis of the current operations and provides a snapshot of how many people are employed, what their cost is to the organization, and what resources are required to maintain current operations. As part of the current operations analysis, the study should provide some details about how long a process takes, what steps are involved, what resources are needed to complete the work, and what the current bottlenecks are. Process efficiencies can be predicted only if the process has been analyzed in sufficient detail to break down individual steps and associate costs with those steps.

- **Business process engineering.** Once the current operations are understood, the next step is to determine where improvements can be made and efficiencies gained. Can a 22-step process involving five people be reduced to 6 steps involving two people? If so, what are the new procedures, process steps, and associated resource costs? In addition to calculating these efficiency gains, the cost-justification process must recognize new or additional resource costs that were not part of the previous system. For example, these costs may include
  - Additional personnel for scanner operations or computer operations
  - Additional communication line charges
  - Recurring costs for training and maintenance

- **Image system costs.** After the current operations have been reengineered and the processes have been defined, the appropriate system resources can be defined. These resources include workstations, communications sizing, servers, software, application development, and project implementation costs.

When the current operational costs have been determined, they can be compared with the projected costs for the image system. The difference, or delta, between current and projected costs results in a positive or negative cost-benefit analysis, as shown in Figure 6–1. If this type of analysis is not performed before the installation of an image system, it will be difficult to measure results quantitatively because previous baselines were not established.

Cost performance indexes (CPIs) provides information on how project costs are performing. The index, (Figure 6–1), is found by dividing the actual cost of work performed (ACWP) by the budgeted cost of work performed (BCWP):

$$CPI = BCWP/ACWP = 42/30 = 1.4$$

For every dollar invested in the project, there is $0.40 ROI.

By the same token, the scheduling performance index provides information on how the project schedule is performing: if you are ahead of, behind, or on schedule. This index, also illustrated in Figure 6–1, is determined by dividing the budgeted cost of work scheduled (BCWS) by the budgeted cost of work performed (BCWP):

$$SPI = BCWP/BCWS = 42/34 = 1.24$$

The project at this point is 24 percent ahead of schedule.

Other useful indexes include

FIGURE 6-1

A project index chart enables project managers to evaluate cost-benefit analyses.

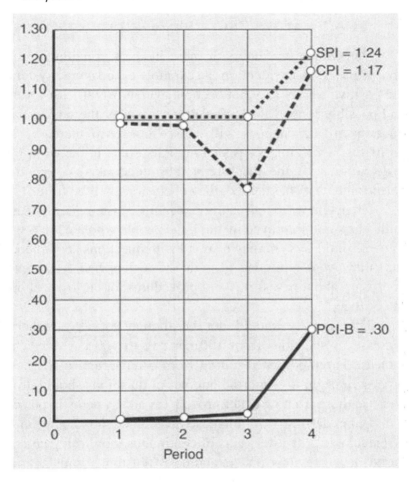

- The percentage complete index (PCI-B), which is calculated by dividing the budged cost at completion (BAC) by the BCWP:

PCI-B = BCWP/BAC = 42/139 = .3, or 30%

- The percentage complete index (PCI-C), which is calculated by dividing the estimated cost at completion (EAC) by the actual cost of work performed (ACWP):

PCI-C = ACWP/EAC = 30/156 = .192, or 19%

Despite the usefulness of these indexes, sometimes ROI on a project is not evident. In the example of the image system, the positive results may not become evident for at least a year and possibly longer. If a complete overhaul of the business is undertaken, the changes will cause short-term increases in problems, which may cause a temporary spike in the work for a department. If the measurement is undertaken before the "electronic dust" has settled, the conclusions will be false.

For example, if the current benefits system is replaced with a new and improved method, the people who are the "customers" of the system may respond with questions about benefits (they were reminded of a question they had forgotten), confusion about new forms and procedures, or curiosity about the change.

This activity should not be thought of as a general increase in questions from 100 per day to 150 per day. The increase is temporary, resulting from change, and if the new processes begin to work, the number of questions should drop because there are now better procedures and systems in place.

Gains derived from increased customer satisfaction may be calculated only after years of continuous monitoring and be based on a previous understanding of customer satisfaction. For example, customer turnover may have been established at 12 percent per year by reviewing the last five years' records. Turnover may have been traced in part to poor customer services such as lack of response, poor response times, and a low quality of response. A new turnover percentage calculation may require a year or more before customer turnover can be analyzed as a result of annual contract renewals and other factors. Perhaps only after several years can it be established that customer turnover has been affected by the new system.

Measuring results should be planned for as part of the original project. A proper baseline must be established, the original figures must be maintained and kept available for several years, and the appropriate resources must be dedicated to a new analysis. A side benefit to revisiting the cost-benefit analysis is that midcourse corrections may be made on the basis of new data and further process improvement may occur.

An Overview of PERT and CPM Analysis

In 1958, the Special Projects Office of the U.S. Navy developed PERT to plan and control the Polaris missile program. PERT is similar to CPM but has a probabilistic approach that provides three time estimates for the duration of each activity.

In working with PERT, especially when it is applied to ePM, the first step is to decide what your tasks are and which tasks depend on which. Providing accurate estimates of task durations is not always easy without good historical data. For this reason the PERT approach uses three estimates for the duration of a task (activity):

- Optimistic time (a): the time an activity will take if everything goes perfectly
- Most likely time (m): the most realistic time estimate to complete the activity
- Pessimistic time (b): the time an activity will take if everything goes wrong

From these estimates we calculate the **expected time** (t) for the task. The time estimates are often but not always assumed to follow the beta probability distribution:

$$\text{Expected time } t = \frac{a + 4m + b}{6}$$

$$\sqrt{\text{Variance}} = \left[\frac{b - a}{6} \right]$$

The project variance is the sum of the variances of each of the tasks on the critical path. The square root of this is the project standard deviation. From the normal distribution equation:

$$z = \frac{\text{due date} - \text{expected date of project completion}}{\text{project standard deviation}}$$

Looking this value up in the normal distribution tables gives the probability of the project being completed on the due date. At the end of this process we have

1. An expected completion date for the project.
2. Knowledge of which tasks are critical to the project. For instance, if they are delayed, the delivery of the final product is delayed.
3. Knowledge of which tasks are not critical. They can be delayed to some extent (the float, or slack, of the task) without affecting the overall delivery of the final product. Resources from these tasks could be diverted to the critical tasks if they start to fall behind.
4. An estimate of how likely it is that the project will be finished by the deadline.

Note that it is not necessarily accepted that the normal distribution curve is suitable for predicting the spread of duration errors, especially in ePM, where estimates tend to be too optimistic rather than too pessimistic. Hence, you very likely will need to skew the distribution curve to correct for this. The formula below has helped me do that:

$$\text{Expected time } t = \frac{a + 3m + 2b}{6}$$

You can perform a PERT analysis to estimate a task's duration in Microsoft Project EPM. After you specify the optimistic (the best-case possibility for the total span of active working time expected for a task, that is, the amount of time from the optimistic start to the optimistic finish of a task), pessimistic (the worst-case possibility for the total span of active working time expected for a task, that is, the amount of time from the pessimistic start to the pessimistic finish of a task), and expected (the total span of active working time expected for a task, that is, the amount of time from the expected start to the expected finish of a task) durations of the tasks in your schedule, Microsoft Project calculates a weighted average of the three durations. You can also use the optimistic, pessimistic, and expected task durations separately to determine the shortest, longest, and most likely project end dates.

What Is a Weighted Duration Average in PERT Analysis

A weighted average is the result of the expected, pessimistic, and optimistic dates and durations analysis of PERT. By default, PERT analysis calculation gives heaviest weight to the expected duration and the lightest weight to the pessimistic and optimistic durations.

You can perform a PERT analysis in two ways:

- By using the default weights for duration estimates if you think that the expected duration estimate is more likely than either the optimistic or the pessimistic estimate or think the latter two estimates are equally likely.

- By changing the way the project weights duration estimates if you think that the optimistic, expected, and
  pessimistic durations have probabilities of occurring
  that are different from the default probabilities of 1 out
  of 6, 4 out of 6, and 1 out of 6, respectively.

In MS Project you can do it this way:

1. On the View menu, point to Toolbars and then click
   PERT Analysis, as shown in Figure 6–2.
2. On the PERT Analysis toolbar, click PERT Entry
   Sheet, as shown in Figure 6–3 (notice the arrow).
3. For each task, enter the optimistic, expected, and pessimistic durations in the Optimistic Dur., Expected
   Dur., and Pessimistic Dur. fields, respectively, as
   shown in Figure 6–4.

FIGURE 6–2

Accessing the PERT analysis tool in MS Project.

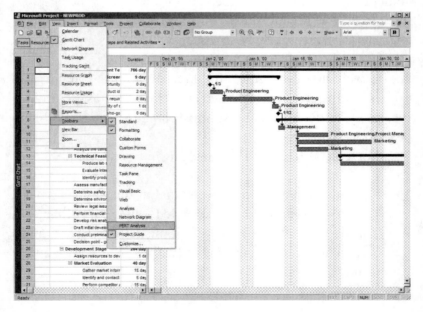

FIGURE 6-3

Accessing the PERT Entry Sheet.

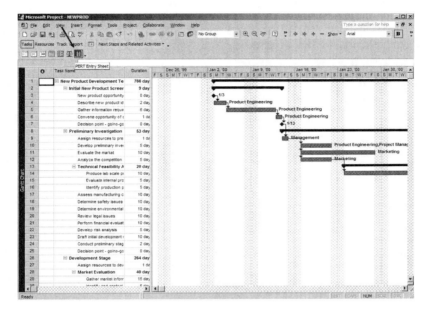

4. If a task's duration is not expected to vary, enter the expected duration in all three fields.

5. Click Calculate PERT to calculate the estimated durations.

6. Microsoft Project estimates a single project duration based on a weighted average of the three duration values for each task.

7. To view the optimistic, expected, and pessimistic durations on the PERT Analysis toolbar, click Optimistic Gantt, Expected Gantt, and Pessimistic Gantt.

8. To view the end dates of the three resulting schedules on the Tools menu, click Options.

9. Click the View tab and then select the show project summary task box, as shown in Figure 6–5.

FIGURE 6-4

Entering optimistic, expected, and pessimistic durations in the Optimistic Dur., Expected Dur., and Pessimistic Dur. fields in the PERT Entry Sheet.

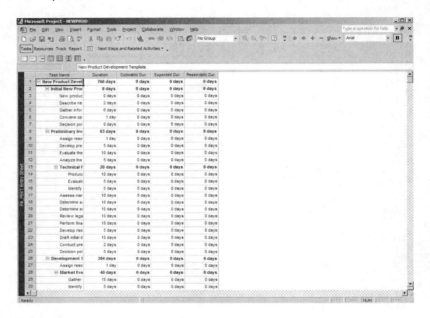

Understanding and Using CPM for ePM

Around 1957 the CPM was developed to assist in the building and maintenance of chemical plants at DuPont. Critical path analysis (CPA) is used to organize and plan projects so that they are completed on time and within budget. A project is structured so that tasks that are dependent on each other are identified; this allows critical tasks to be identified.

CPA (or CPM) is similar to PERT but uses a deterministic model; that is, the duration of the activities and their cost are known with certainty. In using CPA, the first step is to decide what the tasks are, which tasks depend on which, and how long each one will take.

FIGURE 6-5

Selecting the project summary task box in MS Project.

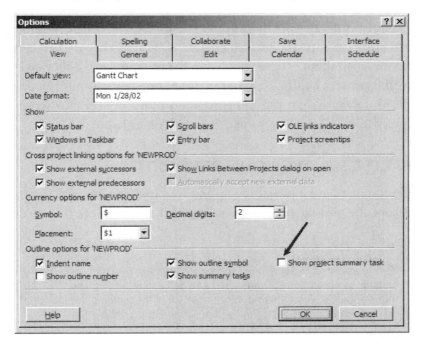

Once we have defined the relationship between the tasks and their durations, we can derive two numbers for each task:

- The earliest starting time for the task (ES). Starting from the earliest (starting) task in the project, the ES of the task is the ES of the preceding (dependent) task plus the previous task's duration. This is calculated for each task.

- The latest starting time for the task (LS). Starting with the last task in the project, the LS of the preceding task is the LS of the task minus its duration. This is calculated for each task.

The difference between these two numbers is the float (or slack) of each task. This approach can then be used to identify critical tasks on the project. These are tasks that by definition cannot be delayed or take longer than their estimate without affecting the time the overall project will take. There is no slack (or float) in them. These tasks give the critical path. Other tasks in the project can be delayed or take longer without affecting the duration of the project (provided that they remain within their float). Figure 6–6 illustrates this relationship.

GANTT CHART: THE VIRTUAL PERSPECTIVE

Gantt charts are a project planning tool that can be used to represent the timing of the tasks required to complete a project.

FIGURE 6–6

Every task on a network must have an ES (early start) and an EF (early finish), as well as an LS (late start) and an LF (late finish). The difference between those durations provides the existing float for each task, and tasks without a float will determine the critical path.

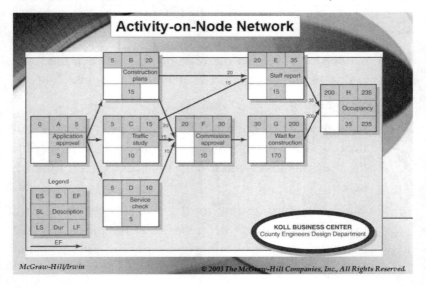

Gantt charts are simple to understand and easy to construct, making them very popular with project managers for all but the most complex projects. Figure 6–7 illustrates a a Gantt chart prepared using Microsoft Project.

In a Gantt chart, as shown in Figure 6–7, each task takes up one row. Dates run along the top in increments of days, weeks, or months, depending on the total length of the project. The expected time for each task is represented by a horizontal bar whose left end marks the expected beginning of the task and whose right end marks the expected completion date. Tasks may run sequentially, run in parallel, or be overlapping.

As the project progresses, the chart is updated by filling in

FIGURE 6–7

A gantt chart is a project planning tool that is simple to understand and easy to construct (Microsoft Project).

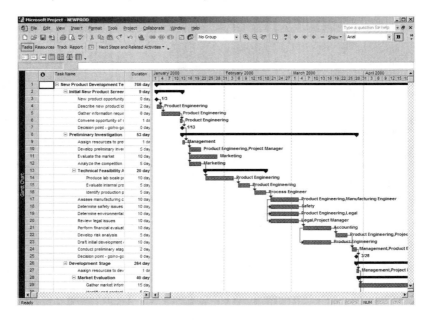

the bars to a length proportional to the fraction of work that has been accomplished on the task, as shown in Figure 6–8. This way, one can get a quick reading of project progress by drawing a vertical line through the chart at the current date. Completed tasks lie to the left of the line and are completely filled in. Current tasks cross the line and are behind schedule if their filled-in section is to the left of the line and ahead of schedule if the filled-in section stops to the right of the line. Future tasks lie completely to the right of the line.

In constructing a Gantt chart, keep the tasks to a manageable number. More complex projects may require subordinate charts that detail the timing of all the subtasks that make up one of the main tasks. For virtual team projects, it often helps to

FIGURE 6–8

By establishing baselines one can easily track the progress of a project on a Gantt chart.

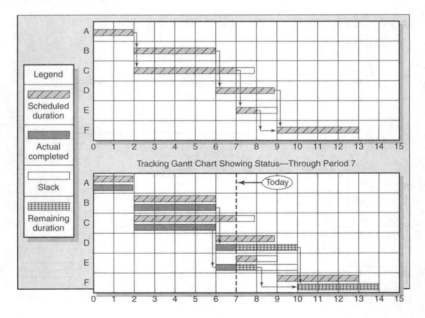

have an additional column containing numbers or initials that identify who on the team is responsible for each task. Microsoft Project makes this process easy by entering the name of the project worker next to the task so long as you provide that information in the task information window (Figure 6–9).

Figure 6–10 shows a Gantt chart with the names of the resources allocated to the particular task (circled).

Often the project has important events that you would like to show on the project timeline but that are not tasks. For example, you may wish to highlight when a prototype is complete or the date of a design review. You enter these events on a Gantt chart as "milestone" events and mark them with a special symbol, often an upside-down triangle.

FIGURE 6–9

By entering the name of a resource in Microsoft Project, project managers are able to track a task associated with its resource directly on a Gantt chart.

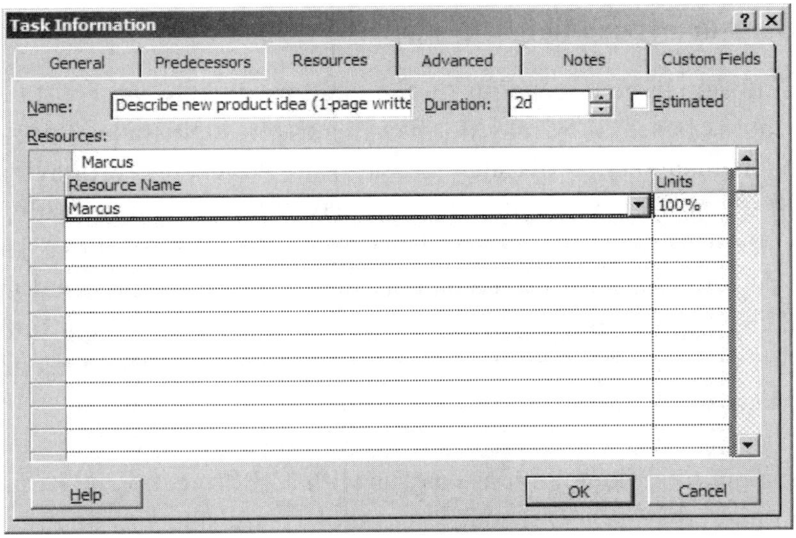

FIGURE 6-10

Microsoft Project allows the association of a resource with a task as viewed on a Gantt chart.

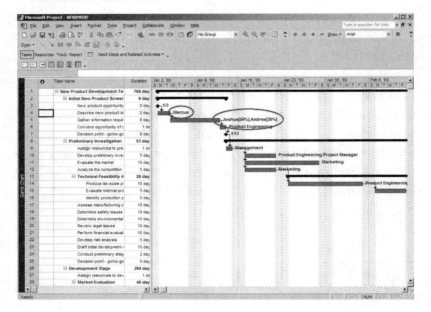

Gantt Charts on Microsoft Excel

Unfortunately, depending on the countries where your virtual team is based, they may not have access to sophisticated project management tools such as Microsoft Project and Primavera Systems. In some countries you may find that the operating system or internal policies don't allow those applications, or you may not have the technical support resource allocated to them. In this case, you may decide that you want to use a simpler approach by asking your teams to generate Gantt charts on Microsoft Excel.

Gantt charts made with Excel are easy to update and maintain (although not as easy as with MS Project, Primavera, or any other project management tool). Here's how to do it:

1. On a piece of scrap paper, make a list of tasks, assign each task tentative start and stop dates (or durations), and list the people responsible for each task. Also list important milestones and their dates. If you have more than 15 or 20 tasks, split the project into main tasks and subtasks and then make an overall Gantt chart for the main tasks and separate Gantt charts for the subtasks that make up each main task.

2. Decide what resolution to use in the timeline. For projects of three months or less, use days; for longer projects, use weeks or months; and for very short projects, use hours. In this example, we will assume you have chosen a resolution of days.

3. Launch Microsoft Excel.

4. Under Page Setup, select landscape orientation and then select the options to center the chart horizontally and vertically on the page.

5. Also under Page Setup, activate the "fit to one page" button. (Note that if the text comes out too small, you may have to print the chart on two pages and paste them together. Even better, adjust the resolution of the date scale or drop less important tasks to make the chart fit on one page.)

6. While you are at Page Setup, set the header and footer to be blank. (It's better to write the title right on the spreadsheet rather than use the header for the title.)

7. Finally, under Page Setup, turn off the option to print gridlines.

8. Set up the cells now. Use the border command to draw boxes around the appropriate cells.

9. Now enter the scheduling data. To make the gray bars, which indicate the length of a task, select the

appropriate cells and then the fill command (one of the buttons near the top).

10. As the project progresses, fill in the gray bars with black to denote the fraction of a task that is complete.

11. You may want to convert this file into a PDF format a post it on your Extranet so that your virtual teams can access it. Alternatively, you can send this file by e-mail.

I hope that you won't attempt to run a project on Microsoft Excel, which, as you will notice, is much more labor-intensive than Microsoft Project. But according to a Microsoft's survey, there are still more project managers using Excel out there in the world than using Project.

▧ CASE STUDY: RAZOR PRINTING, SA

Marcus Goncalves

Three years ago the Razor Printing (RP) strategic management group set a goal of having a color laser printer available for the consumer and small business market for less than $300. A few months later senior management met off-site to discuss the new product. The results of the meeting were a set of technical specifications along with major deliverables, a product launch date, and a cost estimate based on prior experience.

Shortly afterward a meeting was arranged for middle management to explain the project goals, the major responsibilities, the project start date, and the importance of meeting the product launch date within the cost estimate. Members of all the departments involved attended the meeting. Excitement was high. Although everyone saw the risk as high, the promised rewards for the company and the personnel were emblazoned in their minds. A few participants questioned the legitimacy of the project duration and cost estimates. A couple of R&D people were worried about the technology required to produce the high-quality product for less than $300. But in the excitement of the moment, everyone agreed that the project was worth doing and doable. The color laser printer project was to have the highest project priority in the company.

Lauren was selected to be the project manager. She had 15 years of experience in printer design and manufacture, which included the successful management of several projects related to printers for commercial markets. Since she was one of those uncomfortable with the project cost and time estimates, she felt that getting good bottom-up time and cost estimates for the deliverables was her first concern. She quickly had a meeting with the significant stakeholders to create a work breakdown structure (WBS) identifying the work packages and organizational units responsible for implementing the work packages. Lauren stressed that she wanted time and cost estimates from those who would do the work or were the most knowledgeable if possible. Getting estimates from more than one source was encouraged. The estimates were due in two weeks.

The complied estimates were placed in the WBS and organization breakdown structure (OBS). The corresponding cost estimate seemed to be in error. The cost estimate was $1,250,000 over the senior management estimate; that represented about a 20 percent overrun. The time estimate from the developed project network was only four months over top management's time estimate. Another meeting with the significant stakeholders was called to check the estimates and brainstorm alternative solutions if the cost estimates were not accurate. Some of the suggestions for the brainstorming session are listed below:

- Change the scope.
- Outsource technology design.
- Use the priority matrix to get top management to clarify its priorities.
- Partner with another organization or build a research consortium to share costs and newly developed technology and production methods.
- Cancel the project.
- Commission a break-even study for the laser printer.

Very little in the way of concrete savings was identified, although there was consensus that time could be compressed to the market launch date, but at an an additional cost.

Lauren met with the marketing (Connor), production (Kim), and design (Gage) managers who came up with some ideas for cutting costs, but nothing significant enough to have a large impact. Gage remarked, "I wouldn't want to be the one to deliver the message to top management that their cost estimate is $1,250,000 off! Good luck, Lauren."

Your Task

If you were the project manager for this project, what would you do? Explain.

7
CHAPTER

E-Tools for Quality Control

The selection of e-tools for quality control in virtual project management must be well thought out. A glance at the disaster prevention headlines is enough to send a virtual project manager's blood pressure through the roof. Data disasters are on the rise, making for not only distressing but sensational news, especially when millions of dollars and a project's reputation are at stake.

Take a close look and you'll conclude that today's tools for quality control are simply not good enough. Many ePM managers still use manual control, verification, and auditing systems, that are error-prone, costly, and slow, often causing bottlenecks in project operations. *Homegrown* applications often make ePM managers and virtual teams dependent on an already-backlogged programmer. Thus, if you're serious about adopting e-tools for project quality control, your best choice is a standardized, automated system.

This chapter discusses some of the tools available on the market and the types of features you should be looking for. For the most part, these systems should provide an automated quality control (QC) manager and/or wizard that will allow you to model and select the aspects of the project you want to audit. Many of these products provide a standardized, automated method for verifying production input and output. A good system also automates the balancing and control functions you currently have in place for task distribution, allows you to build in even more control points, and writes in calls from new applications. When strategically placed, your network of QC control points and program calls should provide a rigorous QC system.

SELECTING A CONTROLLING TOOL

As project execution advances, it is important to evaluate exactly what has been achieved and what can be learned for the next time. It is also very important to assess the level of quality of the deliverables and whether that level complies with the levels required by the customer and the sponsors. Of course, a variety of tools and techniques are available. Therefore, this chapter will provide a basic review of the most common controlling tools that use familiar techniques such as the work breakdown structure (WBS), critical path or program evaluation review technique (PERT) analysis and scheduling, and scorecards. These tools are well known in the industry and thus are ideal for use in a virtual project management environment.

Using the Work Breakdown Structure
for Planning and Quality Control

In using a WBS for planning and quality control, the question you should be asking yourself is, What must be executed? You can have a virtual team that is very busy, overwhelmed by the tasks at hand but not actually accomplishing anything. That is where the WBS comes in. As shown in Figure 7–1, the WBS divides the project into smaller and smaller units until you arrive at a level where decent estimates of time, resources, and costs can be made and, very important, can ensure an acceptable level of quality for the project.

Overloading project resources with more than they can handle or not having a clear expectation of goals, objectives, and the level of quality of tasks and subtasks will compromise the quality of project execution. Thus, it is very important that your WBS be well defined; the resources be well scheduled and, if necessary, leveled; and progress be controlled. The bottom line is that a WBS should be more than a clerical aid. It is a formidable quality control tool.

Strengthening WBS as a Quality Control Tool

If I were to ask how many tasks your current project should have, what would you answer? While you are thinking about it, how much detail should there be in a virtual project plan?

The mistake many ePM mangers make is to lay out too many tasks, subdividing the major achievements into smaller and smaller subtasks until the WBS is a "to do" list of one-hour chores. It's easy to get caught up in the idea that a project plan should detail everything everybody is going to do on the project. This springs from the misconceived notion that a project manager's job is to walk around with a checklist of 17,432 items and tick each item off as people complete it. This is unrealistic, and in managing projects virtually, it becomes nearly impossible.

This view is usually linked with another fallacy: The project plan should be a step-by-step procedure for doing

FIGURE 7–1

A work breakdown structure for developing a website.

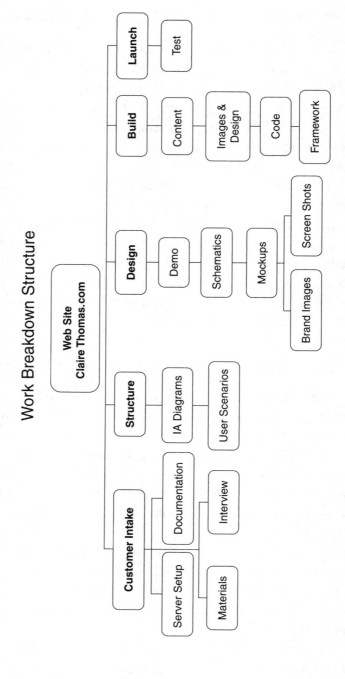

Work Breakdown Structure

everything in the project in case it has to be done again. If the ePM manager is managing the wrong things, this may be handy because we increase the odds of having to do the project again.

Project sponsors encourage these fallacies by marveling at monstrous project plans because they make it seem that the project manager (PM) has thought of everything. Unfortunately, in significant cross-functional virtual projects that involve different backgrounds and environments, there is no chance that the ePM manager will think of everything. The subject matter experts and specialists are the ones who must be held accountable for that. For this type of WBS, my recommendation is never to rely on it as a quality control instrument.

The result of these fallacies is that PMs end up producing project plans with hundreds or even thousands of tasks. Many of those tasks have durations of a few hours or a few days. Can you imagine managing such a project from a distance? Does this level of detail provide better control and lead to successful projects? In my view, a to-do list approach does not produce effective control and interferes with the achievement of a successful end result.

First, the laundry list approach leads to and even encourages micromanagement of the people working on the project, which by definition is nearly impossible to accomplish when the project staff is all over the map. Micromanagement may be appropriate for conventional project management and when you have slackers and laggards working for you, but few virtual project teams are composed entirely of these types of people. The majority of your virtual team members will not thrive under micromanagement. In addition, this style tends to encourage dependency on the project manager rather than the type of independence where people are held responsible for their results. If you find yourself getting too many e-mails, instant messages (IMs), and phone calls from the field to discuss simple project tasks, now you know why.

Second, PMs are consistently more effective when they hold the virtual team members accountable for reaching *measured achievements* rather than completing a list of tasks. How often does it happen that people complete a list of tasks and achieve nothing? When you base task assignments and monitoring on well-conceived and measurable *achievements*, no one loses sight of the desired end result.

Third, the laundry list approach is hard to maintain. People have to report on many tasks, and that decreases the odds of receiving accurate and timely status reports, especially when the medium is the Internet. An ePM manager, with or without clerical support, requires a great deal of data entry to input all the status data. Amid the pressure of ongoing multiple projects, tracking can fall behind and may even be dropped because the effort is too great. This may sound like a stupid and improbable solution, but it happens with alarming frequency even on large and important projects. The logic is: No one is looking at all that detail anyway, so why spend all that time to catch up?

When it comes to virtual project management, as a general rule I like to see the majority of assignments in a project plan have durations between one week and eight weeks. Coupled with this, I advocate weekly status reporting of hours worked and percentage completed and an estimate of the hours of work remaining to complete the assignment. All this should be done automatically through your project management software without the need for conference calls and meetings, at least until there is a chance to review the reports and detect problems. This allows the project manager to maintain good control while placing the responsibility for achievements on the team members.

By using the WBS for cross-functional corporate projects, you have the opportunity to design an assignment and monitoring processes, as well as better control of the quality of those deliverables. As part of this achievement-driven approach, I recommend breaking work down into "packets" of achievement for which you will hold people and teams accountable.

PERT Analysis

Project planning is one of the first major activities project managers need to undertake if they want to control the quality of execution. As Figure 7–2 illustrates, this activity plays a crucial role throughout the project by ensuring that the project trade-offs between scope, time, and cost will not jeopardize the level of quality determined by the sponsors and stakeholders. Hence, it makes sense for virtual project managers to arrive at

FIGURE 7–2

Quality is at the center of trade-offs between cost, time, and scope.

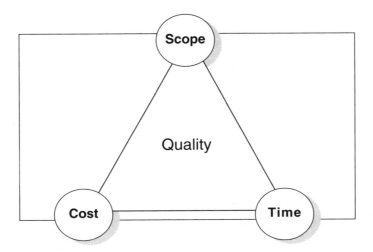

a realistic plan for a project to begin with. Hence, this activity demands great attention from the project manager.

Project planning involves designing the activity (task) plan, resource plan, and schedule within the constraints of a budget. During this phase, a project manager views the project in terms of a Gantt chart or PERT or network diagram and ensures that the plan has a very good chance of achieving the scope within the schedule with the resources allocated. Also, the manager breaks down the (WBS) into smaller tasks to achieve better control.

As was discussed earler, a PERT chart is a critical path method (CPM) chart considered statistically. It can be useful in assessing quality control issues, particularly schedule risk, which usually turns into cost risk.

The essential nature of PERT analysis for quality control is to determine the expected time for each activity by using a weighted average of the most likely along with the best-case and worst-case time estimates that can be imagined. The normal approach to PERT is to weigh the "most likely" four times heavier than the extremes and then sum them all and divide by six. When the expected times have been determined for all activities on the critical path, those times can be summed to determine the expected time for the entire project.

If the standard deviation for a total project is one month, you can consult a standard normal distribution table to see that one standard deviation includes 84 percent of the population. Therefore, the probability that the project will be completed no more than one month late is 84 percent. The probability that it will be completed at least one month early thus is for 16 percent. You can use the standard deviation for the total project to evaluate probabilities for different outcomes by converting a completion date to standard deviations from the expected time and then using the table to find the probability of occurrence.

Although this is an interesting concept, it is used only for projects with frequently repeated tasks and highly standardized methodologies. In all other projects, there are so many other unknowns, uncertainties, and instabilities that PERT analysis is insensitive to the most relevant issues driving the schedule risk. In other words, it may be pointless to do statistical analysis if you already understand where your problems are.

The Use of Critical Path Analysis for Quality Control

Critical path analysis (CPA) uses a deterministic model; that is, the duration of the activities and the cost are known with certainty. Although a practicing project manager may not agree with the deterministic nature of the tasks in a project, that is the way CPA functions.

The stepwise CPA approach to project planning is as follows:

1. Split the project into subprojects and split the subprojects into activities or tasks.
2. Identify the duration needed to complete a task.
3. Identify the resources needed to complete a task.
4. Identify how this task depends on other tasks.

A PRACTICAL APPROACH

Throughout a project life cycle, databases, applications, and system performance and availability are critical factors that directly affect the bottom line. Project managers in general and ePM managers in particular are facing increased pressure to compete and deliver enhanced performance for project processes; when those processes are executed virtually the pressure is intensified by the growth in data and the increased complexity of application architectures. Information technology (IT) organizations that support virtual teams are also seeing an increase in the number of applications they are required to manage, tighter budgets, and demands for increasing levels of customer service.

How does a project remain on schedule and profitable (under budget) in today's challenging marketplace? One way is through quality control and performance testing of project enterprise systems. Performance quality control and testing in this context is something that project managers don't really worry about, but for virtual project management, such controls become imperative as they refer to the process of systematically evaluating the performance of virtual applications under stress to identify potential bottlenecks and assess scalability. The idea here is to predict the performance of (virtual) applications and fix bottlenecks before costly problems occur in production.

Testing applications by using traditional methods is a time-consuming, error-prone process that places a heavy burden on the performance engineer who is tasked with delivering accurate results quickly. Ideally, performance testing should mimic production activity—including users, activities, and data—under test conditions in which the amount of load applied against the application can be varied. Traditional testing methods do not offer a streamlined way to generate accurate results with a granular level of detail in a short period of time, which is always of the essence in project execution. A goals-based approach to performance testing dramatically accelerates and streamlines the testing process, making it easier for performance engineers to do their job.

Goal-Based Quality Control Testing

If you are going to keep a project on schedule, within budget, and within scope and meet quality requirements, you must have a way to measure where you are for each variable of interest. This is, of course, much easier said than done. When you are doing work that has a tangible nature, you can measure progress fairly well, but when you are trying to measure knowledge work from a distance, it gets more difficult.

Goals-based QC testing gives ePM managers the ability to ask critical question about project performance before the quality control process begins. This approach to QC promotes a proactive methodology by enabling QC professionals to set thresholds and parameters for the project to ensure that the outcome meets all the defined quality level requirements. This ability dramatically accelerates the QC process as tests can be aborted once thresholds are exceeded. Further, QC is of little use unless project activity under productionlike circumstances can be reproduced accurately. Simulating project tasks realistically can be quite complex owing to the variety of variables involved.

When goals for QC are set, the QC test will answer the business question "Which level of quality?" much more directly and require less analysis. With a goals-based approach, you can identify the goals of the QC test and then set the criteria accordingly.

Developing Project Metrics

The most common approach used by ePM managers and their virtual teams is to understand the project mission, goals, and objectives; brainstorm metrics; and then decide what metrics can help them achieve better project execution. Virtual teams then should review the metrics with the ePM manager to ensure that they are in synergy with the overall strategy of the project, and an iterative approach may be utilized.

Care should be exercised in determining what is measured in a project. Over the course, schedule and cost variance must be tracked, but metrics should be based on what in fact needs to be measured to improve the project management process rather than on what fits the current measurement system or template with project management tools or best practices. Metrics need to be scrutinized for the value they add in understanding a process.

For instance, the fact that a software installation has been successful does not necessarily means it is providing users with the expected feature sets and benefits. Therefore, measuring installation task completions alone is not indicative of success; customers' satisfaction with the new system must be measured. There will be cases in which despite project closure, actual indicators of success may take a year or more to be assessed, and your project metrics should reflect that condition.

Therefore, there are some guidelines on developing metrics that should be followed. Otherwise, you can fool yourself. Metrics tend to encourage project workers to behave in ways that make the measures most favorable. For that reason metrics must be chosen to encourage the behavior desired by the virtual project organization. Otherwise, you will encourage your teams to do what you don't want them to do.

That's why one of the crucial elements of the project charter in the define phase of a project is the selection of project metrics. The project metrics selected should reflect the voice of the customer (customer needs) as well as ensure that the internal goals selected by the organization are achieved. The metrics selected should be simple and straightforward and meaningful. They should create a common language among diverse team members.

When drafting metrics for a particular project, you should consider how the metrics are connected and related to key business metrics. Typically, no single metric fits all the requirements for a particular situation.

The approach I use for virtual projects is to understand the problem statement, brainstorm metrics, and finally decide what metrics can help the virtual teams achieve better performance. I tend to involve all the project leaders and key technical team members in this process to make sure we are not missing or overlooking any important aspect that needs to be measured during project execution. The virtual teams and local teams then review the metrics with our executive management to ensure that they are in synergy with the overall strategy of the project, and an iterative approach may be utilized.

Be careful when determining what is being measured. Metrics should be based on what needs to be measured to improve the process rather than what fits the current measurement system. Metrics need to be scrutinized for the value they add in understanding a process.

Balanced Scorecard Approach to ePM Metrics

Many e-project management professionals, especially those with six-sigma expertise, advocate the use of a balanced scorecard approach for the selection of project metrics as a way to ensure that the project meets both customer and business needs. The balanced scorecard approach includes both financial and nonfinancial metrics, as well as lagging and leading measures across the four areas or perspectives:

- Financial
- Customer
- Internal processes
- Employee learning and growth

Lagging measures are those which are measured at the end of an event; leading measures are those which help the organization achieve the objectives and are measured upstream of the event.

Most balanced scorecard metrics are based on brainstorming. However, brainstorming can have limited success in establishing sound metrics that have a good balance between lagging and leading measures.

Typical brainstormed balanced scorecard metrics utilized in virtual project management are summarized in Table 7–1. The primary issue in utilizing a scorecard is that it may not

TABLE 7–1

Example of a Project Balanced Scorecard

Financial	Customer
• Inventory levels	• Customer satisfaction
• Cost per unit	• On-time delivery
• Hidden factory	• Final product quality
• Activity-based costing	• Safety communications
• Cost of poor quality	
• Overall project savings	

Internal Business Processes	Employee Learning and Growth
• Defects, inspection data, defects per million opportunities (DPMO), sigma level	• Six-sigma tool utilization
• Rolled throughput yield	• Quality of training
• Supplier quality	• Meeting effectiveness
• Cycle time	• Lessons learned
• Volume shipped	• Total trained in six sigma
• Rework hours	• Project schedule versus actual date
	• Number of projects completed
	• Total savings to date

reflect the actual strategies applied by the team for achieving breakthroughs in the project.

However, instead of utilizing the balanced scorecard approach described above, the virtual teams can employ a more effective method by answering the questions listed in Figure 7–3. This approach helps virtual team members understand the objectives of the project from each of the four perspectives.

Once the project teams have brainstormed each of the four

FIGURE 7–3

The four balanced scorecard perspectives.

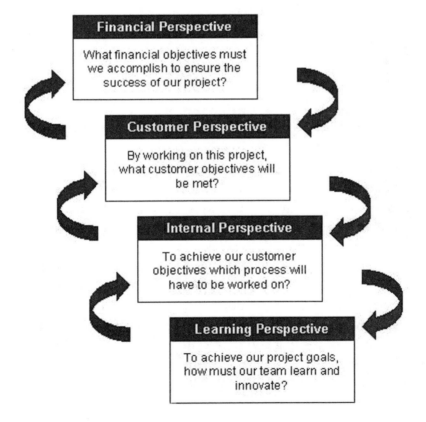

FIGURE 7–4

A strategy map applied to project strategies.

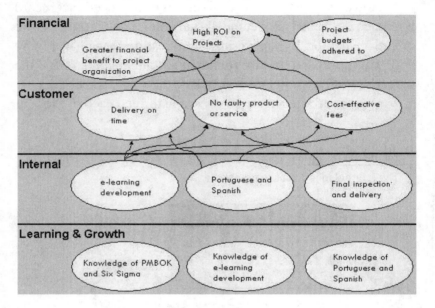

perspectives, the various objectives that must be met by the project will be clearer. These objectives can then be mapped in a strategy map thats cuts across all the perspectives and projects of the organization. The arrows help in understanding the cause-and-effect linkages in the strategy. Figure 7–4 shows a strategy map used in this way.

Once the strategy map for the project is determined, the team can begin brainstorming appropriate metrics for each of the objectives and, while doing so, maintain a balance in the selection between leading and lagging measures. This kind of approach ensures that a virtual team will select a set of metrics that are aligned with the strategy used on the e-project. Metrics selected in this way not only ensure that appropriate metrics are developed but also help the team in project planning and create a sense of direction for the team.

Tapping into Collaboration Tools

As a virtual project manager, to control the quality of your deliverables you have to reach certain goals, including but not limited to the following:

- Decreasing project cycles
- Keeping contracted services within the budget and on schedule
- Preventing delays from claims or changes
- Producing quality deliverables
- Increasing your stakeholders' (and customers') satisfaction

Innovation is essential if learning is to take place from a distance. But to take advantage of new ideas and technologies in virtual project management, ideas must be turned into knowledge and that knowledge must be turned into a tangible deliverable—action—as a direct component of the project. The fact that your team generates an abundance of new ideas and those ideas are being turned into knowledge does not mean you have found an edge in your ePM practice; you still must assess the quality of the deliverables.

In fact, raw and unfiltered information flowing through ePM communication channels is often of limited value. In such a scenario, knowledge management can help you assess the quality of the communication and knowledge base available to your virtual teams by providing meaning to any data that have been collected. Knowledge management (KM) can also help ensure that this information is shared across the virtual teams, the organization, and its constituents. Unless raw knowledge is interpreted, the information generated from it will remain unutilized. In addition, to improve knowledge interpretation and sharing, ePM managers must get better at collaboration. Again, KM can simplify the process of sharing knowledge, but if the value proposition of doing this is not made clear, it will not get done.

More specifically, KM strategies can be of great value in ePM by allowing for the collection, management, and dissemination of best practices. In addition, KM enables a focus on data warehousing and/or data mining to anticipate project needs and customer trends. Further, KM can be a successful tool for document management. Of course, this is only a small sample of options, but KM should be seen as a powerful tool for promoting collaboration and ultimately knowledge sharing inside and outside project teams, thus improving the level of quality of virtual team deliverables and project outcomes as a whole.

The choice of technology you make in promoting collaboration, and therefore learning, will depend on the business processes and requirements that are the targets of your project implementation. In ePM, because of the nature of distant project teams, learning does not occur for its own sake; it should attend to the design and pursuit of very clearly defined needs. Technology will enable it but not deliver it. Project enterprise portals, for example, have been the preferred KM delivery framework for ePM activities. But without concomitant changes in the way your virtual teams work and carry out their tasks, improvements in collaboration are only a possibility, not necessarily a reality. Learning—and collaboration, for that matter—requires action.

In "Simplicity, Speed and Self-Confidence: An Interview

with Jack Welch,"[1] Ram Charan discusses GE's quality control process, which was modeled after a New England town meeting. "Work-Out," as Welch called the process, had two main practical goals: one intellectual and the other practical. The practical goal was to get rid of bad habits accumulated since the establishment of GE. Thus, a good way to control the quality of project deliverables proactively is to get rid of the bad habits that make them happen in the first place.

The intellectual goal aimed to redefine the relationship between virtual project managers and virtual teams by making those leaders virtually present in front of their own people several times a year to let them learn what and how their people thought about the business, themselves, and their leaders. Work-Out is a great example of project management in action. You see creation and interpretation processes at work here. You also see an opportunity for retention of knowledge and change in behavior, with great chances for meaningful results. Notice that technology is not strongly emphasized.

An example, relying more on technology tools that of is Procter & Gamble, which is using what it calls the Plumtree Corporate Portal to control the quality of content from 1 million Web pages and thousands of Lotus Notes databases in an enterprisewide knowledge base. The strategy is creating one view of a business with hundreds of organizational units worldwide. Not only is the portal organizing access to documents in an enterprisewide Web directory, it is also integrating information and services from other systems.

Knowledge management portals can be a tremendous help in PM as an effective strategy to deliver a customizable, multidimensional interface to enable searchable access to data, reporting, and applications. These portals can include not only content management and quality control tools such as search and retrieval, access to budgets, WBS, and general information about the project as well as a repository for documents, websites, and databases but also collaboration and group productivity tools.

Several vendors, such as IBM and Microsoft, have knowledge portal product offerings. Lotus's Discovery Server offers a knowledge portal that enables the management of personal and community information and activity, as well as tools for user profiling and expertise location and content tracking and analysis. The following is a scenario in which this tool does an excellent job in proactively (not correctively) helping to control the quality of virtual project outputs.

Suppose you have a developer in India working on an application that requires JavaScript. She is not familiar with JavaScript and wants to make sure the quality of her coding is not jeopardized, and so she decides to search the project's enterprise resources to speed up her development efforts. Using a Web browser, as shown in Figure 7–5, the developer goes to her enterprise knowledge map (K-map) for help. The K-map displays the top-level categories of information in her organization, much as the home pages of websites such as Yahoo do.

The K-map is a graphical user interface that shows information resources from disparate systems in a single view that can be searched or browsed. The information presented in the K-map is automatically generated and maintained on the back end by the Lotus Discovery Server and modified by systems administrators.

The K-map, as shown in Figure 7–6, displays multidimensional categories consisting of documents, people, and virtual places or repositories of information. Rankings for documents and people help the developer decide which resources are most relevant.

The developer decides to search specifically for resources identified with "JavaScript," as depicted in Figure 7–7. Using

FIGURE 7-5

Lotus's Discovery Server is an enterprise portal that can be used for proactive quality control tasks.

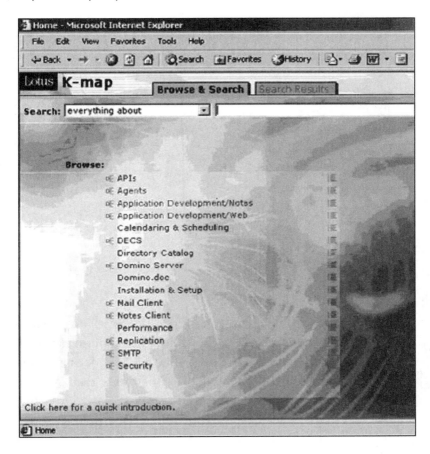

the drop-down refinement list of search criteria, the developer decides to search for "everything about" Javascript.

The K-map displays the search results, and the developer can look at tabs of information resources. Here she finds categories, documents, people and places that contain information related to JavaScript (Figure 7–8).

FIGURE 7–6

Lotus's K-map displays multidimensional categories that consist of
documents, people, and virtual places or repositories of information.

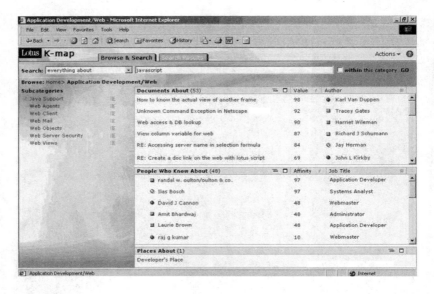

Documents refer to multiple types of files from various
locations in a virtual project organization that contain text such
as Lotus SmartSuite or Microsoft Office files, Web pages, and
Lotus Notes databases. These data repositories can even be
based on several Intranets all over the world so that your virtual
teams can tap into specs, standards, norms, best practices, and
other project-specific data anywhere.

The developer in this example can quickly scan the document summaries derived by the Discovery Server to help
decide if they are relevant and worth opening. She can also
click on the column headings to change the view and see other
information about the document, such as its author and from
which remote office or headquarters the document was
retrieved. A ranking is derived by the Discovery Server based

FIGURE 7-7

Lotus Discovery Server's search criteria drop-down list.

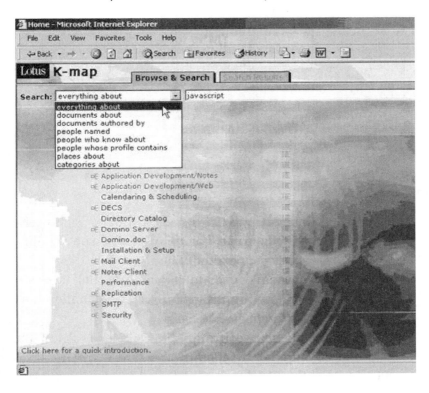

on its advanced metrics and analysis services that relate user activity to documents to determine value. Figure 7–9 illustrates this process.

To save time spent on trial and error, the Discovery Server allows the developer to find someone who has experience with JavaScript to answer a few quick questions so that she can rapidly get under way. The developer can view all the people associated with JavaScript and their "affinity" rankings (how strongly each person is related to the topic), and this information is again derived by the Discovery Server.

FIGURE 7-8

Lotus Discovery Server's search results tab.

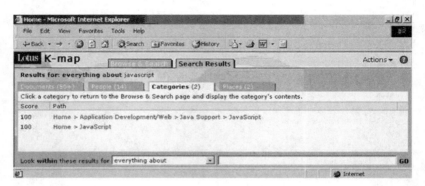

Based on the people awareness icon next to each user's name, the developer can immediately tell if a person is online and available to be contacted. As Figure 7–10 shows, one symbol indicates a user is available, another indicates that he or she is unavailable, one shade shows the user is not online, and another shade signifies "do not disturb."

Last but certainly not least, the developer looks at the places found by the Discovery Server associated with Java-Script. Because the developer's organization also uses Lotus K-station and the Discovery Server recognizes and can index the K-station community places (virtual team workspaces), the developer has the benefit of finding entire repositories of information related to JavaScript. Built-in security features display only the information that she has access to see.

She can, for instance, quickly link to a discovered community place that might contain any combination of discussion forums, document libraries, bookmarked Web pages, and more related to her topic of interest.

Another very useful feature is the user's profile, (Figure 7–11). Clicking on the user's name launches a profile with

FIGURE 7-9

Document search results in the K-map.

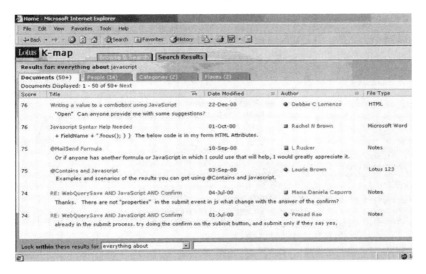

FIGURE 7-10

People search results in the K-map.

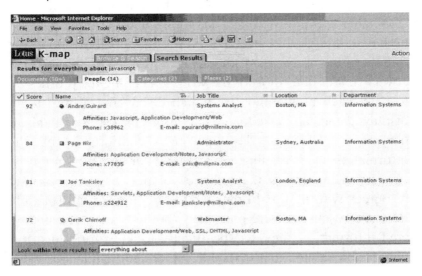

FIGURE 7-11

Lotus Discovery user profile showing contact information.

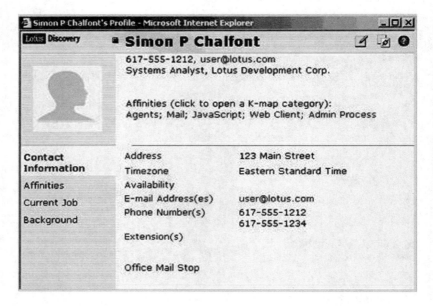

contact, job, and background information, as well as a person's associated "affinities" to various topics and the time zone the user is in so that the developer won't awaken someone in the middle of the night to ask about JavaScript. Although the Discovery Server does most of the work in keeping the profiles up to date, each user authorizes which discovered affinities are displayed and can make manual additions or deletions in his or her profile. Thus, the developer feels comfortable that the information she is reading is public and current.

By using the K-map, the developer was able to find resources with minimal time spent searching for information. Relevant resources were presented via the K-map that uncovered information she was specifically looking for and information she did not know existed. This added tremendous value to her specific task of application development. She found expertise that could minimize trial-and-error time. Leveraging the project's know-how, the developer avoided mistakes she might have otherwise made, increasing the quality of the deliverables.

This is just one example of low information technologies, in particular knowledge management tools, can add value to everyday business activities to reduce redundancies and increase speed in a more user-friendly way than ever before. This includes both internal uses by project team members, as well as making similar capabilities appropriately available to external business partners, vendors, suppliers, and customers to enhance their experience in finding information that relates to the project.

Peer-to-Peer Collaboration

A novel way to promote collaboration and manage virtual projects is through the use of peer-to-peer (P2P) collaboration technologies. Some Internet collaboration infrastructure based on P2P architecture enables the connection of a project's internal people with virtual teams, business partners, independent contractors and customers, and supply chain and distribution channels regardless of their function or geographic location. These capabilities give ePM managers the means to design and assemble virtual service communities.

Independent software vendors (ISVs) such as Novient's services provide applications that enable the optimization of organizations' service processes by matching available people and skills to project requirements and automating the service delivery process. All activities in the project organization, especially knowledge capture and dissemination, must be optimized both technologically and organizationally. That is the case because if faster time to market is to be a realistic proposition for competitive businesses, new knowledge of market conditions, customer needs, and internal capabilities and capacities must be generated in real time.

CASE STUDY 1: AUDITING TIME AND COST— A MATTER OF QUALITY

Marcus Goncalves

The ability to exceed the customer's expectations is fundamental to the success of any project, and the existence of effective and well-documented quality procedures will raise the credibility of the project team and the confidence of stakeholders.

The design of a complex engineering system, from the realization of a need (for a new system or improvement of an existing system) through production to engineering support in use, is known as systems engineering (especially with military or space systems) or new product development (with commercial systems). Either way, the engineering of complex systems is carried out in a series of sequential phases or stages. A task group formed from U.S. engineering societies, coordinated by the National Society of Professional Engineering (NSPE) in cooperation with the National Institute of Science and Technology (NIST), agreed to establish auditing procedures throughout the life cycle of a project.

Nonetheless, the work to be carried out to accomplish the project's goals is based on established processes. Those processes are defined and described in process descriptions and work models as well as in recognized industry standards. If special routines are required, they must be documented along with any agreed deviations from established process descriptions, in particular for industrial and mechanical engineering environments.

In creating a complex system, hundreds or thousands of engineers, technicians, and other workers may be involved in creating designs, reviewing them, manufacturing or constructing in accordance with them, and inspecting to assure that what has been made agrees with what was specified. However, no complex system is specified perfectly to begin with, and the needs of the user may change during the design phase; therefore, design changes are inevitable.

Control systems for drawing and/or design release and configuration management are essential to ensure that everyone knows what the official design (configuration) is at any instant yet change can be managed effectively. Quality control and quality assurance are examples of such control systems.

Quality control includes the checking, measuring, and auditing necessary to prove that the product of the project complies with the agreed specifications or the desired level of quality. Quality assurance includes the auditing and reviews necessary to prove that the quality control processes are working.

Audits are called by different names in different organizations. Generally, customer audits are carried out to make sure that the performing organization can fulfill the requirements and stipulations of a contract or to evaluate whether that organization has the capability to complete a project. Project management audits may be instigated by the project manager or sponsor to verify whether the project is organized effectively, with the right competence and quantity of resources, and whether it is being carried out correctly.

Reviews normally focus on a project deliverable and take place at recognized milestones or intermediate measurable events. A milestone review checks the status and quality level of the results achieved against predefined milestone criteria. Reviews are normally the responsibility of the project manager.

Milestone Review Process

Milestone review process steps include the following:

1. Collect data, such as milestone criteria and progress reports.
2. Prepare checklists from milestone criteria.
3. Convene a meeting with all the people responsible for achieving the results included in the milestone criteria.
4. Compare the results achieved with the milestone criteria, highlighting any deficiencies.
5. Evaluate the results of the review.
6. If the results meet the milestone criteria, the milestone is passed and the project can go on to the next phase.
7. If there are only minor deficiencies, the project manager may decide to pass the milestone with an action plan to clear the deficiency list.
8. If there are major deficiencies, the review should not have taken place.

The auditing process also involves configuration management, which is used mainly in development projects.

Configuration Management

Designing a new system or product is a very complex undertaking. With global corporations and organizations racing to bring new ideas and products quickly to market, the ability to control and organize diverse teams working on a joint design project is critical. Thus, configuration management is making inroads into all aspects of product and system development.

Configuration management is the discipline of identifying the elements of an evolving system in order to monitor changes made to the elements and maintain traceability of the changes through the system's evolution. The purpose of configuration management is to ensure that the status and location of all versions of the project's product are known and recorded and to make sure that unauthorized changes are prevented.

The Internet has helped provide the communication infrastructure that allows companies such as Boeing and Daimler-Chrysler to develop new products and implement design changes to new and existing products without teams ever meeting.

Configuration management consists of four main concepts:

- *Baselines.* The configuration at any point of reference. All modifications and changes between one reference point and the next are controlled using the change control process. The baseline and the changes form the new baseline.

- *Change control.* All changes between one baseline and the next are subject to the formal rules defined in the change control process.

- *Formal approval of changes.* Changes that do not affect the cost or schedule of a project are normally approved within the project team. Changes that do affect the cost or schedule must be approved by the project sponsor. The levels of authorization normally are stated in the project plan and the quality plan.

- *Traceability*. Configuration management makes it possible to trace the changes of a product and trace the changing relationship between products.

Control of Nonconforming Product

Products that do not meet specifications need to be dealt with in a formalized way. They need to be marked and segregated to prevent them from being installed, used, or delivered. Such control can be performed through the following process:

I. Planning Quality Activities
1. Analyze the project tasks with regard to quality.
   a. The scope of the quality work within the project
   b. The policies and procedures to be used
   c. The processes, methods, and tools to be used
   d. The internal and external standards to be followed
   e. Customer-specific requirements
2. Investigate quality routines in subcontractor organizations.
3. Write a quality plan.

II. Executing the Quality Activities
1. Implement and control project activities to assure quality.
2. Make all audits, checks, and inspections.
3. Identify risks that may prevent successful completion of the project.
4. Initiate preventive measures.
5. Compare the output of the project with the specified deliverables.
6. Report observations and experiences.

III. Concluding Quality Activities

1. Report any experiences gained that might be useful in succeeding projects.
2. Suggest improvements to the project's methods and processes.

Value engineering activities are always encouraged in—and often required—of contractors by the U.S. Department of Defense (DoD) and NASA. Practitioners share their experiences with the Society of American Value Engineers (SAVE) and can earn the title Certified Value Specialist by passing an examination.

Discussion Questions

1. What are the reasons for dividing the systems engineering/new product development process into phases or stages?
2. What are the principal reasons configuration management is necessary?
3. For an engineering design or project management system you are familiar with, describe the drawing release and design review process.

▧ CASE STUDY 2: ARE YOU MANAGING PERFORMANCE?

Marcus Goncalves

When times are good, many of us spend an extensive amount of time supporting our line managers in the motivation, reward, and retention of the key people who are critical to the success of our projects. As far as other mechanical engineers are concerned, we tend to assume that no news is good news. It's only when we encounter a tougher economic climate that we start to question the contribution each member of the team is making toward the success of the project. Why have these things not been addressed before?

Unsurprisingly, most of us are disinclined to confront people with their shortcomings in an open, honest, and constructive manner. We would rather put this task in the "too difficult" file. We need to make the connection between team and individual goals while realizing that our primary instinctual goals for ourselves are best served if the team is successful. The situation can be aggravated by creating avoidance management when professionals don't realize that they are typically not experts in marketing, manufacturing, quality assurance, and finance. They should realize that other departments have functions and needs that are not clear or easily understood by technical professionals, much as other departments have difficulty understanding the needs of technical professionals.

What are the consequences of avoidance management? One option is to encourage those identified as below par to leave the project and move on in a discreet and dignified way. However, there is no getting around the fact that a stigma is attached to anyone who arrives for an interview out of a job or having been made redundant. As a result, employees prefer to hang on and then resort to litigation. Why? Quite simply, they know that there is usually insufficient evidence on which to terminate and that to avoid costly tribunals and court cases, we are more often than not prepared to throw money at the problem and agree to a compromise agreement with confidentiality clauses and a satisfactory reference.

The net result is that underperformers are rewarded with a new and better-paid job elsewhere, much to the annoyance of the high achievers we are trying to retain.

As project managers, we have a duty to anticipate these

issues and encourage our line management and project sponsors to assume responsibility and take action. Here are some questions you might want to consider:

- When hiring a new resource on your project, do you follow up on employment references?
- Do you check how far a new hire is living up to expectations?
- Do you ask project leaders to review regularly the performance of their teams, particularly those not yet covered by employment protection as it applies in your country?
- Do you query appraisals conducted through rose-colored spectacles?
- Are your project managers trained to ensure that assessments are consistent?
- Do you talk regularly with all project managers about performance?

If you want to affect the bottom line in any project where human resources are the greatest cost, make sure to invest as much energy in weeding out the rare poor performers as in looking after the stars.

Discussion Questions

1. Define in your own words what constitutes the successful completion of a mechanical engineering project to develop a new product. How important is staffing for such a project?
2. This case discusses typical reasons for project failures and includes lack of accountability in the form of avoidance management. In your own environment,

what do you think it means, and how could it be prevented?
3. Between which two company departments is an attitude of working together most critical to the success of
the project and the company?

🔖 CASE STUDY 3: THE BLAME GAME— HOW NOT TO MANAGE PROJECT TEAMS

Ed Hartnett

In any engineering organization things go wrong. Product is
shipped that doesn't meet customers' expectations. Defects,
perhaps severe ones, are missed in testing and discovered in the
field. Documents and manuals contain mistakes. The list goes
on and on.

There are two possible responses to such a crisis. Some
project managers will ask: "What can we change to make sure
this kind of problem doesn't recur?" Other project managers
will ask: "Who was responsible for this mistake?" They will
begin to play the blame game.

A Game with No Winners, Only Losers

The blame game is fun to play. It allows a project manager to
find an outlet for everyone's anger and frustration. It provides
hours of entertaining conversation and redirects uncomfortable
responsibility.

The only real problem with the blame game is that it is
impossible for anyone to win. Temporary victories are possible. When the CEO asks for an explanation of a screw-up, it's
comforting to point the finger at one of the engineers and say:
"He did it!"

Unfortunately, that solves nothing. The mistake still has to be corrected, the customer is still unhappy, and now the engineer who made the mistake is unhappy too. The mistake is likely to happen again.

If the CEO has even the brains of an oyster, the blame game won't work for long. Soon will come the realization that this project manager can't deliver the goods.

Who Makes Mistakes Anyway?

Some engineers make very few mistakes. These are the engineers who do as little as possible. They decline to rock the boat. They certainly never try to improve anything. They follow the herd, well to the rear. Since they never initiate, they can never be blamed. These engineers look forward to their paychecks and don't spend much time worrying about the quality of the product. After all, it's not their problem.

Other engineers like to make things better. They are always looking to improve the product and produce it more cheaply. These engineers are constantly making decisions. They are the ones on the cutting edge of progress. Nothing but the best is good enough for them. These are the engineers who make the most mistakes. They are also the engineers who are responsible for all the progress. In an organization that plays the blame game, these engineers are the biggest losers.

What Would Captain Kirk Do in a Situation Like This?

As an old trekkie, I'm quite familiar with the adventures of Captain Kirk and his diverse crew. Although there are plenty of things he could be criticized for, such as his ceaseless violations of the Federation Prime Directive, there was one thing that Kirk knew how to do well: accept responsibility.

In how many episodes did we hear Kirk explain that the captain is responsible for the actions of his crew? When things went wrong on the Starship *Enterprise*, Kirk never turned to Spock and asked: "Who screwed up this time?" He instantly turned his full attention to resolving the current crisis and took full responsibility for any damage. There's a good lesson here for project managers.

Who Is Really to Blame?

When a mistake is made by anyone on the team, it is far more accurate to blame the project manager. After all, the project manager is supposed to understand that people are imperfect. He or she is supposed to devise processes and systems to catch mistakes. If that's not the job of a project manager, what is?

Since it's the project manager's job to establish the work process, it's also his or her responsibility. If a defect works its way through the process, the process is broken and needs to be fixed. If instead of trying to fix it the project manager decides to play the blame game, the process will remain broken. Look for more defects in the next release.

Engineers very quickly learn to cope with the blame game. After all, they are good at solving problems. There are two solutions to the blame game problem from an engineer's point of view: Stop trying to improve anything or find another job. The second solution is usually the better one.

Here's a Dollar; Go Buy a Clue

Nothing destroys respect for a project manager faster than the blame game. It may take only one round of play to lose the respect of everyone on the team. Only a few more rounds are required to lose the respect of upper management as well.

Next time a defect is discovered in your product, instead of blaming the engineer responsible, go out and buy a book or two about the process of professional engineering. Spend some time working on test plans. Set up a work review process to catch future mistakes. Do something useful.

Most important, take responsibility. Apologize to the entire team for the process defect that caused the product defect. Pull a Captain Kirk.

You'll find that you can not only improve your product but also gain respect from your team. Not only will they be inspired to avoid this kind of mistake again, they will be inspired to think about process improvements and taking risks.

Until the genetic scientists manage to create perfect people who never make mistakes, we will have to learn to cope with them. Stop playing games and get to work instead. When it comes to process improvement, there's always plenty to do.

Discussion Questions

1. Do you agree with the statements the author makes in this case? Does the blame game really go on in organizations?

2. Why should a project manager take responsibility for his or her group's actions, if in fact he or she was not the one executing the failed task?

3. Would group rewards instead of individual rewards be in line with the management style advocated in this paper? Should a project manager emphasize group rather than individual rewards?

8

C H A P T E R

Integrating Speed, Change, and Radical Innovation with ePM

As has been discussed throughout this book, the virtual project manager, or ePM manager, is one of the many emergent professions in the knowledge and information age. New technologies have eliminated the need to make space and times coincide, but they also have imposed new rules and new conditions. This means that in regard to their degree of awareness, these professionals operate within working structures that require new means of organization and communication.

Distance project management has become both an opportunity and a challenge for them, and taking control of this factor requires both knowledge management and project management practice. This entails to continuing training needs to secure the professionalism, specialization, and retraining of e-project managers, e-leaders, and virtual team workers.

In informal surveys I have conducted with project management graduate students at Boston University as well as in my own practice, I have found that up to 98 percent of project managers have not received any training in virtual project management, e-leadership, e-project organization, and the management of virtual teams or a virtual project management office (ePMO).

However, although some professionals I interviewed were not aware of ePM or virtual project management, most of them had heard about the practice and had been working in a mixed environment not by choice but as a result of budget cuts, difficulties in traveling, or a heavy workload. In any event, they all felt they could benefit from training in virtual planning, communication, and human resources management despite the fact that they considered that type of training to be secondary. Most of them lacked the qualifications for these disciplines and consequently acted rather intuitively. Besides, they argued that they did not have the time to learn more and had not found the proper material or training offer.

This chapter attempts to provide answers for these needs and improve the qualifications of professionals in the areas of virtual project organization, quality management and control, and management and coaching of virtual teams.

BECOMING AN EFFECTIVE ePM MANAGER

The role of a virtual project manager is neither a professional profile nor a new profession. Instead, it is a complementary and intrinsic role of higher technical and managerial jobs in the new technologies sector because of the new work methods that these tools provide and impose. In other words, it is not a profession strictly speaking but a specialization of the conventional project manager role that has seen the discipline evolve into a more ubiquitous, synchronous, and pervasive form where the role of project manager has to deal with activities that are being developed on a distributed and delocalized basis through the use of new technologies, many already discussed in earlier chapters.

To be successful, ePM managers must be able to integrate speed, change, and radical innovation. Figure 8–1 shows a typical ePM environment.

DEVELOPING AND MANAGING VIRTUAL TEAMS

In developing the core task of managing a project, the efficient management of the work being performed by the different virtual teams is a key factor in ensuring the quality of the final

FIGURE 8–1

A typical ePM environment.

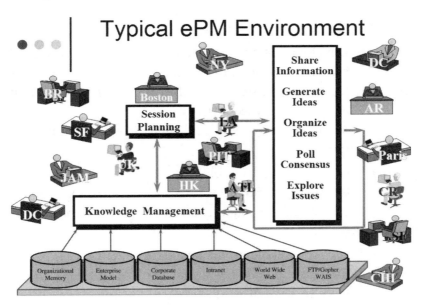

work. Individual local work and the work of a virtual team should be homogeneous throughout the project stages, and the final result should match the initial expectations.

Therefore, special attention should be paid to the development of the virtual team. Responsibilities should be distributed according to the participants in the project, and their *scope* and *level* should vary according to the following:

- The importance and scope of the virtual teams, their purpose, and the activities being performed
- The degree of delegation and autonomy
- The virtual project workers in the remote project offices
  - Work teams
  - Permanent or transitional collaborators
  - Local workers
- Their status in the project organization

Their responsibilities should pertain to

- Research and development
  - Development or participation in the initial design of products, services, or projects
  - Designing, setting up, and maintaining virtual teams and remote project offices
  - Technological monitoring and/or updates and innovation
- Internal and external relations
  - Commercial relationships and maintaining contact with clients during the development of the product or project
- Leadership and team management
  - Organization and performance of work teams
  - Coordination of work, tasks, and actions

- Encouraging and training the virtual team
- Monitoring production processes and making decisions about the necessary changes
- Solving technical and human problems
- Evaluation of results from qualitative and quantitative analyses
- Responsibility for the final quality of products and/or services

These responsibilities do not differ much from the conventional project management approach. However, circumstances make a difference. The presence of the digital component affects project development, as is discussed next.

Training Is an Important Factor

One of the biggest problems in virtual project management is that project professionals are not savvy about the technologies that enable it. This is not to their detriment, as project managers in general are not information systems and technology professionals and most of the project management literature available in books and in magazine format does not cover the subject. While writing this book I surveyed about 60 professionals about the technologies I outline in the book. For the most part, they were familiar with e-mail, instant messaging (IM), and Microsoft Project. Only 3 of the 60 knew what Microsoft Project EPM was, and among those, only 1 had worked with it.

Therefore, there is a tremendous need for training in virtual project management, in particular on the technology side. The challenge to train professionals in these technologies is actually greater as result of the dramatic pace of technological innovation and the wide variety of tools available on the market.

Virtual project managers therefore must keep up with the technological resources available, as this industry is characterized by a never-ending flow of information and innovation. Specific training is being made available for professionals in large organizations, but very few training and/or consulting organizations are focusing on training ePM managers. I applaud the American Society of Mechanical Engineers (ASME) for its forethought in making such courses available as part of its curriculum: There is a course in virtual project management available throughout the year across the United States.

How Virtual Teams Differ from Conventional Ones

When the members of a virtual team congregate through technological means such as Intranets, Extranets, Web portals, IM, or phone conferences or through conventional means such as getting on a plane and flying to a remote office, their responsibilities and tasks usually involve the following:

1. Participating in designing and setting up the virtual workspace
   - Analyzing the needs and requirements of the clients
   - Analyzing suppliers' offers
   - Preliminary assessment and evolution of the virtual project space, such as the website, the discussion boards, and the chats, together with the virtual team
2. Organizing and securing the operation of the virtual project offices
   - Setting up the organizational guidelines and the operational rules for the end users
   - Optimization of results in the work environment
   - Organization and management of the work schedule and activities

- ○ Management of economic resources related to the space
- ○ In some cases, performing administrative management tasks such as hiring, budgeting, and invoicing.

3. Coordinating the cooperative work, actions, and activities related to the virtual project
   - ○ Defining the roles of the main participants in the virtual project teams
   - ○ Establishing the actions and exchanges pertaining to organization, operation, maintenance, coaching, and training
   - ○ Organizing virtual (at a distance) or face-to-face project meetings
   - ○ Securing the monitoring and advancement of the project work
   - ○ Defining and communicating commitments as necessary
   - ○ Evaluating the results of actions in the virtual project offices and making the necessary changes in the virtual teams
   - ○ Acting as a spokesperson with clients
   - ○ Representing the work team before third parties

4. Securing project management and ▸communications technology, maintenance, and support
   - ○ Solving or participating in the solution of technical problems
   - ○ Securing the technological maintenance and innovation

5. Training and coaching
   - ○ Training the virtual team members in communication tools such as e-mail, IM, discussion boards, newsgroups, and Microsoft Project EPM and other project management tools

- Training the virtual team members so that they can participate effectively in the common virtual project workspace
- Acting as mediator between the virtual staff, vendors, collaborators, partners, stakeholders, and customers
- Helping virtual project leaders share the same values, criteria, and conditioning and orientation guidelines.

6. Evaluating the results
   - Analyzing and summarizing actions and reactions from clients, stakeholders, and project workers
   - Doing quantitative and qualitative analysis
   - Proposing solutions

There are also general tasks and functions that must be taken into consideration. In spite of the diversity of situations and activities involving the whole virtual project team, the tasks and roles outlined below should be part of everyone's job description:

- Internal and external communications
  - Commercial relations
  - Representation and public relations
- Technical
  - Consultancy and design of work
  - Planning of tasks and activities
  - Organization of work teams and the virtual workspaces where they meet: designing and setting up operational procedures and guidelines
  - Coordination and coaching of virtual teams
  - Monitoring and control of the state of advancement of the work

- ○ Securing the quality of the processes and the results
- ○ Providing technological support to the virtual team: orientations on the use of technologies and solving technical problems
- ○ Securing innovation, mainly technological innovation
- • Administrative
  - ○ Human resources management
  - ○ Technical and financial resources management

In the case of organizations where the distribution and organization of teams already have been set up to a great extent, you will find that the professionals who set up these teams typically are not the ones who manage them. Several project staff members exchange and/or share roles and act as virtual workers in some projects and team coordinators in others.

Allotment of Working Time According to Functions

As for the time allotment for the different virtual tasks assigned, it is typical to find the following main tasks performed by virtual teams, as depicted in Figure 8–2:

- • Business relations and communication with clients: up to 35 percent of the time
- • Project definition, planning, and organization: 25 percent
- • Progress, performance measurement, and quality control: 15 percent
- • Coordination and communication with virtual teams: 10 percent
- • Solving technical problems: 10 percent

FIGURE 8–2

Allotment of working time for virtual team workers according to functions.

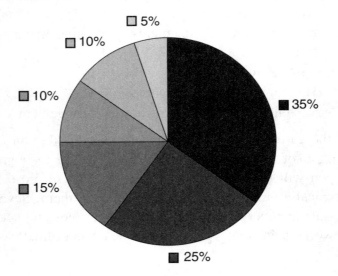

☐ Business relation and communication with clients

☐ Project definition, planning, and organization

☐ Progress and performance measurement, and quality control

☐ Coordination and communication with virtual teams

☐ Solving technical problems

☐ Management of common virtual workplace

• Management of the common virtual workplace: 5 percent (although this increases for activities concerning Internet service providers and portals)

These data show that most of the time is devoted to communicating with the clients, although communicating with the virtual teams is also a very important task. Note how little time is devoted to the revision of activities. This does not mean that revisions are not important; as we all know, they are very important. But owing to the nature of the working environment, a lot of time and thought is spent during the initial stages of the project.

On my own projects, once I feel comfortable with the project leaders and know that they understand the work that needs to be done, are comfortable with their own teams, know they can ask for help at any time, and know they are allowed to make mistakes but should always take advantage of the communication technologies they have at hand and the vast technical resource available to them online and on the phone, I get out of the way.

Types of Virtual Teams

In the old days, during the time of old team management models, the motto was "If in doubt, go travel to sort it out." However, this is highly inefficient and expensive, especially in a rapidly growing global organization. Many corporations are at the limit of what they can manage without huge structural changes unless they develop a different way of working.

I often find that senior executives are traveling twice as much now as they were two years ago (despite economic problems and the impact of September 11, 2001). Many are already spending up to six weeks a year at 35,000 feet, in addition to dealing with the hassles of flight delays, taxis, hotels, and jet lag. So what happens next year? The model of team management followed by most corporations is unsustainable and will be a number one survival issue.

Therefore, virtual teams that can bridge the distance gap

will win a clear competitive advantage, traveling less but with greater impact during each visit and backed up with regular videoconferencing, shared-space technologies, chat, e-mail, telephone conference calls, and other digital tools. Forget old-style video links in boardrooms. Think wireless everywhere, anytime: video links that can start as spontaneously as a tele-phone call.

To achieve those results, however, you must understand the different types of virtual teams and their characteristics so that you can take full advantage of their potential. There are four types of virtual teams, as shown in Figure 8–3:

- Local
- International
- Interactive
- Collaborative

FIGURE 8–3

Types of virtual teams and time versus place framework.

	Place	
	Same	Different
Time Same	Boston (Local)	Mexico (International)
Time Different	Los Angeles (Interactive)	Argentina (Collaborative)

Local

Local virtual teams are those which are located in the same time zone and geographic location. The boundaries of what you call local depends on your perspective. A virtual team in Florida may be considered local because it meets the two criteria: same time and same place. In this case we are considering the *same country* as the same place, whereas others may consider the same *state, town*, or even *building* to be the same place. When there are two teams in the same building, to consider them virtual, they need to be be physically separate or virtual in relation to another team. Of course, these distinctions are mostly semantic.

International

International teams are located abroad from the local team, in another country. These teams often are more complex to work with as cultures tend to be different, along with currencies and languages. In this case, in selecting a location for your international virtual team, make sure to develop an assessment matrix for site selection (Figure 8–4).

Before establishing an international team and remote project office, you must understand your firm's competitive position in its global industry. Make sure to assess your firm's strengths, weaknesses, and available resources and management's attitude toward implementing an international remote team. Questions you might want to ask include the following:

- Why would you or your sponsors establish a virtual team abroad?
- Does your firm have adequate core competencies regarding an alliance or merger project (language, cultural symmetry, political understanding, etc.)?

FIGURE 8–4

Assessment matrix for virtual team site selection.

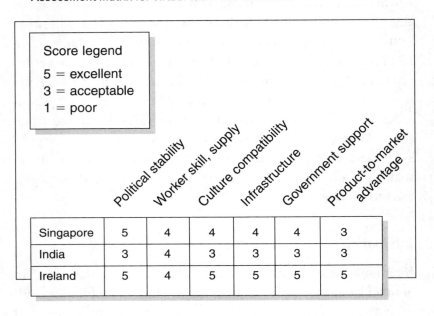

	Political stability	Worker skill, supply	Culture compatibility	Infrastructure	Government support	Product-to-market advantage
Singapore	5	4	4	4	4	3
India	3	4	3	3	3	3
Ireland	5	4	5	5	5	5

Score legend
5 = excellent
3 = acceptable
1 = poor

- Are you opening a remote office in light of competitive demand? If not, what is the reason?
- Do you have the financial resources available?
- Do you have multicultural exposure?
- Are you comfortable with the risk levels?

There are many other situations you must consider (Figure 8–4), which include the following:

- **Legal/political**. Are you prepared to operate within the laws and regulations of the host country?
- **Security**. In some countries the crime rate is much higher than what you are accustomed to in the United

States. The growing presence of organized crime has discouraged foreign firms from setting up operations in the former Soviet Union. In setting up projects in Angola, a common practice is to hire tribal bodyguards.

- **Geography**. This is often an underestimated factor. I once provided consulting for the Institute of International Research in Dubai in the United Arabic Emirates, and it was a shock to deplane at a temperature of 105 degrees at 8:30 A.M. The capital of Bolivia— La Paz—is in such a high altitude the most foreigners need a day or two to acclimate to the atmospheric pressure, which makes it difficult to breathe.

- **Economy**. How business is conducted in a country can affect your project. As was mentioned earlier, this is one of the hurdles I have operating in South America, especially in Argentina, where inflation is very high and the economy is unstable.

- **Infrastructure**. Can the country provide you with the services required for your project? This includes adequate transportation, communications, electricity, technology, and education.

- **Culture**. Are you ready to accept and respect the customs, values, philosophies, and social standards of the host country? Will religious factors affect the project? How about local languages?

Of course, this is just a brief summary of issues you must consider when planning to set project operations overseas. It underscores the complexity of working on international projects, but it should give you some idea of where to start. Great resources about every country can be found at the Central

Intelligence Agency website at www.cia.gov as well as the Chamber of Commerce in the cities in the countries you are contemplating. Also, don't forget to check the Centers for Disease Control (CDC) for health information at www.cdc.org.

Interactive

Interactive groups can be in the same locations or not too far from each other and take advantage of many similarities, such as language, culture, time zone, technology, and background, that allow them to establish a very interactive relationship. Distance does not necessarily prevent a virtual team's interactivity. For instance, you may have an interactive relationship between a team in the United States and another one in England.

Interactive groups can be very distinct and differ from local organized groups. The decision to use interactive groups in ePM is an important step in the process of converting a virtual project into a *learning organization*, at the heart of which lies the commitment by ePM managers, team members, stakeholders and sponsors, vendors, other professionals, and organization members to make the project a success. All the parties involved should be inspired—an important function of an effective project leader—by the promise of a new project paradigm in a knowledge organization in which virtual projects are not jeopardized by ethnic, cultural, socioeconomic, or religious background. I have discovered in my own practice that coaching groups on the basis of equality and dialogue or the principles set out by dialogic learning is a way to ensure more learning as well as solidarity among all the diverse team participants.

Collaborative

Collaborative teams enable you to organize the work breakdown structure (WBS) and organization breakdown structure
(OBS), speed decision making, and enhance relationships with
project sponsors, stakeholders, and peers. Virtual team collaboration has captured the imagination of many professionals,
enabling teamwork across distances, time, and geographic
zones.

Boundaries between the team members of virtual teams
are minimized by electronic communication. By the nature of
their distributed existence over the globe, virtual teams can be
supported by information communication technologies (ICTs)
such as Blackboard and Web Board that support chat, forum,
and other collaborative tools. In virtual teams, ICTs enable
interaction between the participants and also have an impact on
team dynamics.

Technology is one of the aspects of virtual collaboration.
A variety of cultural and organizational issues also play crucial
roles in the success or failure of virtual collaboration, as was
discussed in earlier chapters.

DRIVING FORCES BEHIND VIRTUAL TEAMS

There are several driving forces behind virtual teams, varying
from technology and economics to competitive advantage and
professional growth. Figure 8–5 outlines some of the main
ones, but let's take a look in more detail at some of the other
forces:

1. More flexibility and adaptability than conventional
   teams
   ○ The ability to work together with virtual teams,
   instead of working in the same office or having to

FIGURE 8-5

Driving forces behind virtual teams.

Driving Forces Behind Virtual Teams

- Conservative E-Commerce Project facts: (Source www.cutter.com)
  - 50% of new software projects are web-based
  - 20% of them are critical
  - 31% of IT budget spent of Web Projects
  - 95% should be done "within a year"
- Other Facts
  - Globalization
  - Downsizing/Rightsizing
  - Telecommuting
  - Partnerships and Alliances
  - Increasing Outsource trend
  - SWAT/Focused teams
  - Increasing competition, etc.

---

work overseas, with flexible hours and the opportunity to work with professionals with whom you otherwise wouldn't be able to collaborate.

○ Setting up virtual teams that will be able to collaborate and communicate even after the project or product has been completed, as this type of communication does not rely on space and time, which may allow virtual team members to work together again.

○ Allows for the setup of virtual teams consisting of many professionals whose lack of availability or mobility would not have allowed them to work together.

○ Optimizing contacts between colleagues and collaborators.

○ Greater chances for innovation, since experts who

otherwise would be unavailable may be incorporated within the virtual teams.

2. Better profitability of human, financial, and technical resources
   ○ Allows the coordination of several projects to be executed simultaneously, without the need for much traveling.
   ○ Enables the detection, preparation, and management of projects with external collaborators in an easy way, improving project working skills and timeliness.
   ○ Project results can be delivered immediately via electronic means, and the feedback process can start immediately.
   ○ Communication can be operative 24 hours a day even with differing working hours and time zones.
   ○ Once the initial technical investment has been made, general costs can be minimized (for instance, communications, trips, venues, infrastructures) on every scale.
   ○ It is easier to provide services to more clients without increasing production costs.
   ○ The time spent traveling and commuting decreases and can be reallocated for project work or relaxation.
   ○ Flexible and autonomous management of working hours results in more satisfied virtual workers and better quality in the working environment.

3. Performance
   ○ Better selection of professionals because they are not limited to the local market.
   ○ Easier and autonomous access to a wider variety of knowledge bases, information, and resources otherwise unavailable because of their remoteness.

- ○ Technical support and solutions can be provided almost immediately.
- ○ Problems can be spotted more easily through automated software.
- ○ Communication standards accelerate and multiply without additional costs or strain.
- ○ Decisions can be made more easily because of the flow of information and feedback.
- ○ The distribution and allotment of tasks improve, as well as their monitoring and follow-up.
- ○ Information is automatically registered and made available as a type of collective project memory.

4. Improved professionalism
- ○ The professional satisfaction and motivation of virtual team members increase because they can participate more actively in the decision-making processes and take on new responsibilities.
- ○ Virtual team members can work more autonomously and make contributions and suggestions more easily.
- ○ Customer relations improve, especially for those overseas, as there are many ways of keeping them informed and participating in the project in a very interactive fashion
- ○ There is better planning and management of working hours.
- ○ Working hours become more flexible on a local and an international scale.
- ○ Virtual access technologies enable better organization and prioritization of urgencies.
- ○ Virtual presence helps save time lost to physical interferences and interruptions.
- ○ Time is saved when tasks are better coordinated in a global perspective.

DIMENSIONS OF VIRTUAL TEAMS

Virtual teams can be classified in four dimensions. Although some scholars propose three dimensions—time, space, and culture—others identify people, links, and purpose as the characteristics that distinguish a virtual team from a traditional team. There are other definitions, but I prefer to stick to one that is more business-oriented, as illustrated in Figure 8–6:

- Stability of membership, which can be stable or fluid
- Clarity of team boundaries, which can be unclear or clear
- Time frame in which to operate, which can be immediate or long-term

FIGURE 8–6

Typical characteristics within the dimensions.

Two Virtual Team Examples

	Project or Product Team	Action Team
Stability of Membership	Fluid	Stable/Fluid
Team Boundaries	Clear	Unclear
Timeframe	Longer-term	Immediate
Regularity	Frequent	Infrequent
Task	Nonroutine	Nonroutine
Decision Authority	High	Moderate
Complexity	High	Moderate

- Regularity of activity, which can be regular or infrequent

Another approach is to divide teams into subtypes and distinguish virtualness as a characteristic. In this context, there are four classes of teams:

- **Pure**: Team functions virtually, without control of any one organizational method.
- **Transitional**: Team functions as a combination of hybrid and mono forms.
- **Hybrid**: Team functions in a multiorganizational culture.
- The team members all function in the same organization.

One gets the feeling that everything old has become new again with the Internet. Recently developed technology has greatly enhanced the possibility of geographically dispersed employees working together on common projects. This thread of thought is woven into related areas, such as corporate structure with virtual companies and virtual enterprises. Some concepts are taken from the older topic of telecommuting. Still others come from CASE tools that allow collaborative engineering. Most of the concepts from these ideas are shared, as is the literature.

INTEGRATING QUALITY WITH ePM: A CDPM APPROACH

I believe that unless the project team is involved in assessing and selecting the project to be undertaken and unless the customer—whether internal or external—plays a major role in managing the project, the project will fail. The team must be part of the early design of the project. We offer a way to accomplish project selection from a quality analysis process with the customer and offer some concepts on how the customer can be integrated into the project team function.

Customer-driven project management (CDPM) is a concept that provides excellent resources to increase the quality of ePM. Here, I borrow some of the concepts that Bruce Barley and James Saylor developed in *Customer-Driven Project Management: Building Quality into Project Process,*[1] which I recommend you read. I then add the virtual project management approach, based on the best practices we have accumulated over the years at MGCG.

The beauty of CDPM lies in its focus on total customer satisfaction by integrating two very effective management approaches:

- Total quality management (TQM)
- Project management (PM)

The combination of these two disciplines allows ePM managers to put real value into customer-driven programs and projects throughout the project life cycle.

This approach blends and broadens those two disciplines into a new way of executing projects; in particular, I take advantage of it for the execution of virtual project management. The approach uses the customer's voice as the driver of the project deliverable. It stresses total customer satisfaction, continuous improvement, people involvement, and measurements from total quality management. It uses project management approaches to emphasize the provision of a successful deliverable. It targets new patterns of relationships and new processes between and within organizations to meet the challenges of virtual project management.

Customer service is difficult because all customers are different. This situation is complicated further when we consider that in virtual project management the customers can be indeed very different, speaking different languages and having a different culture and different expectations. All customers want different things, and so no single solution is the right solution. You have to be highly skilled in your communication and people-handling skills to come out of customer interactions on the positive side. And although you probably do that very well, the more options we have to choose from, the greater our likelihood of success is.

To illustrate, let me share one of my war stories. A few years ago I had an excellent project assistant, named Bogale, who worked with me on a London-based project. He was Ethiopian and had lived in London for a few years when we met there and decided to work together. I recalled having a speech delivered at the University of Kent in Canterbury and discussing with Bogale the importance of customer service even when one is delivering a presentation. We talked about body language, handshaking, and eye contact. Despite the fact that he and I had been working together for a few months, this was the first time we had met. Although I immediately trusted him and never had to question the veracity of any of his reporting over e-mail and Microsoft Project, I realized that during the whole afternoon we spent together before I left that Bogale never looked me in the eye. I could detect him looking at me when I was not looking at him, but if I looked him in the eye, he would avoid eye contact.

I thought about this the whole way to Kent, and it bothered me so much that after my speech there I shared the experience with a friend of mine at the university, Professor Abhaya Parmanand, who smiled and commented:

> You are always evangelizing that customer-driven project management is very important, and I have always been impressed with your international experience, but it surprises me that you

are not being able to provide a good customer service to your assistant. After all, he is your customer as well, you know? I recommend you learn more about his culture, and your clients, before you pass judgment.

Needless to say, Professor Abhaya was not about to tell me what was going on but led me to believe I was being blindsided by a very important issue in international (virtual) project management customer support: the cultural factor. He suggested that I talk to Bogale about it on my return and left it at that. Sure enough, I invited Bogale for tea on my way back the next day and decided to share with him my thoughts about our conversation and his lack of eye contact the day before.

Can you believe Bogale kept looking down the whole time I was telling him that the day before I got the impression he was hiding something from me by not looking at me eye to eye while I was talking to him? What nerve, I thought. To my surprise, he began to explain his behavior by apologizing first and then telling me that in Ethiopia it is a sign of respect to look down when someone with authority or well-deserved respect is talking to you. I never felt so dumb in all my life. Worse, Bogale extended to me tremendous customer service by apologizing first, providing me with the information I clearly needed, and complimenting me as well. It goes without saying that I was speechless and red-faced. I learned that customer service means different things to different people in different countries.

Leveraging Customer Value

One of the advantages of virtual project management over the conventional approach is that it allows for customer value leveraging. By tapping into every customer expectation at the point at which that expectation can be translated into project development, virtual project managers can develop a real-time relationship with the customer to ensure that the customer's voice is part of every project dialogue.

The presumption here is that customer value comes primarily from the growing confidence the customer gains in a project relationship in which the virtual project team is working in his or her interest. This is the focus of the so-called boutiquelike consulting firms, among which I would include MGCG, as opposed to the major department storelike company embodied by the big consulting firms. Without this leverage through constant communication and access to the key gateways in the virtual project management process, today's customers lack the assurance that a project is progressing as the customer expects it to.

Unless you are in constant contact with the customer and are listening to the customer's concerns and feedback (which doesn't mean allowing a project to be plagued with scope creep because of the customer's ever-changing desires), all you have is a list of specs that may not attend to the customer's needs.

Especially when managing projects from a distance, you need that level of interaction with the customer, as written specifications never fully capture the vision of the customer as that vision is informed by project progress and learning. The Internet allows this process of interaction with the customer to be more transparent, less intrusive, and more time-effective. In my practice, on every e-project I manage, one of the first initiatives I take is the creation of an e-mail distribution list for that project. The list is geared mostly to the customers and sponsors, but it also circulates to all project leaders, who in turn, at their own discretion, circulate it to every project worker on their teams.

We use this distribution list to communicate informally

the accomplishment of any major achievement in the project, circulate news or distribute Web links to news and articles that support our approach to project execution, and convey local environmental, political, or economic issues that may affect the project. This keeps the people on the list educated and abreast of the external and internal factors affecting project development, on both the positive and the negative sides.

The Use of Supply Chain Management for CDPM Advantage

The role and impact of supply chain management (SCM) in CDPM can be substantial. It can stretch from suppliers and vendors, to each virtual team remote office, through production, all the way to the distribution of products and services to sponsors and customers. American Cystoscope Makers, Inc. (ACMI), for example, uses enterprise resource planning (ERP) and manufacturing resource planning (MRP) systems to help track and verify the effectiveness of its supply chain management.

In long-duration projects where multirelationships with vendors, customers, and project teams are long-lasting (Figure 8–7), SCM can help project managers, especially ePM managers, partner for success, allowing the flow of knowledge forward and backward along the supply chain and focusing on the customer as part of a value-oriented supply chain. It is very important that project sponsors understand the cost savings to the project and support project managers in this long-term endeavor as a strategy to enable project development to become more efficient while cutting wasted cost and building valuable relationships with suppliers, customers, and vendors. In addition, SCM enables better control of project tasks, such as logistic planning, forecasting, scheduling, sales, buying, building, and warehouse control.

FIGURE 8–7

Supply chain management enables project organizations to partner for success, allowing the flow of knowledge forward and backward along the supply chain and focusing on the customer as part of a value-oriented supply chain.

Supply Chain Management

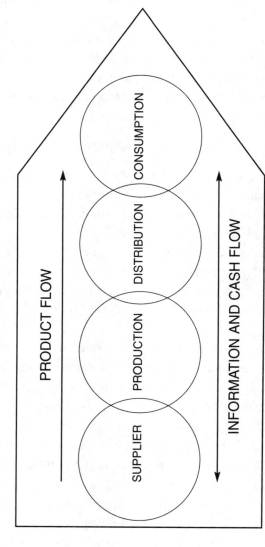

PRODUCT FLOW

SUPPLIER   PRODUCTION   DISTRIBUTION   CONSUMPTION

INFORMATION AND CASH FLOW

VALUE-ORIENTED SUPPLY CHAIN
INTERRELATED VALUE-ADDED PROCESS

Supply chain management involves the integration of all activities in moving and storing products beyond the boundaries of the project organization. It is the key to manufacturing-oriented project value, and project managers must rethink the way they manage change programs and implement information technology. Although the use of SCM in long-term project management is a bit foreign to some project managers, I believe that those who don't embrace it won't be around in five years.

Although SCM has proved beneficial within single-project enterprises, the true advantage lies in effective planning, decision making, and optimization of the entire supply chain, from raw materials suppliers to the consumer, and involves multiple companies collaborating with different trading partners, as shown in Figure 8–8.

FIGURE 8–8

Value-oriented supply chain as an interrelated value-added process.

Supply Chain Management

**Effective Supply Chain + Partnerships =
Competitive Advantage = Increased Sales**

Using ePM to Promote Quick Turnaround

One of the main advantages of applying project quality management to ePM is the capacity to limit the duration of project tasks to the direct work needed to accomplish them. Tom Peter's original concept of a bias for action has evolved in our ePM practices into what I call turning knowledge into action, a new impetus for turning any piece of knowledge a member of the virtual team has into something actionable (thus our corporate motto, "turning knowledge into action one client at a time") with quick turnaround, quick victories, short timelines, and more real-time exchange of product and service designs before we move into the production or service mode.

The duration of a task involves two factors: the time necessary to do the work and the elapsed time it takes both to do the work and to achieve other objectives, such as document approval. Elapsed time involves turnaround times on project documents, approval cycles, negotiation of regulatory issues, and other factors that push schedules out to the right, slipping key tasks into the critical path. Virtual project management changes this process by providing a method for electronic exchange of technical and adminsitrative documents with the customer and vendors, electronic signatures, and instant communication on project issues from the same graphic or text material.

THE USE OF CONTINUOUS IMPROVEMENT FEEDBACK SYSTEMS

Developing and implementing a system for the submittal, processing, and turnaround of customers', project workers', stakeholders', and sponsors' suggestions for improvement can be one of the most positive informal total quality management systems you can have in a project. But to develop an effective system, you must assess some of the variables that exist so that you can select the best system for your project. Here are some questions you should ask:

- Does your virtual project organization have a human resources–based performance recognition system?
- Does your virtual project organization have an infrastructure that will support a database to facilitate the collection of improvement opportunities?
- Does your virtual project organization currently have the mind-set that ideas for improvement are a way to improve project deliverables and develop best practices and that recognition for them is a standard behavioral norm?
- Does your virtual project organization currently recognize employee-based improvement via financial, job-based, or corporate communications rewards?

These questions should provoke discussion between you and your project team to establish the realities of not just implementing but recognizing value from the outcome of this program.

You may also want to explore some of the rewards and recognition programs in the marketplace. You'll find that several companies offer software, infrastructure, and processes to support rewards that are built around the variables you wish to measure. Some organizations utilize them from a human resources standpoint, others use them from a production or productivity standpoint, and others use them to recognize improvements made within a process.

It may also behoove you to read up on the Japanese principle known as *Kaizen*, which means small incremental improvements. Many U.S. and international companies have adopted this method. Its premise is that small incremental improvements made by each virtual project worker inevitably add up to a greater organizational sum.

In regard to the build-out of a system, the simple development of a database that is managed and observed by a continuous improvement committee is a great start. That committee prioritizes it and then presents it to a steering committee that allows management and executives to evaluate the potential improvement opportunities and set projects in place.

I believe this approach to continuous improvement is the most efficient because your virtual project organization will have bought into a homegrown solution to improving the business. Attaching a reward and recognition system to this type of program can be done simply by adding a column in the corporate newsletter, putting postings on the bulletin board, or sending an e-mail to acknowledge the receipt of an individual's suggestion and indicate whether it was accepted and implemented. Once a program like this has been implemented for a while, you will begin to see morale shift and individuals will take a more entrepreneurial and inclusive approach to participation. It is also beneficial to have more detailed quarterly follow-ups on the portfolio of improvement projects to expose your organization to the outcome.

Keep in mind that the best continuous improvement programs are internally built, are open, allow for creativity, and, most important, have the organization respond to the participants. Your next step might be evaluating what the cultural norms are within the organization and ensuring that they represent or will accept the mind-set of excellence.

A WORD ABOUT *KAIZEN* AND ITS CONTRIBUTION TO CDPM

Kaizen means "improvement," a continuing improvement in personal, home, social, and working life. When applied to the workplace, it means continuing improvement involving everyone: managers and workers alike.

The business strategy behind *Kaizen*, which I strongly recommend for virtual project management improvements, involves everyone in the project organization working together to make improvements *without large capital investments*. This includes but is not limited to eliminating waste in all all organization systems and processes.

Although continuous improvement embraces quality enhancements in products and services, the scope of *Kaizen* extends well beyond that as it seeks to include improvements in all aspects of the project's activities, from the processes and relationships it develops for taking in materials and components from downstream suppliers, through all its internal value-adding processes, to the way it interacts with its distribution systems and final customers.

With *Kaizen*, you need to become an involved leader, guiding project workers to improve their ability to meet project expectations of high quality, low cost, and on-time delivery. I strongly recommend that you read Masaaki Imai's *"Kaizen: The Key to Japan's Competitive Success,"* which discusses the subject in much more detail.[2] However, here are the 10 basic tips for *Kaizen* practices in dealing with customers and attempting to improve ePM customer-driven results:

1. Discard conventional fixed ideas.
2. Think of how to do it, not why it cannot be done.
3. Do not make excuses. Start by questioning current practices.

4. Do not seek perfection. Do it right away, even if for only 50 percent of target.
5. Correct it right away if you make a mistake.
6. Do not spend money for *Kaizen*; use your wisdom.
7. Wisdom is brought out when one is faced with hardship.
8. Ask "Why?" five times and seek root causes.
9. Seek the wisdom of ten people rather than the knowledge of one.
10. *Kaizen* ideas are infinite.

❑ CASE STUDY: PROGRESSIVE LEADERSHIP BEGINS WITH A PROGRESSIVE LEADER

Marcus Goncalves

Progressive leaders work from the inside out. When faced with business challenges, they first look at their own internal capacity and assess where they need to change and develop their inner qualities. They view problems as opportunities to expand their inner development to further their own purposes and the purposes of others in and beyond the organization.

Progressive leaders consider the welfare of their workers and customers first. By looking after their well-being, they develop a sense of purpose and meaning that surpasses the quarterly earnings report. Progressive leaders have nothing left to prove. They are interested only in creating an environment where others—their workers and customers—can access and develop their dreams and inner potential.

Progressive leaders have poise. They emanate a sense of confidence and strength that arises from being comfortable with themselves. They have nothing to prove and therefore can be a collaborator, a teacher, a leader, a friend, and a mentor to others. They are an example of warmheartedness in a cold business world. They operate from a stance of wisdom that is developed from accessing their own and others' struggles in business and life. They are well rounded because they are curious about how problems work and how people can overcome problems from a perspective of inner transformation.

The path to becoming a progressive organization is often a circular one and must begin with an assessment of the culture and the mind-set behind the leadership. What are the beliefs that are the foundation of the organization? What are the values and ethics? It is the definition of these values and ethics that separates an exemplary company from an ordinary one. People look to create meaning in their lives. Many people attempt to separate their work lives from their personal lives, thinking that work is where one earns a paycheck to do the things that bring meaning. They often see work as duty. There are others, however, who seek to have an impact by developing exemplary organizations that better the lives of their workers and the world around them. These organizations are committed to a creating deeper meaning through the work they perform.

Progressive leaders should seek out mentors who can act as a thinking partner, assisting their organizations and its leaders along the path to progressive leadership by doing the following:

- Conducting vision and planning processes
- Auditing the organization: appraising the culture and its resources
- Assessing nonwinning mind-sets that contribute to losing strategies
- Managing change
- Training in how thinking works and becoming one's own coach

Genuine Communication

I believe it is only through genuine communication that leaders can articulate the nuances of the future and thus invite others to participate in achieving their goals. To be successful in the twenty-first-century economy, progressive leaders who strive to foster collaborative dialogue as opposed to endless circular discussion must be created and nurtured. Only progressive leaders are able to understand that genuine communication is a key to success. Genuine communication helps organizations understand that the problems that arise among people are generated by a misunderstanding of each other's intentions, ideas, and meaning.

Communications workshops are a dime a dozen, and most have no lasting impact on the organizational culture into which they are introduced. This is the case because communication is not a technique; it is an expression of thinking. Improving communication in the workplace—or anywhere, for that matter—arises from improving the thinking skills and subsequent listening skills of the participants. Improved communication arises from a stance of accountability in regard to

- One's listening mind-set
- The effects of one's speech
- Generating an outcome that is new
- Stepping outside the predictable patterns
- Perceiving your colleagues in a new, more helpful light

Progressive leaders are those who are able to look outside their immediate workplace challenges and take a greater view where the benefits are broadened and stretched far beyond the executive or the company. When you acquire progressive leadership, you create more than profit; you bring forth change and immeasurable returns in the outside world. This is the key to obtaining the extraordinary future that sets an organization apart, that creates a sense of common purpose, a sense of belonging and partnership and community, and a sense that personal values and ethics are aligned with those of an organization.

Therefore, to become a progressive leader you must push yourself to be creative in your thinking and be introspective within your organization. You must push yourself to see how your passions for your work can create greater value in the outside world. The bottom line is that profits and growth are about performance, and performance is about people, and successful people are about a good greater than themselves.

Discussion Questions

1. The path to becoming a progressive organization is often a circular one. Explain how you can apply this concept in your project leadership environment.
2. Improved communication arises from a stance of accountability. Among the stances listed above, which one is the most challenging for you, and why? Which one is the easiest?
3. To become a progressive leader you must push yourself to be creative in your thinking and be introspective within your organization. Do you believe your work environment supports this process? If not, what do you believe is the alternative?

9
CHAPTER

The ePM Office

Large organizations with several locations may find that virtual project team members are geographically scattered, as we discussed in Chapter 8, particularly with international teams. Project management offices (PMOs) must learn to manage these virtual teams as they become a more important part of the project organization's workforce. Nonetheless, I don't see PMOs playing a major role in initiating or promoting virtual teams. Instead, their primary role seems to be to enable virtual teams to operate effectively.

To implement an efficient virtual project management office (ePMO), you need to identify the main purposes and functions of the PMO. All PMOs have similar functions—to provide support to project implementations—but depending on the specific environment, your ePMO may need more or fewer functions than others do.

Therefore, you must develop a framework that fulfills the functions of an ePMO. This framework will allow you, as a project manager, to review a checklist of best practice items and choose those which are appropriate for your type of project. Structured in a manner that is similar to that of any PMO implementation, this ePMO framework is based on project life cycles and is developed in an iterative process. Project initiation, is the first phase you need to address. Each quarter, another life cycle phase should be developed and tools should be added. You also need to create an ePMO website and make sure it remains dynamic, with tools and examples being added continuously.

As ad hoc and informal approaches to managing projects continue to be less than effective in meeting time-to-market goals, the need for a project management office becomes more compelling, and at a certain state the PMO evolves into a virtual project management office. This chapter provides an approach that addresses the immediate needs of an organization and at the same time considers longer-term ways to improve project management and develop an effective set of policies and procedures. You will see how to achieve immediate value while positioning yourself for the long run. The approach is based on the results of successfully implemented PMOs and ePMOs within organizations and has been refined through consulting experiences and industry research.

THE EVOLUTIONARY APPROACH TO THE PMO:
THE VIRTUAL PMO

Project management offices have become a major vehicle for managing projects in both the public and private sectors. As the practice of project management has grown, so has the demand for a systematic method of implementation. Organizations have acted quickly to acquire project scheduling software, send employees to project management training programs, and even establish project management academic degree programs.

But when should you use a PMO or an ePMO, for that

matter? You should create and maintain an ePMO to support the following functions:

- **Project administration**
  - Design and implementation are done by separate contractors, many in different and remote locations, often overseas.
  - Multiple contractors are necessary since the virtual project's site locations are overseas, in a foreign country, because of the complexity or size of the projects or as a condition of the bid process; a single contractor does not have the expertise to do the work and management of multiple contractors. A centralized view of the solution is required, and the project may call for the use of local (foreign) resources. The ePMO can also prequalify contractors for multiple projects, both nationally and internationally.
  - The client organization is diverse, and it may be difficult to get cooperation unless it is managed actively.

- **Project management process**
  - Conditions or scope may change throughout the project. Extra expertise is necessary to manage this change.
  - There may be limited resources to accomplish multiple tasks, often at remote sites.
  - There may be multiple projects under the same program umbrella or multiple initiatives utilizing the same resources.
  - Time to market is a critical factor in completing the project.

- **Remote project sites**
  - Services are implemented across diverse geographic regions.

- **Project communication plans**
  - It is necessary to provide consolidated reports and a single source of communications to the client.

For these reasons and because of the need for additional expertise, ePMOs should be staffed by ePM management professionals who serve the organization's project management needs both when colocated and remotely. The duties and functions of project offices vary from organization to organization, depending on the nature of the projects (virtual or not), size, and available resources, although in recent years these differing roles have converged. Nonetheless, ePMOs and PMOs usually attend to very standardized roles that are needed in every project (Figure 9–1).

Project management offices and ePMOs today carry out some or all of the following functions:

- Supply project management support to the project team and the virtual teams by assuming administrative chores for project scheduling, report production and distribution, project management software operation, and maintenance of the "visibility room" and the project workbook.

- Provide the organization with project management and ePM consulting and mentoring, by serving as internal project management consultants, providing the organization with the expert insights it needs to execute projects effectively. These consultants usually are housed in project offices.

- Develop and maintain conventional project management and ePM methodologies and studies for the organization by developing common methodologies and standards as well as promulgating them.

FIGURE 9-1

Main roles of a project management office.

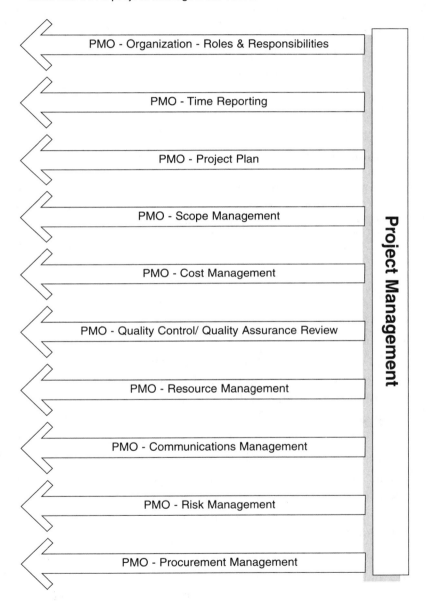

- Provide conventional project management and ePM training to the organization by training employees and project workers in project management principles as well as providing training material and instructors.

- Provide the organization with managers and ePM managers who can run projects by housing professional project managers who can be assigned to projects as needed.

The Need for a PMO

Unless your organization carries out projects only occasionally, you probably don't need to develop systematic capabilities for a PMO. In this case, establishing a project office would be similar to fishing in a small pond with a bazooka. However, as your organization becomes more projectized and directs more of its energy toward implementing projects, an ad hoc approach—the first level of the Capability Maturity Model Integration (CMMI) model—to project management leads to inefficiency. With more projects, a project office becomes a must.

When you decide to establish a PMO, you should be able to develop a consistent approach to implementing projects. In addition, I recommend configuring the PMO to serve the whole organization, as it can play an important role in integrating the several groups within it, spanning many functional activities. Another side effect of PMOs is that they tend to nurture project management professionalism, as an organization's employees and project workers who are engaged in project work are more likely to achieve and maintain the highest level of insights into and attitudes toward project management.

Today's project offices have antecedents in the project offices of the defense and construction industries, which have always been project-focused and organized to centralize project management activities in a single place. However, these traditional project offices were different from those which are emerging today. They generally served the needs of a single, large, complex project. Figure 9–2 illustrates the progressive benefits of a PMO.

You probably have noticed that companies today are managing projects more informally than ever before. Although informal project management has some degree of formality, the emphasis is on managing the project with the minimum amount of paperwork. Nonetheless, in developing a policy for project management, four elements are essential to success:

- Effective communication
- Effective cooperation

FIGURE 9–2

The progressive benefits of a PMO.

Global Recognition

Profitability Improvement

Productive Project Teams

Organizational Improvement

Culture Shift to Project Management

Staff Professionalism in Project Management

Predictable, Reusable PM Tools and Techniques

- Effective teamwork
- Trust

As Figure 9–3 shows, project management has evolved over the years. As companies have become more mature in project management, the emphasis has shifted to guidelines and checklists instead of life cycles and formal policy and procedures.

The Challenge in Developing Policies and Procedures

Does this picture look familiar? Your staff is working harder than ever before, yet projects seldom are completed on time. The most frustrating thing is that no one knows why this occurs or what causes the unexpected delays and cost overruns. The immediate response is to increase control, review policies, and reexamine guidelines.

FIGURE 9–3

Evolution of policies, procedures, and guidelines in project management.

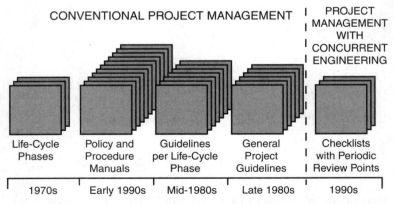

Evolution of policies, procedures, and guidelines. *Source:* Reprinted from H. Kerzner, *In Search of Excellence in Project Management.* New York: Wiley. 1998, p. 196.

Too much control inhibits productivity, and this explains the tendency for more informal controls in today's PMOs. However, as Figure 9–4 shows, the challenge of project informality is that each organization's group has a different way of discussing progress, and lack of consistency makes communications confusing. Unfortunately, this is part of the process every organization and PMO must go through.

A reasonably structured method for managing projects is needed, and so you take the conventional and safe path and decide to implement a PMO with consistent project management practices. You soon realize that this poses a different problem, since you have very little time and limited resources and need project improvement now. To top it off, competitive pressure is strong, and you feel the need to focus on product development, not another process change.

The inevitable question surfaces: How can you implement a PMO and improve project management practices while, continuing with product development and business operations?

Advantages of a PMO

Running projects today is a complex task that includes activities such as designing and implementing solutions and services as well as managing change. With multiple hardware and software vendors and a diverse range of partnerships and alliances, today's infrastructure landscape is more complex than ever. In addition, as you try to manage multiple projects for the same program initiative, more complexity is added to the equation.

This is when a dedicated PMO can provide the facility and processes to deliver projects on time and within the budget by managing program schedule, scope, and resources while watching the cost and quality. A PMO provides expertise

FIGURE 9-4

Project management growth concepts and definitions.

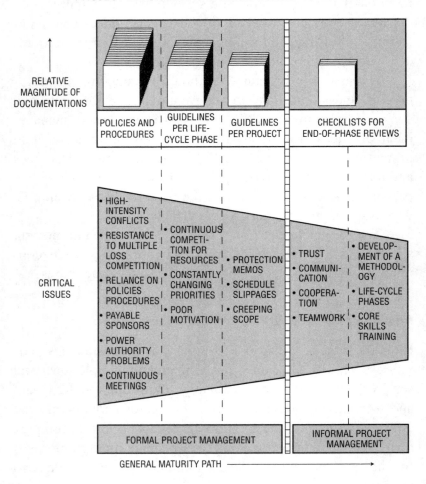

PROJECT MANAGEMENT GROWTH CONCEPTS AND DEFINITIONS

tailored to your business requirements while taking responsibility for all projects in your program. It also provides the extra focus and resources that complex projects demand.

One of the main advantages of implementing a PMO is

that it can coordinate multiple projects under the one umbrella and be the center of excellence that supports project managers in the implementation of the functions required to achieve success in a project.

The PMO, as was discussed earlier, should be staffed by project and program professionals and should consolidate project resource plans, financial reporting, project schedules, change, risk, and quality information into master documents to deliver projects on time and within the budget, direct and monitor projects to ensure quality, and disseminate project information. As Figure 9–5 shows, the PMO should provide a team of qualified staff, project management tools, support, mentoring, project portfolio management, and quality assurance.

The PMO keeps critical projects on time and within the budget by providing accountability at every stage, from planning to acceptance. It identifies and resolves issues before they add time to already intense time-to-market pressures. The PMO provides expertise tailored to your business requirements along with the extra focus and resources that complex projects demand, maintaining project momentum by contributing in the following areas:

- *Consolidated administrative support.* Program management office personnel can make the lives of project team members easier by doing administrative chores such as project scheduling, report production and distribution, project management software operation, and maintenance of the program's "war room" along with project and program documents. The PMO receives, consolidates, and distributes information for all the projects under the program umbrella.
- *Project management consulting, mentoring, and training.* The program manager will oversee the operations

FIGURE 9–5

An organization chart of a typical PMO.

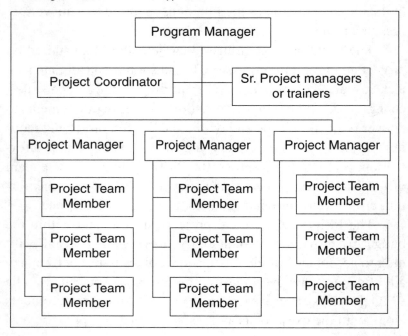

of each individual project and project manager, offering
mentoring, support, and training as needed. Advanced
training can be coordinated or provided by the program
manager, and each project will undergo periodic quality
assessment reviews at project milestones and at closeout.

- *Resource allocation.* With limited resources, it is
  critical to have the right people at the right place doing
  the right jobs. The program manager is in a position to
  assign the project managers and project team members
  to match program needs with specialized skills,
  availability, and geographic location as well as balance

the workload of project managers and project team members. By doing this the program manager ensures that resources are used efficiently in all the projects under the umbrella of the program.

- *Vendor management.* Many details need special attention when one is purchasing hardware, software, and services from any vendor. The program management office provides objective accountability to identify and resolve issues that can delay the specification and delivery of the right equipment to the right place at the right time. The program manager has the authority to hire and fire contractors, assign the contractors to particular projects, and manage contractor issues centrally.

Development of a Top-Level Policy Overview

To avoid the danger of turning management flexibility into chaos, you must make a conscious effort and plan to focus on immediate value and business necessities. The key is to keep the project policy and its implementation simple, focused on value, and structured with a plan. Your project management (PM) policy should jump-start the PMO implementation, beginning with a tactical focus and considering immediate concerns, business necessities, and minimum needs. For the time being, eliminate every unnecessary issue. You can always add them later; after all, a PM policy is a dynamic document.

Although the focus is on the short term in the beginning, longer-term solutions should be considered and preliminary steps should be undertaken to lay the groundwork for broader, more complex issues. Long-term solutions address permanent maturity efforts that will result in long-term value to the organization and ensure that you achieve your time-to-market time frame not just once but again and again thanks to repeatable processes. To accomplish this, we recommend a four-stage approach:

- Stage 1: Establish of a foundation.
- Stage 2: Start with short-term initiatives.
- Stage 3: Roll out with long-term solutions.
- Stage 4: Provide support and improvement.

To provide you with an overall rational for developing a PMO, Table 9–1 outlines the main functions delivered by a PMO.

The Four Stages of PMO Policy Development

You can divide the development of a policy for the project management office into four phases, as is discussed next.

Stage 1: Establishing the Foundation

In this stage you define the PMO policy and determine your immediate concerns and long-term objectives. As appropriate, you start with an assessment of your

- Current capabilities
- Short-and long-term goals
- Objectives

You should then baseline your assessment against the project management maturity model shown in Figure 9–4. This will help you identify the baseline positioning of project management in your organization and aid in planning future tasks and activities.

Next, you must hold a series of meetings with key stakeholders and subject matter experts to understand current capa-

TABLE 9–1
_____

The Main Functions of a PMO

* Matches business goals with appropriate technology solutions
* Provides increased resource utilization across the organization, matching skills to project needs across all projects in the program
* Manages and enforces project priorities
* Provides centralized control of all projects under the program umbrella
  ○ Increases communication and coordination across projects
  ○ Manages and controls scope, change, cost, risk, and quality across all projects
* Provides increased client satisfaction with project-related work and operational support
  ○ One place to go for all project status and communication
  ○ Support staff for project services
* Reduces time to market
* Reduces project costs because common tasks can be managed at the PMO level
* Reduces project risk

bilities, challenges, issues, and goals. Based on the discussions, an assessment report should be developed that captures the current state and future vision along with an improvement plan that recommends short-term initiatives and long-term solutions.

After developing the top-level improvement plan, you should determine the PMO's functions and staffing, identify stakeholders (make sure to include key management, mentor programs, and pilot projects), and prepare a communications strategy. This phase ends with the PMO having the go-ahead to proceed with funding and with immediate staffing needs approved.

Stage 2: Starting with Short-Term Initiatives

In this stage you start the PMO, put in place short-term initiatives, and initiate the mentoring effort. PMO start-up includes staffing the office for near-term needs, initiating communication activities, and making the organization aware of the PMO and its responsibilities.

You then should initiate two efforts to demonstrate the immediate value of the PMO within the organization: short-term initiatives and project mentoring. The short-term initiatives are solutions to immediate concerns and take care of issues brought to the surface by key stakeholders. These are items that can be implemented quickly while taking care of organizational top-priority concerns. Some examples are

- An inventory of your projects (new product development, information technology, business enhancements, etc.)
- Deployment of a project management methodology
- Summary reports and metrics
- Project reviews and brown bag training lunches
- Support for new projects and projects in need
- Project planning or project control workshops
- Identification and deployment of one or more pilot project initiatives
- Templates

In conjunction with the short-term initiatives, you should undertake project mentoring. This is an excellent way to provide immediate project management value to projects that are in the start-up phase or are in need of support without waiting for the implementation of formal training programs or process rollouts. Stage 1 ends when the short-term initiatives are in place and the team is ready to focus exclusively on the longer-term solutions identified in Phase 2.

Stage 3: Rolling Out with Long-Term Solutions

There are increasing benefits to organizations as their project management capabilities mature. Stage 3 focuses on improving and streamlining the processes, developing people, and putting in place a more permanent support structure for project management. In this phase you will develop long-term solutions, continue the mentoring effort, conduct additional pilot tests as appropriate, and gradually roll out the fully functioning PMO. Some examples of critical success factors are

- Process and methodology tailoring and continuing development
- Development of a training curriculum
- Detailed reports and metrics development
- Resource management
- Tool deployment
- Project manager career progression and certification
- Project portfolio management
- Organizational change and transition planning.

All these items take time to develop, and the deployment should be done incrementally, starting with pilot tests on select projects. The assessment and improvement plan devised during stage 1 provides the overall long-term goals and objectives for the PMO, and this phase develops, pilot tests, and rolls out the methods, standards, training, and support activities to achieve the overall goals.

Stage 4: Supporting and Improving the PMO

In this phase the PMO should be operating and supporting the organization. The PMO should be conducting day-to-day activities, refining project management activities, and expanding its involvement where appropriate. Training and other initiatives should continue under the direction of the PMO. In addition, key stakeholders should be providing feedback on the PMO's efforts and its activities should be refined continually.

Best Practices: PMO Implementation Activities

In our experience with small, medium-size, and large organizations in both the private and public sectors, we have found a series of activities that work as well as many others that don't work in a PMO implementation. The following is a list of best practices to help your implementation.

When developing your project management policy and implementing the PMO,

- Keep it simple
- Focus on value
- Plan
- Secure executive sponsorship
- Communicate

Keeping it Simple

First and foremost, be realistic and work the basics. If your staff members cannot explain why they are doing a particular project and cannot identify their 60-day plan, focus on those areas first. Do not worry about a sophisticated estimating process yet; focus on understanding the project goals (a project charter) and developing basic plans.

Once you identify these basic needs, stay focused and do not do too much too soon. Employ the minimum PM essentials, such as project management plans, schedules, metrics, and reporting. You should start up the PMO to help project teams. Don't try to optimize every aspect of project management.

Focusing on Value

This point goes hand in hand with the first one. Determine the organization's most pressing concern and fix it. Find out what hurts the most and focus on it. Talk to key stakeholders at all levels in the organization. Try to fix one key concern at each level. Sometimes the immediate fix is an interim solution that is done inefficiently, such as manual reports, but at least those reports provide information and insight with some degree of confidence.

The key is that whatever you choose to include in your policy, make sure to link the goals of the PMO to the organization's goals and make provisions for how the PMO and project management practices will help meet the organization's goals.

Planning

Although this process may be painful and may appear to be nonproductive, take the time to plan up front. The plan will help set expectations and facilitate communications. Establish incremental goals to show progress and results to the organization. Identify specific short-term and long-term solutions and explain how in some cases an interim solution will set the stage for a long-term objective (for example, a report that is done manually). Make sure to include enough time to conduct pilot tests and train individuals before setting in place the new process or tool.

Securing Executive Sponsorship

No matter what you do, without executive sponsorship, you will fail. Make sure you understand who cares, who will be most affected, and who makes decisions. Get those people involved from the beginning. Find out their needs, expectations, and goals. Identify their concerns and work to address them. Remember to keep it simple, focus on value, and plan. Understand the problems at different levels. Identify an executive cheerleader and encourage as much cheering as possible. Establish a project board and plan regular status review meetings.

Communicating

The best idea goes nowhere if you keep it to yourself, surprise everyone at the last minute, and expect the idea to be accepted and practiced. People don't like these kinds of surprises. Explain what you are doing and, most important, why. Let everyone know how the PMO and the new business practices will help. Package a "story" and spread it around. Communicate the same message over and over, tailoring it to the different levels of the organization. Communicate your goals and successes via different avenues, such as a project board, status review meetings, brown bag sessions, e-mail, and communiqués. Get the word out.

What to Avoid

Just as there are key activities that work in a PMO implementation, there are factors that hinder progress. Below are some of the activities you should avoid. At a minimum, recognize what is going on and change your behavior and approach.

This is a summary list of don'ts in setting up a PM policy and developing a PMO:

- Do it all at once
- Procrastinate

- Forget key stakeholders
- Demand before providing
- Work in a vacuum

Don't Do it All at Once

There are three major factors in a PMO implementation: people, process, and tools. Obviously, changing all three at once is a very complex undertaking that is to be avoided if possible. Change the tool environment but keep the process the same or change the process but use the same tool environment. A phased approach makes this feasible. Don't do it all at once: You may not be able to deliver, and people will get confused.

Don't Procrastinate

Once you make the decision to implement a PMO, move on it. Don't hesitate or only partially support the idea. You will lose support and focus, and the organization will stop believing in the concept.

In addition, if you take too long to implement the PMO, you may encounter organizational changes and upheaval. Such adjustments may result in changes in your executive sponsor and other key stakeholders. Priorities may change, and the effort may lose support and funding, resulting in an unsupported attempt that won't work.

Don't Forget Key Stakeholders

Earlier, we mentioned the importance of executive sponsorship. Executives are not the only key stakeholder-in or customer-of the PMO. There are other customers, including project managers, project teams, functional and resource managers, and line managers. As with the executives, get these stakeholders involved from the beginning and determine their needs, expectations, and goals. Understand the problems at different levels; otherwise, you may overlook a key concern.

Don't Demand before You Provide

A PMO must be viewed as an entity that helps and supports, that provides services to ease project management administration and facilitate smart business practices. All this results in an improved track record of project delivery. The PMO should never be in a position of always demanding information and seldom providing services. You will not be successful by always demanding; you win by providing.

Don't Work in a Vacuum

In a PMO implementation, a team approach wins. The office is intended to serve multiple customers, each with personal experiences and ideas to share. Incorporate other people's ideas, acknowledge them, and give credit where it is due. Learn from others' experiences; don't reinvent the wheel. Find out individual requirements and needs and design accordingly and appropriately. Don't work in a vacuum or you'll miss a lot of good stuff.

Final Words for Success

A decision to develop a PM policy and implement a PMO does not need to be followed by a lengthy, drawn-out implementation. You can't afford it, time is short, and you are faced with limited resources, competitive pressure, and the need to do business. The way to develop a PM policy and implement a

PMO is to focus first on immediate value and business necessities. You should design an implementation approach that takes care of these immediate concerns and in parallel lays the groundwork for longer-term solutions.

The key is to keep the implementation simple, focused on value, and structured with a plan. Don't try to do it all at once. Build an office that provides services to ease administration and put in place smart business practices. The net result will be a structured, consistent method for managing projects and an understanding of project performance, resulting in overall better project performance.

THE ePMO ENVIRONMENT

Although many organizations have a strong track record of delivering major information technology (IT) projects that are on time and within budget and meet requirements, the success rate and project efficiencies can be improved. In this global economy the extent and format of project execution and reporting vary by organization and by project. Similarly, project management best practices are scattered across the horizon and projects often don't even have a centralized repository for project documents and resources.

An approach recommended by the Gartner Group to address project reporting and management processes is the development of an ePMO. The five key goals of the ePMO are

- Standard methodology across multiple project sites and geographic boundaries (consistent tools and processes)
- Resource evaluation (validation of business assumptions and life cycle costs)
- Project planning (competency center and library of project plans)

- Project management (consistent practices and an enterprise model and a source of project managers)
- Project review and analysis

The office can take many forms, ranging from a project repository that is a central source of methodology and standards to an enterprise project office that directly manages and oversees projects wherever they occur within the enterprise.

Many of the benefits of the project office approach can be achieved by establishing a virtual project management office. The initial effort should include the development of a project repository and the sharing of best practices.

It's a Virtual World Out There

We live in a virtual world. Instead of visiting a bookstore, we go to Amazon.com or Barnes & Nobles.com over the Internet. Rather than stand in line at the bank, we do our banking electronically. Technology gives us the opportunity to communicate and virtualize project management offices.

In late 1980s Digital Equipment Corp. (DEC) was initiating a project that would enable project teams to be put together with team members coming from headquarters in New England, manufacturing in Texas, and the design shop in California. Back then attempts to run a virtual project management office were hampered by technical limitations, but since DEC's first efforts more than two decades ago, those limitations have largely disappeared.

Today's focus on the development of ePMOs has shifted from grappling with technical feasibility to resolving management issues. Some of the challenges associated with implementing ePMOs are obvious. For example, how do you handle the fact that team members may reside in different time zones, something frequently mentioned in this book as one of the main obstacles to ePM execution?

Other challenges are more subtle. How can project offices ensure that geographically dispersed virtual team members have a common level of competence and a reasonably uniform understanding of the processes underlying a project? This issue is further complicated when team members come from different cultures where education levels and perceptions of how the world works vary.

Configuring an ePM

The PMO is situated physically in the home office. It supports the efforts of the people in the field in several ways, including maintaining project management methods and standards as well as maintaining a reusable library that contains templates, algorithms, and processes that have been developed on other projects and are available for use on current efforts. Finally, the PMO also acts as a liaison with the organization's functional groups, such as the finance, information systems, and engineering departments. Thus, if team members in the field need support from engineering, the PMO can arrange to have it provided through an ePMO setting, as shown in Figure 9–6.

Virtual organizations are based on communication. The entities they are composed of—individuals, committees, workgroups, geographically dispersed companies, and globally active enterprises—depend on the fact that distance and time zones do not hinder work. The advantages provided by the more flexible form of virtual organizations should not be vitiated by personal alienation, lack of necessary processes, or technical systems, that are difficult to use.

Therefore, technology for project management and col-

FIGURE 9–6

ePMO infrastructures allow virtual teams to gather and deliver
information and execute tasks virtually.

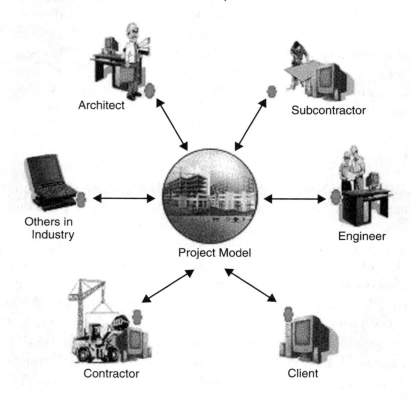

laboration in distributed ePMOs allows virtual teams to work.
In an ePMO environment all systems or technologies should
emphasize collaboration and management, but each one from a
different angle. Figure 9–7 provides a list of collaboration technologies and how they apply to and can be used in the ePMO
environment.

In developing an ePMO environment, keep in mind that
working with virtual teams in distributed environments often
means that the teams are geographically dispersed but access a

FIGURE 9-7

Collaboration technologies and how they can be used in the ePMO environment.

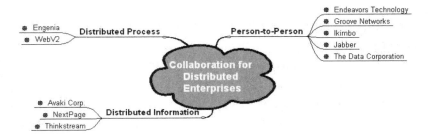

central website for their project work. This may be all right for some projects, but nor for all. An alternative to this centralized structure is the peer-to-peer (P2P) approach, where the team environments are distributed across the team members' PCs or laptops, with no central sites necessary. By using the applications TeamDirection Project and Groove Workspace as an example, I want to show that the operation of project management in such distributed teams does not have to be more difficult than it is in normal projects if you have the right tools.

KNOWLEDGE MANAGEMENT IMPLEMENTATION

Since biblical times it has been known that the best way to transfer tacit knowledge is through face-to-face communication. According to G. Van Krogh in *Enabling Knowledge Creation*, 60 to 95 percent of knowledge transfer, both explicit and tacit, occurs via oral communication. But today's business environment leaves relatively little time for face-to-face contact. Thus, project managers, especially those managing virtual projects, are faced with the challenge of facilitating the transfer of tacit knowledge among their teams and partners.

There are several alternatives worthy of imitation. British Petroleum, for example, developed a virtual teams project that uses a mix of technologies, including videoconferencing and shared chalkboards, to connect teams at different sites around the globe. At MGCG we have used similar strategies with the Bank of Brazil and the Ministry of Health of Costa Rica. The Foxboro Company, in partnership with Boston University, allows employees and affiliates to participate in virtual classes delivered by broadband videoconferencing. Another example is PricewaterhouseCoopers, which uses similar resources to let teams from the firm's knowledge centers share their thoughts, experiences, and war stories. Audio and video recorders are used to ensure that all comments are captured.

Knowledge management can help in programs like this, as mapping the information flow within the organization is necessary and must be the first step. It is very important that processes, technology, structure, and culture be adapted to reflect a knowledge-sharing environment. These elements are key to ensuring that critical information links are maintained, updated, and managed effectively so that the right information not only gets to the right person but gets there quickly.

Another problem project managers must be alert to arises when they attempt to manage knowledge. Again, knowledge managers can be tremendously helpful here as knowledge is not data that one can store and retrieve in a database; it is not information either. Knowledge is understanding, and one gains knowledge through experience, reasoning, intuition, and learning. IT technology-based initiatives such as data mining and warehousing are therefore, only half solutions in this context. Individuals can expand their knowledge only when others share their knowledge. Consequently, when one's knowledge is combined with the knowledge of others, there is innovation and new knowledge is created. Projects in general can derive great benefits from this process.

Project management should involve systematic approaches to finding, understanding, and using knowledge to achieve project objectives. Thus, managing knowledge creates value by reducing the time and expense of trial and error in a project and preventing the reinvention of the wheel. Knowledge management (KM) adds value to project management when shared knowledge is put to use and reused. An effective KM program within PM can substantially affect the bottom line of a project by increasing the return on investment (ROI) and reducing the total cost of ownership (TCO) for business intelligence.

We are entering a new millennium, with the U.S. economy now nursing a hangover, having flopped after two years of Y2K and dot-com-induced indulgence. Companies are looking for ways to increase revenues and maximize profits. Companies have cut back on advertising, travel, and training budgets, among other things. In the process, many KM programs have been cut back, if not terminated. In project management, KM is almost unheard of. It is not surprising that in this climate companies are examining every project more closely, but restricting KM implementations as a productivity tool under PM can be a big mistake.

Knowledge management can increase the ROI of any project management initiative tremendously by streamlining and sharing intellectual capital within the teams and among the project sponsors and stakeholders. Yet many project managers are scrambling to recalculate the ROI of projects that previously won approval on the basis of an implementation's strategic merit. Stakeholders and sponsors want to see hard numbers to confirm a project's value.

Such tangible results are very difficult to quantify in PM these days, as not all knowledge acquired in these projects take the form of a best practice. In fact, the most valuable knowledge is the knowledge people have in their minds; tacit knowledge. This form of knowledge is the most difficult to access because people are often unaware of the knowledge they have or its value to others. Thus, one of the main goals of KM within project management is to attempt to make tacit knowledge explicit, thus allowing it to be shared and used by others. More than ever before, project managers must partner with knowledge managers and be a different breed, armed with visionary skills, strategic thinking, ambassadorial skills, and willingness to take high risks.

CASE STUDY 1: FOCUS ON VALUE

A few years ago a banking institution in Brazil decided to deploy project management methodology in its IT organization. The deployment plan focused on three key PMO areas:

- Deployment of a standard project management process and methodology
- Project management tool development and deployment
- Training for the staff affected by the project management initiative

Regular meetings were established to communicate developments and expectations with two primary career groups: the project managers and the project planners. A standard approach to managing projects was developed, deployed, and taught to all the project teams. Project brochures were distributed listing the "top 10" projects and their deliverables, milestones, and quality metrics. Entire project teams received performance bonuses based on delivery against the top 10 goals.

Directors and vice presidents routinely participated in project reviews and led meetings to discuss the value of the divisional PM initiative. As a result, planning was sufficient for all stakeholders to understand expectations for the project. Most of the top 10 projects were delivered on time and satisfied or exceeded the quality metric goals. Experience was developed to enhance delivery quality in future projects.

Lessons Learned

Mentoring support was critical in the first phases of PMO deployment because of the severe lack of internal PM competency. Methodology efforts were started and redirected on three occasions because it is critical to deploy an effective methodology and integrate that tailored methodology into PM training initiatives.

❧ CASE STUDY 2: REDUCING TIME TO MARKET FOR COMPETITIVE ADVANTAGE

A start-up software development company wanted to decrease the time-to-market period for its new products. The PMO decided to modify its project management practices in an effort to reduce time to market. The PMO put in place a mentoring program, project planning and estimating, project tracking and control, and additional project coordination and communications avenues.[1]

The PMO ensured that the PM methodology was established and followed. The organization started planning and showing the impact on key milestones. Regular meetings were held to address issues. The PMO enabled comprehensive resource capacity planning and project prioritization, resulting in better planning for resource demand. The attention and focus placed on project management caused project teams to pay closer attention to detail and use better discipline in meeting deadlines. The net result was a reduction in the launch cycle of the flagship product of three months, resulting in the receipt of the Best Enterprise Product award at Comdex Fall 2000 and subsequent acquisition of the company by Symantec few months later.

Lessons Learned

The main lessons learned include the following:

- Project methodology buy-in at the business unit level is critical. Those buying in saw their time to market improve, while others who didn't "pay for the service" languished and their time to market got worse.
- Take small incremental steps and show results continuously (keep it simple and focus on value).
- Get an executive sponsor high in the organization.

❑ CASE STUDY 3: IF ONLY WE KNEW THIS BEFORE

An automaker was adding a new type of car to its offerings. A new technology customer convenience unit was planned as part of the rollout. With four years of development and production expected, a subcontractor was chosen to build the units. One year after the contract, the subcontractor was asking for a delay in delivery and more money. At that point the technology was a generation old.

On assessing the problem, we found that performance and technical specifications were severely lacking from the start, especially the performance specifications. No requirement was levied on the subcontractor regarding the specific project reporting requirements and delivery milestones. There was very little accountability for schedule delays, and cost overruns were included as part of the contract. How did they get to that point?

During contract negotiations, the automaker failed to include specifications with sufficient detail to include operating performance characteristics and requirements. No provision was established in the contract for the subcontractor to plan and control the development project adequately or to report its ongoing status to the automaker. Many delays, technical complications, and overlooked deliverables built up to create a project disaster.

Lessons Learned

The automaker did not do sufficient project planning or require it from one of its key stakeholders: the subcontractor. The automaker did not react until the damage was already done and then wanted to put project controls in place. In the end no one was happy: A poor deliverable was produced, the new vehicle delivery was delayed, costs were overrun, and protracted litigation ensued.

CASE STUDY 4: SOMEBODY OPENED THE FLOODGATE

A semiconductor company saw the need for standard PM practices and a central office to manage ongoing efforts. The project budget was expected to increase significantly, and management recognized the need to manage the resources intelligently. The organization was going from an informal PM environment to one with more structure in process and tools. Both process and tools were being changed at the same time, and most project managers did not welcome the change.

The PMO effort progressed smoothly until the project managers were asked to change their tool environment and be more disciplined in drafting project management plans. The leadership was focused on other pressing issues and did not have time to support the PMO initiative. There was rebellion on one side and lack of interest on the other. The initiative was pushed to the back burner and significantly decreased in scope and importance.

Several factors contributed to the situation: organizational changes and upheaval, changes in priorities, doing it all at once, and lack of executive sponsorship.

Lessons Learned

A few of the main lessons learned were the following:

- Keep things simple and focused on value to preserve the initiative during the organizational changes.
- Put in place a strong communications program to obtain buy-in from all key stakeholders.
- Introduce the tool environment and new processes in an incremental fashion.
- Secure and repeatedly work to keep executive sponsorship.

10

CHAPTER

Concurrent Projects and Change Management

The function of the project management office (PMO) has shifted dramatically in the last several years. Once a back-office and support operation, a PMO, and now a virtual project management office (ePMO), is vital to mission-critical project management, especially when it involves distributed systems such as enterprise resource planning (ERP), customer relationship management (CRM), e-commerce, and supply chain management. With the increase in global competitive markets and economies, now more than ever projects need to be completed on time and within the budget. The entire virtual project enterprise depends on ePMOs.

Concurrent project management enables companies to pay heed to the call, placed on them by competition, to find ways to improve productivity and shorten the time to market with products of higher quality and lower cost. However, tradition is deeply ingrained, and so most project management professionals are set in their ways and do not know how to convert to concurrent project execution. They often find that resistance to change is strong, that inertia in the product development that is underway—in the older, sequential, traditional way—is too great, and that the forces that cause the older methods to be followed are still there.

To be competitive and have effective project management practice, we must drive higher-quality products and services to market faster at a lower cost. Simply put, in a company that depends on high-technology products in a competitive marketplace, we must address the issue of survival and properly implement modern product development methods to compete well.

This chapter provides a short observation of a trend that is relying enormously on the functionality, features, and expertise of a well-implemented ePMO and ways we can take advantage of it: the implementation of concurrent projects. The basic purpose of the chapter is to provide insight into the concepts and discipline of concurrent project management. We show how to get started in this discipline and how to implement concurrent project management techniques.

AN OVERVIEW OF CONCURRENT PROJECT PLANNING

Concurrent project planning lays the foundation for success in project management. Quality project planning enables project managers to derive useful information for making decisions to achieve safety, time, and budget goals. Poor concurrent project planning prevents project management from using an analytic process to achieve those goals. It is the "garbage in, garbage out" axiom at work. Therefore, the planning stage for any project should be given as much attention as possible.

Manual Concurrent Project Planning

Concurrent project planning in many industries is still a "start from scratch" labor-intensive effort for every new project. Planners analyze each logical work element by defining the necessary steps (tasks), estimating their duration and resource requirements, and laying out a logic network for sequencing (scheduling) them. Given sufficient time, experienced personnel can produce the highest-quality plans with the manual planning process. Unfortunately, business pressures and time constraints do not always give planners the luxury of manually planning to the best of their abilities.

Concurrent Project Planning with Project Templates

With the advent of computers and project management software, reusable project files (project templates) have become a valuable tool for concurrent project planners. Project templates increase productivity and help standardize estimates from project to project. The bulk of the data entry, estimating, and scheduling effort is already done. Planners can focus on customizing previous (historical) efforts.

However, the use of project templates does have some pitfalls. An organization needs to give planners adequate time to review and customize project templates or it will suffer from cut-and-paste syndrome (CPS). CPS inevitably leads to errors such as including the wrong (old) steps, forgetting necessary new steps, and overlooking schedule logic and/or using labor-hour estimates that are not customized to the current situation.

Concurrent Project Planning with Estimating Modules

Dynamic estimating modules incorporate the benefits of project templates while avoiding their potential pitfalls. These modules can be thought of as large, flexible project templates that incorporate many different scenarios. Estimates and resource requirements are stored as estimating formulas instead of fixed amounts. Schedule logic is "supernetworked" to allow flexibility in including or excluding ranges of tasks while maintaining logic network integrity.

To use dynamic estimating modules, planners enter the required parameters into the project estimating software. The appropriate task lists, durations, resource assignments, and predecessor schedule logic are extracted and calculated from the estimating modules in accordance with the supplied parameters and then exported into the main project file.

Evolution of the Concurrent Project Planning Process

Over time the benefits of using dynamic estimating modules will multiply. Since estimating formulas and schedule logic are captured in the estimating modules, there will be no drop-off in quality when new or inexperienced planners arrive on the job. Dynamic estimating modules will give larger companies the means to standardize planning and estimating by using their best practices across the enterprise. These modules are the next step in the refinement of the project planning process.

Finally, keep in mind that concurrent project management is based on a simple premise: Instead of the traditional method of the old manufacturing model, where a design team dumps an unworkable process onto a production group, these groups work together from the beginning or conceptual phase all the way through production and product delivery.

MANAGING CONCURRENT PROJECTS

The question project management (PM) professionals have when it comes to concurrent project management is how to implement these new methods. Managing multiple projects that start and end at different times can be difficult. Projects often have to be prioritized and shoehorned into an annual budget with limited resources to manage them. An integrated approach is required to optimize the use of resources and predict resource requirements and expenditure accurately.

Another issue for most professionals setting out to practice concurrent project management is which model to implement. Many of them have told me that they have attended meetings of one sort or another, heard the experts speak, sat on subcommittees, and discussed the matter at great length, yet they do not know where to begin. The question is still asked: We know we should be practicing concurrent project management, but how do we get started and how do we followup with it successfully?

To be successful, you need to be able to delegate and manage unrelated projects that draw on common resources and/or the variety of projects producing an integrated outcome by blending common resources and dissimilar contributors.

Here are three principles of project integration that I use and recommend:

- The application of consistent PM methodology
- The establishment of an ePMO or PMO
- The use of the correct tools for the effective management of projects

It is important for us to orient ourselves properly for addressing the overall subject of concurrent project management and understanding the various relationships necessary in implementing the associated disciplines. Figure 10–1 provides focus in this regard, showing that concurrent project management happens through a cross-functional team.

The cross-functional team is best established by combin-

FIGURE 10–1

Hierarchy of organizations and cross-functional teamwork.

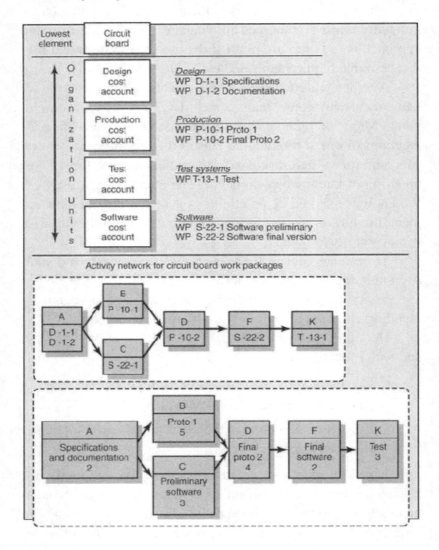

ing personnel in a functional and matrix organization. That is, the project leader may have a long-term assignment in marketing, for example, and is assigned management of the cross-functional team for the duration of the project. Other members of the team are drawn from marketing, manufacturing, and engineering.

The concept of team building and consensus management involving simultaneous design, product engineering, manufacturing, and quality control and concurrence by all is what I call concurrent project management. The Institute for Defense Analysis (IDA) in its Report R–388 defines it as follows:

> Concurrent project management is a systematic approach to the integrated, concurrent design of products and their related processes, including manufacturing and support. This approach is intended to cause developers, from the outset, to consider all elements of the project life cycle from conception through closure, including quality cost, schedule, and user requirements.[1]

Concurrent Development of E-Project and Quality Processes

The essence of concurrent project management is the planning, scheduling, and carrying out of the project and quality processes concurrently with the design of the product or service by the virtual project workers, with the concurrence of everyone. It is important that the project planning be done concurrently with representatives (I call then deputies) from all virtual project teams.

Concurrent ePM can be construed to have an additional meaning: The concurrence of all virtual project workers to buy in to good new project development management, excellent design concepts, and productive implementation. Figure 10–2 depicts this type of project organization, which is known as "projectized" as the whole organization is a cross-functional one built around projects.

In any PM development, higher quality, lower product cost, and often much faster time to market result from concurrent PM practices. The cross-functional product development team identifies and plans the development or manufacturing processes, the tooling and other manufacturing requirements, and the quality engineering and assurance requirements early on. The major difference between a project organization focused on concurrent project development and one that is not is that the cross-functional team carries out many of these activities together, as a team, as opposed to conventional proj-

FIGURE 10–2

A concurrent PM organization is referred to as projectized as the whole organization is a cross-functional one built around projects.

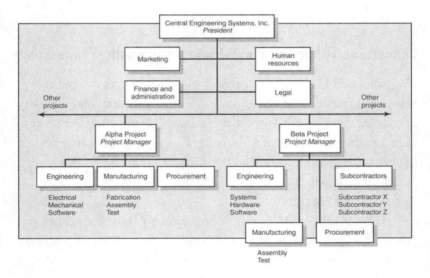

ect organizations, where the tasks are carried out by each assigned department alone.

I have found that a major reason for schedule slippage, the bane of project management, is that the schedule was unrealistic to begin with. This is avoided in the cross-functional team approach. I have seen overwhelming evidence that companies that are successful in developing projects on time and under budget consistently implement concurrent project management.

For instance, suppose marketing and manufacturing are not involved with research and development (R&D) during the engineering design of a product. Suppose we are not careful and fall vulnerable to a more traditional and sequential approach, which is common in many project organizations. The result is that the specifications continue to change too much for too long. Figure 10–3 illustrates this scenario by showing two different product definition graphs.

The conventional, traditional approach to PM, typical in many project organizations, is shown in line A. The product specifications are not detailed enough at the outset, there is a lack of substantial quality function deployment input from the customer and/or user, and manufacturing involvement is not deep enough at the outset of new product development. In addition, marketing and manufacturing are not involved deeply and effectively enough during the R&D phases. The result, as schedules continues to change—as inputs from these other groups eventually surface when they finally get involved with the project tasks—is that the project falls victim to scope creep.

In line B, with the concurrent project management approach, there is deep and effective involvement by all functions in the cross-functional virtual team's work, which is often

FIGURE 10-3

Change in product definition over time.

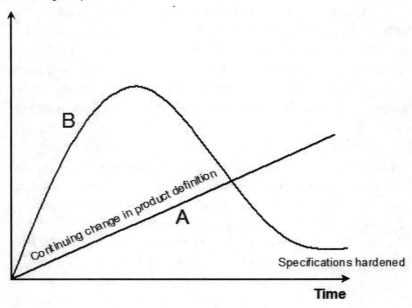

seen as a waste of time, a lack of focus, or unnecessary by conventional project managers but in reality is a vital stage of effective project execution, especially in virtual projects. Product specifications are formed very dynamically in a rapid state of virtual flux in the very early stages of planning. These contributions may arrive via instant messaging (IM) sessions, phone conferences, e-mail, or formal documents. Since in this case there is strong input from all virtual project team groups, the project's specifications are detailed and hardened early on.

The reason line B does not end at zero as time increases is that I want to leave room for creativity even after the specifications have been firmed up. I recognize that there will probably be some changes desired, and I do not want to stifle creativity.

CHANGE MANAGEMENT IN CONCURRENT PROJECT MANAGEMENT

As was discussed earlier in this chapter, most professionals are set in their ways. Thus, it is natural for us to resist change. However, to shift from sequential project development to concurrent, it is essential to change the whole outlook and approach. Therefore, a change in human behavioral patterns is a major requirement. Ways to effect a change in organizational behavior to dissolve the traditional interface barriers between departments must be addressed. Table 10–1 provides the 12 principles for managing change. If you keep those principles in mind, your journey should be a little easier.

In virtual project management in particular, as the speed of change continues to increase, change management is a fundamental competency needed by human resources (HR) professionals. Virtual team members need to know who to go to.

TABLE 10–1

The 12 Principles for Managing Change

1. Thought processes and relationship dynamics are fundamental if change is to be successful.
2. Change happens only when each person makes a decision to implement change.
3. People fear change if it "happens" to them.
4. Given the freedom to do so, people will build quality into their work as a matter of personal pride.
5. Traditional organizational systems treat people like children and expect them to act like adults.
6. "Truth" is more important during periods of change and uncertainty than "good news" is.
7. Trust is earned by those who demonstrate consistent behavior and clearly defined values.
8. People who work are capable of doing much more than they are doing now.
9. The intrinsic rewards of a project are often more important than the material rewards and recognition.
10. A clearly defined vision of the end result enables everyone to define the most efficient path for accomplishing the results.
11. The more input people have into defining the changes that will affect their work, the more they will take ownership of the results.
12. To change the individual, change the system.

Therefore, effective communication, full and active executive support, employee involvement, organizational planning and analysis, and a widespread perceived need for the change are very important.

Implementing change in an organizational environment that is already virtual project–oriented, and has a high level of trust is a huge plus. Understanding and responding to the range of human emotions during times of intense change, are also critical: Remember, many of these project workers are working out there by themselves. In this virtual project management world, with resources stretched thin and performance expectations high, project leaders must motivate the virtual workers concurrently, with HR, which must exert leadership to prove its worth as a business partner and show that it can provide value to the organization.

Typical challenges you will find in dealing with human behavior change as you attempt to shift the project organization to a concurrent one include but are not limited to the following:

- **Management of polarities**. This is the art of preserving order amid change and preserving change amid order. Concurrent project management will test your organization's ability to respond and adapt quickly while providing increased stability in the middle of change. If this process is successful, it is a great leverage point for achieving sustainable competitive advantage.

- **Cultural shift**. This is all too common in ePM organizations that often deal with multiple foreign cultures in a single project. But the challenge also includes the internal organization's culture shift, such as from directive to participative project management styles or from hierarchical to team-based project management and decision making.

- **Structural shifts**. This is another common challenge in concurrent PM as the project management structure shifts from more centralized to more decentralized operations (and back again).

- **Strategic shifts in focus**. This is typical in concurrent project management, as the strategy not only shifts from conventional to concurrent project execution but also may shift from quality improvement to cost cutting or from a product focus to a customer focus and vice versa.

Many change efforts follow a predictable pattern that is likely to lead project organizations down paths filled with frustration, resistance, and ultimately preservation of the status quo. After compelling arguments are developed for why change is needed, a plan for getting from "where you are now" to "where you want to be" is viewed as the solution, with implementation of the strategy seen as the last step. However, if your vision of the future—where you want to be—consists of a shift from one pole of a polarity to the other, your efforts are guaranteed to generate resistance.

The following is a list of steps to help you have a smooth transition from conventional to concurrent project management and be able to deliver your project successfully:

1. Select the project. Develop the virtual project team as was discussed earlier in the book. Make sure all members of the virtual teams have an attitude of owning the project. This will assure successful implementation and integration.

2. Define the internal or external customer's requirements from the start, not forgetting to include all the virtual teams involved.

3. Define the scope of the virtual project and the out-

come desired. As part of this definition, determine where the project begins and ends. What is the first step? What is the last?

4. Define measurable goals, milestones that will enable you to know what the project has accomplished. Define your budget for the project. Determine the staff and working schedules: Will you need a second shift to interact with a team in a different time zone? I have had to implement a second-shift working schedule for some of the professionals in a development team so that they could interact with an Indian-based virtual team.

5. Determine how you will communicate progress and accomplishments and gather input from organization members who are not on the team. Will you use electronic newsletters, an e-mail distribution list, updates via the project management application tool, conference calls, webcasting, or a combination of these methods?

6. Flowchart the current process or, for a specific project, list the steps necessary to accomplish the project. I strongly recommend the use of a good project management application tool such as Microsoft EPM, Primavera Systems, or Kickstart.

7. Measure how the current e-project is performing right now if this is an ongoing project. Study the data to adjust your goals and expectations.

8. Determine whether additional information, resources, or people are needed to complete the project. Bring the people and resources identified into the group.

9. Create an action plan to complete the project's steps. Assign the appropriate people to complete each step. Create a due date for when each step will be accom-

plished. Make sure people have the time they need allocated to the project.

10. Determine an ongoing method to track whether the steps are accomplished as planned. Hold periodic meetings, set up a centrally located planning calendar, widely distribute meeting minutes, or list the steps on a public whiteboard.

11. Implement the action plan. Document the methods used to accomplish each step. You want to be able to share the steps and goals and duplicate the successful ones if this is an ongoing or periodically repeated project.

12. Determine how the team will measure, record, and track the effectiveness of the project implementation and planning process for the future. You can rely on an integrated approach by using the critical path method (CPM) and earned-value method (EVM) to plan, schedules, and track progress and costs against the planned budget across multiple projects. Progress reporting can be tailor-made for all levels of the organization by using a single source of data to ensure that all the team members are working together toward the common goals.

We discussed the concept of CPM in earlier chapters but have not mentioned EVM. The earned-value method is considered an advanced project control technique for the integration of schedule and cost. However, prevailing project control, including the EVM is an effective tool only under the limiting assumption that every activity (or cost account) is independent.

EVM lacks flow and value generation concepts in that value is created only if what a customer wants is made when the customer needs it. Thus, EVM does not differentiate between value-generating work and non-value-generating work. The study suggests a new cost measure, customer earned value (CEV), which can differentiate between value-generating and non-value-generating work. With the use of CEV, managers can get information on work-in-process inventory levels and coordination ordination between trades. CEV motivates trades to consider the internal customer's needs; therefore, it can contribute to improvements in workflow.

The critique of EVM and the creation of CEV are part of an ongoing research effort, the next step in which will be the development of a methodology for implementation of the CEV concept.

13. Using the data collected, evaluate the results. Did the project meet expectations and satisfy planners and participants? If not, why not? Document this for future projects.

14. Celebrate the accomplishments of the team.

15. Determine how the lessons learned and the steps experienced during this project can be applied to projects in the future. Find a method for integrating best practice steps for project management.

ORGANIZATIONAL CULTURE: THE HEART OF THE PEOPLE[2]

Leaders everywhere know that the culture in an organization is pivotal to its success and vitality. They know it is intimately tied to leadership. They also know it is "how things get done" because the culture drives the norms, beliefs, and behavior of the organization. What they don't know is how to refine and change a culture that has inherent weaknesses or does not fit the world today, and they do not necessarily know what they as leaders should do about the changes that need to be made. Figure 10–4 depicts the culture wheel, which was devised by Carla Carter of Carter and Associates.

Leaders in the era of total quality management (TQM) found that all the tactics for installing mission and vision, improving process, and measuring results meant nothing if the people in the organization did not buy into a new way of operating and could not see a future state that was significantly

FIGURE 10–4

The culture wheel.

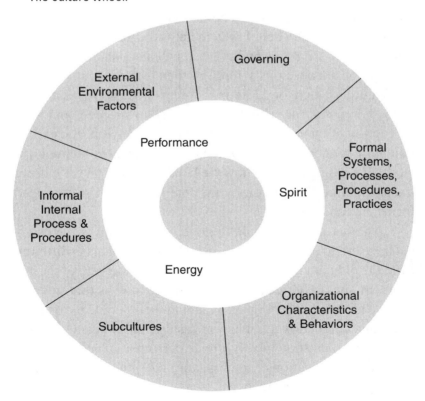

better. What those leaders sometimes did not realize was that there was a pressing need to look specifically at culture and systems as part of the foundational underpinnings of change needed for greatness. They also did not see clearly the need to focus on fully deploying and then integrating and linking change efforts into a cohesive whole that fit the vision of the future. That lack of understanding led to false starts and confusion, not performance excellence. In the end people were often discouraged even though they had worked hard at the tasks they had been asked to embrace.

How Cultures Are Formed

How leaders believe things should get done is a key driver of culture. The leader's belief system helps the people picture how things ought to be overall. Leaders establish culture consciously or unconsciously through their personal motives and the resulting behaviors. External forces also can forge culture change. Leaders care about what it takes to succeed, and their perception of those needs will affect their behaviors and expectations. The most obvious external factor today is technology. Nothing is going to affect how we behave more than the current transformation brought on by the Internet and other advanced forms of technology.

Another good example in government today is the external pressure to perform "more like a business." This is different from the old paradigm of operating as a good steward of the citizens' monies. The result of this new pressure is that government leaders are coaching and teaching their people to run their programs competitively, measure results, build business cases for change, plan strategically, create customer value, and so on. There are ramifications for the culture and, therefore, management systems and/or practices.

How does culture affect the management system? By determining how an organization does its work, how it structures work groups, how performance is managed, and what results leaders consider priorities.

Why Culture Is Important Right Now

Culture provides consistency for an organization and its people, a critical need in organizations where leaders change as a result of job rotation, mergers and acquisitions, and so on. Knowing "what matters around here" helps people feel they are working with some stability and predictability in a changing world. It also provides order and structure for activity in that the "internal way of life"—its boundaries, ground rules, norms, communication patterns, and conditions for reward and punishment—is understood.

Culture also determines the location of power within an organization. In more traditional cultures, power rests with management; in more nurturing cultures, power is more widespread.

Culture may also affect who can report to whom. It also often limits what the organization's strategies can be. It is because of the pressing need for change today that many organizations have to refine the current culture, which thwarts innovation and excellence.

This may be the case for many organizations at this point in time. Changes have been implemented in the last decade, but too often deployment is a problem. Employees' complaints are being heard—and at times not heard—because of the need for better communications about expectations, the rules of the game, the integration of initiatives with daily service delivery, the big picture, and so forth. Many of the issues being brought to the surface by today's workers have cultural implications.

Yet changing the culture has not often been an initiative, resulting in a sense of complacency or discouragement.

Why Culture Is Hard to Change

Organizations are systems; that is, the members are not autonomous entities that just happen to be together. Instead, people are a part of a larger whole, and anything of significance that occurs to that larger whole, can affect each and every member.

It may take time and money, but a technology system can be updated and changed. And despite the fact that people may know that the new system will be faster and more effective, there will be resistance to it. Thus, the heart of the matter is people.

It is clearly understood in private industry that a merger or acquisition could take place, which would mean a change in leadership. This could lead to an erosion of belief in such important values as continuous improvement. Why change if my job might not be around in another year or so? It could also thwart important new endeavors such as the recent development of knowledge-sharing strategies. Does this preclude change and imply dependency on the status quo? Of course not, but it does imply the need to begin to create a sense of urgency and actively involve the middle managers in the organization. Figure 10–5 lists the sources of complacency or discouragement.

In another sector—the political arena of government—it is accepted that leaders change with the next election. This strongly supports a key government workforce belief that this too shall pass. What does this mean for any kind of change? It means that making change in government may well be more difficult or take more time than is the case in private industry.

FIGURE 10-5

Sources of complacency or discouragement.

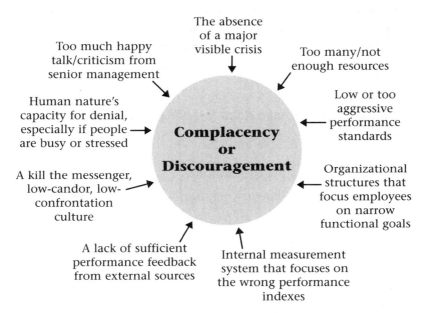

Does this preclude change in government? Of course not; there are many exciting examples of major turnarounds and/or transformations in government today.

Since the idea that change is constant is becoming more evident, people need help in understanding the vision and their part in it. They also need to be involved in making change happen. They also need education and support to help them overcome myths such as the following:

- If I get upset, maybe I can stop this.
- It might impact others, but it won't impact how I do my job.
- I'm not in a position to make these changes work; that is senior management's job.

Given people's natural resistance to change, a leader *must* think that the change needed is worth the pain. He or she must also be willing to stay the course, for it may feel at times like navigating through or even drowning in whitewater.

Figure 10–6 depicts some behaviors that reflect the culture.

People Need to Assume Accountability for Change

With a little help, people can learn the following:

- They need a positive attitude.
- They have to take ownership of some of the change.
- They need to choose battles carefully.
- They need to be tolerant of management mistakes.

FIGURE 10-6

Types of behaviors that reflect the culture.

Norms of Group Behavior

Somewhat Visible

☐ Employees respond quickly to customer requests.
☐ Managers involve lower-level employees in decision making.
☐ Managers work at least one hour past the official close of each work day.

Shared Values

Invisible

☐ Managers care about customers.
☐ Managers prefer a smooth environment and avoid conflict.
☐ Employees are concerned more with quality than quantity.
☐ Managers value hitting the budget at all "costs."

Somewhat Hard to Change

Extremely Hard to Change

- They need to keep a sense of humor.
- They need to determine if what once were strengths are now obstacles.
- They need to support management in its vision of the future.
- They need to help in inventing the future.
- They need to manage stress and pressure.

Leaders Need to Assume Accountability for Change

With a little help, leaders need to do the following:

- Clearly articulate a vision of the future.
- Create a burning platform or sense of urgency to help people jump ship.
- Solicit others' input and involve others in getting there.
- Educate and explain the changes that must happen.
- Hold people accountable for progress toward the new state by tracking their utilization of what they learn and what they are asked to do.
- Consider both task and work changes and emotional needs, carefully crafting the human side of change so that it is inculcated into the fabric of the organization.
- See the whole picture and develop implementation plans for change that accept the idea that the execution is as important as the plan for change.

Carter's Approach to Culture Change

Working with an internal steering/design team, the external consultants gather and assess initial information that will act as the foundation for change. The following nine steps are key to determining the issues and the underlying foundational changes that need refinement or adaptation to help the organization thrive.

Phase 1

1. Understand the current cultural state and the key issues thwarting performance and spirit in the workplace.
   a. Gather information that currently exists; create an initial issues map.
   b. Validate issues with a representative sample of employees and customers by using a quiet, focus group technique.
2. Establish a sense of urgency.
   a. Discuss approaches to change that have been attempted and review their success.
   b. Develop a new approach that touches the heart of the people.

Phase 2

3. Develop a concrete vision of the future state.
   a. Conduct a large search conference to communicate the vision and develop potential strategies for achieving it.
   b. Determine what strategies for action will be adopted when.
4. Communicate and gain buy-in for the vision.
   a. Determine the vehicles to use to inform and continuously reinforce the vision of the future state.
   b. Determine specific ways that management and the steering/design team can begin to role-model expected behaviors.

Phase 3

5. Empower broad-based action for change.
   a. Identify obstacles to change and get rid of them.
   b. Identify structures and systems that are sapping the performance capability of the organization; create action plans for change.
   c. Develop reward and recognition programs and processes for encouraging new behaviors, innovation, and idea sharing.
6. Generate milestones to celebrate change.
   a. Plan for visible improvements in performance and spirit.
   b. Create milestones and short-term wins.
   c. Reinvigorate the change effort and reward people who make the wins possible.
7. Review progress and plans; evaluate the newly forming state to fit with the strategic vision.
   a. Conduct a progress review with employees, customers, and other key stakeholders.
   b. Assess leadership and each member's progress toward the new behaviors; assess the effectiveness of change sponsorship.
   c. Review the steering/design team's progress and effectiveness as a change agent.
   d. Highlight individuals' progress toward the new state.

Phase 4

8. Continue ongoing initiatives to adapt the culture to the future state.
   a. Formally review plans for action; create milestones and continue the effort.

    b. Add new and innovative ideas to the plan based on employee and customer input or other external environmental factors.

    c. Celebrate visible improvements.

    d. Stay the course.

9. Anchor new approaches and efforts in the desired culture (future state).

    a. Link new initiatives with the future vision, ensuring that people see how the pieces fit.

    b. Continue to refine programs, processes, and systems to fit the strategic vision.

    c. Change the statute, if necessary, to support the vision.

In our experience phases 1 and 2 are best achieved with support from outside experts. Once the strategic effort moves into phase 3, senior management, the steering/design team, and the internal consulting staff have enough momentum that they can carry the torch effectively with much less external support.

CULTURE CHANGE CONCLUSION

There is much that can be said about the stages of change. Your organization may have been endeavoring to make significant changes over the last several years. It is likely that progress has been made, but perhaps it has not been easy. Employees may not be clear about how all the initiatives fit into the big picture. The actual future state may not be understood. Communications may have been fragmented. Perhaps deployment has been fragmented.

It is crucial to understand that large-scale change takes time. To think that just two or three years is enough to internalize culture change is to misunderstand the nature of large-scale change. Change of the size and significance envisioned by today's leaders requires a long-term commitment.

If your organizational culture change is only a few years young, it probably has shallow roots. Do the people in the organization realize this? Do they buy in to the nurturing and watering it will take not just to adopt but to internalize the change? Do they believe that they can be a force in moving the organization to new heights?

If your organization culture change is five or more years old, perhaps the deployment has been weak. Strong sponsorship and management is needed throughout the journey. Has your organization built in the strategies and tactics needed to institutionalize the future state, or has it taken it for granted that it will continue to deploy on its own? A model offered by Darryl Conner, one of Carla Carter's team's gurus in change excellence, may assist you in diagnosing where, in the stages of change, your organization currently is (Figure 10–7).

◪ CASE STUDY 1: FOSTERING CULTURE CHANGE

Marcus Goncalves

The board of directors and the executive staff are responsible for the climate they create in the organization. That climate has a major impact on the organization's ability to share knowledge across time and space. In my management consulting practice I have seen this as the most difficult aspect of knowledge transfer. By default, people have always taught themselves to collect knowledge as a way to achieve power or as a method for professional self-preservation. What is taught in colleges and universities is that knowledge should be acquired and used, but we have never learned how to share it.

FIGURE 10-7

Stages of change commitments.

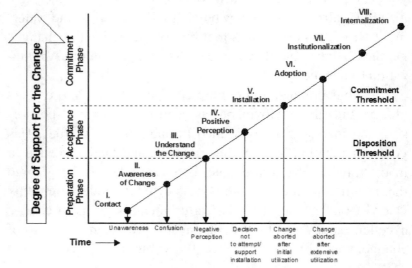

Stages of Change Commitment

Source: Daryl R. Conner, *Managing at the Speed of Change* (New York: Villard Books, 1993).

If businesses are to be successful in the knowledge economy of the twenty-first century, we must reverse that tendency. In this new economy, the most powerful individuals will not be those who build their own information islands but those who are willing to become a source of knowledge to their peers and the organization as a whole by proactively sharing what they have. Continuity and trust, which are necessary to accomplish proactive knowledge transfer within the company, must be promoted. Further, the same climate of continuity and trust should be fostered with customers.

Aside from collaboration within the many groups in a learning organization, knowledge transferring also promotes the building of relationships of continuity and trust with customers. This fringe benefit of knowledge transferring is possible only if it is done by the individuals of the organization. Thus, those with account responsibility, for example, are automatically involved with the customer by the nature of their position. Software engineers and product developers, as well as applications experts and industry specialists, should also be involved in this process, provided that they are effectively engaged on the front line. This is true for everyone in the organization. Actually, the number of people in the organization involved in relationships with customers can determine the momentum of the whole organization not only in terms of how efficiently it is becoming a learning organization but also in terms of how proficiently it is exercising the transfer of knowledge.

Another important aspect to consider is the quality of the people you, as a learning organization, can bring to this relationship with partners, supply chains, and distribution channels, which will determine the level at which your organization can operate in this relationship. The higher the quality of the individuals engaged in knowledge transfer, the higher the quality of the knowledge that can be brought to bear on any problem that your customers and coworkers bring to you. But do not underestimate other levels of the organization, as every individual independent of his or her role can effectively contribute to this knowledge management initiative.

For example, at Buckman Labs, the managers had a goal of having 80 percent of the organization effectively engaged on the front line by the end of 2000. Such a level of knowledge sharing and transferring assumes different shapes according to the organization in which it is implemented. It may translate, as in Buckman's case, into finding a way to get as many people as possible creating and transferring as much knowledge as possible in the best way to have a positive impact on the customer. Some organizations may focus on making sure that there is a high level of interaction between the organization's people and paying customers with a measurable frequency and duration. For others, it might be ensuring that the majority of their people actively use their electronic forums, Web portals, and e-mail or even ensuring that they get their accounting right, which may include profit recovery activities, so that their groups measure up to the new corporate goal.

My advice is that regardless of the nuances, idiosyncrasies, and specifics of any learning organization, the goal of knowledge-transferring strategies is to bring the full weight of the knowledge that exists in the hardware, software, and people, in a relevant and useful manner, to bear on the requirements of the customer. I believe that many learning organizations, especially those which realize they must adopt a generative learning attitude as opposed to an adaptive one, are doing a lot of these things already. But if they can get all their people to exercise knowledge transfer at all times, a tremendous power can be unleashed. The goal here is not to go after definitions, numbers, procedures, or any other quantifiable business goals. It should be about involvement, commitment, creativity, passion, and ultimately the freedom to do everything the organization can and use all of the knowledge it has to make sure that the people have done their best to satisfy their customers inside and outside the organization in every way.

Knowledge transferring will be successful only when you are able to engage all your people fully and effectively with a technological system and in cultural surroundings where they can all be comfortable. Only then will you have addressed the collaboration and knowledge-transferring issues of your organization.

◥ CASE STUDY 2: ANTICIPATING AND PROMOTING CHANGE

Marcus Goncalves

Although everyone would agree that the twenty-first century holds many unknowns, to manage ePM effectively and support sponsors and customers, ePM managers must realize that ePM is characterized by vast and dynamic changes. New technologies, in particular the Internet and PM technologies, as well as new regulations, directives, and resource restrictions, will be the catalysts of change. Why do I believe ePM managers are the ones to hold the flag of organizational change? What can ePM managers do to prepare for and implement effective and lasting project organizational change? As Figure 10–8 illustrates, in many ways we are starting from scratch, with a whiteboard, repositioning and replacing all the pieces.

FIGURE 10–8

The coupling of ePM and concurrent project management is forcing ePM managers to restructure their project organizations from scratch.

Strategy in itself is a powerful tool in bringing clarity to any project organization, as it can help integrate and focus energy, efforts, and resources across boundaries. My emphasis is on charging ePM managers to lead change in organizations because these professionals can take advantage of knowledge strategies in which three other critical leaders in the organization are brought together as members of the changing management process: the CTO or head of IT, the COO or head of HR, and the CEO. By bringing together these leaders, who rarely have sat at a strategic table together except at staff meetings, project organizations are able to bring an integrated, focused, strategic force to their efforts.

The optimal structure of ePM efforts in change management will vary enormously with the size of the organization, the degree of change, and the challenges being faced. One concern project leaders have in charging ePM managers with change management projects is the fear that new bureaucracies may be created in the project. Thus, to be successful in this endeavor, ePM managers must not add red tape to an organization attempting to morph itself into something new, as the e-business process will definitely be affected by the changes that have an impact on policies, procedures, and the existing bureaucracy. In addition, ePM managers must possess excellent entrepreneurial traits and be influential and persuasive enough to meet the business challenges of the knowledge economy. These activities, with advanced software application and business intelligence tools, are best taken care of by information technology (IT) professionals and the CTO/CIO, with the cooperation of the ePM manager, of course.

Therefore, as opposed to launching corporatewide concurrent ePM initiatives without clear business objectives at the outset, one of the main roles of ePM managers in change management is to identify the business competencies that can be enhanced by concurrent ePM as organizations develop different project strategies, depending on whether they are competing on cost, product innovation, CRM, partner relationship management (PRM), or even supplier relationship management (SRM).

Another key challenge ePM managers are equipped to address is the need for systems that integrate knowledge, technology, and people. This has been pointed out by Jim Bair, research director with the Gartner Group, who comments that we now have technologies at our fingertips, particularly the Web, that promise to enhance access to information and make it pervasive and ubiquitous. Bair argues that organizations must incorporate people into their knowledge management (KM) efforts. He also contends that firms should place more emphasis on capturing the knowledge and expertise of their employees and then make sure that it is shared. "It is the uncaptured, tacit expertise and experience of employees that will make a big difference,"[3] he adds.

Any organizational theory will tell us that to change an organization, leaders must first understand how an organization operates. That requires an understanding of the organization's culture, how it was developed, and how it was analyzed. Further, leaders must be able to view the organization from several points of view to understand how it really functions. ePM managers can play a major role in this process by helping leaders unfreeze, restructure, and refreeze the organization's culture as necessary—or, if you prefer, remove, reshape, and reposition the cheese inside the organization to promote innovation.

I believe that ePM managers, with the help of KM professionals, are the most appropriate professionals to move the *cheese* (have you read Dr. Spencer Johnson's *Who Moved*

My Cheese?) because of their exposure to KM techniques, knowledge technologies, and the generators of knowledge: people.[4]

This is a time-consuming process that requires a great deal of effort and consistency. Often senior managers, in particular CTOs and CIOs, underestimate and misunderstand it and try to address these cultural issues with total quality management implementations, which can be expensive, lengthy, and ineffective. The U.S. Air Force, for instance, overestimated its TQM implementation, and as a result, more than six years have gone by and it is still working to complete its cultural change. Although changes may be implemented fairly quickly, it takes consistent leadership commitment at all levels to complete the institutionalization process.

Organizational change can be seen as a double-edged management sword. Any major economic, social, or professional event in an organization can disrupt the flow of business and other functions within that organization. When changes occur, they can promote unity and tighten integration throughout the organization or unleash a backlash of unrest and turbulence. Changes in a large organization can affect an entire industry.

For instance, when we look at the sharp decline in crude oil prices in 1998, we see that that event caused a significant reduction in business opportunities for oil service companies. More recently, the burst of the dot-com bubble brought hard changes to marketing companies and the whole concept of real estate on the Internet. The knowledge economy is being characterized as an economy that capitalizes on change, and unless organizations get ready for it, the price to be paid can be very high, as this new economic condition calls for boldness, innovation, and risk taking.

One of the best places in the world for me to spend time in

is Brazil. After I visit my family and friends, I am always amazed by the Brazilian economy and how it positions itself within the global market. What I admire is the willingness and ability of Brazilian entrepreneurs to adapt to change. With the economy in a challenging and ever-evolving position, in particular as neighboring Argentina's economy collapses, it is amazing to see how promising that market is. As I write this chapter in early 2002, one of the best ETF funds available at iShare is a Brazilian fund whose symbol is EWZ. How can that be? How do Brazilian leaders pull this off over and over? The answer very likely is heavily focused on innovation, as executives respond to the challenge by trying to improve their marketing focus and selling their way out of the downturn. They see the moving of their cheese—by global market forces, inflation, and hyperactive cultural changes—as an opportunity to innovate and to reinvent themselves. The same goes for Mexico, one of the leaders in the use of smart-card technology. I am convinced that Brazilian entrepreneurs are always aware that they must change or adapt to new market forces when the market environment changes in order to bring business success. That is why I believe it is the scariest markets that prove the mettle of a fund and its managers.

KM professionals should use their deep knowledge about KM, communities of practice, and organizational change to help project organizations navigate the maze of change and reorganize their organizational groups, much as a football coach reorganizes the team over and over, as many times as necessary, to deal with the game at hand. Thus, the organizational positions, reporting lines, and responsibilities of all executive staff, senior managers, and departmental groups must be modified according to the challenge to address the situation. In Spencer Johnson's analogy, that is when the organization must move the cheese.

Changing One Step at a Time

Changes in a virtual project organization take not only time but also many steps. In the process, any attempt to shorten the steps or develop shortcuts will only produce a false illusion of speed and unsatisfactory results. Change is at the core of the gap between know-how and how-to in any organization, and I believe that gap often exists because leaders know how to implement a change but do not feel confident about how to implement it.

Therefore, ePM managers and KM professionals must help executives and leaders realize that change is not just necessary to bridge the gap but is also the only constant they can count on in turning knowledge into action. Whether it is bridging the gap between the know-how about a new technology and the how to (Figure 10–9) incorporate that technology or the know-how of achieving compliance with a new regulation and how to implement it, change is the bridge that makes it possible. Know-how must generate strategies, but only change strategies can provide the execution plans for how to create effective and lasting organizational change to meet these challenges.

Changes can come in many forms and from many forces, originating from both inside and outside the organization. Bridging a knowledge gap within a project organization always requires the implementation of new organizational structures, realignment and often consolidation of roles and responsibilities, and even the revision and restatement of the company's mission. Thus, change is always at the core of bridging knowledge gaps, of turning knowledge into action. The problem is that often leaders and senior executives have a tendency to postpone change, typically through actions such as "crossing the bridge when you come to it," which often turns into not

FIGURE 10–9

Knowledge provides the know-how, whereas action provides the how-to; change enables the gap between these two forms of knowledge to be bridged.

crossing the bridge at all or, worse, burning the bridge. That is why expensive consulting recommendations seldom lead to change, as executives, despite knowing what needs to be done and often even before hiring a consultant, are not ready to embrace the changes that will come about as they begin crossing the bridge from knowing how to actually executing.

As John Kotter[5] states, one of the major mistakes project organizations make is not establishing a great enough sense of urgency in changing: "Most successful change efforts begin when some individuals or some groups start to look hard at a company's competitive situation, market position, technological trends and financial performance."

Surprisingly, according to Kotter, more than 50 percent of the companies he saw failing in the change process did so because they did not have enough of a sense of urgency. Executives underestimated the hardships that come with changes, in particular taking people out of their comfort zone, or overestimated the sense of urgency they had placed in the process. Lack of patience, immobilization in the face of downside possibilities, concerns about defensiveness in senior employees, lowering of morale, and short-term business results are all reasons for not embracing change, not wanting to cross the bridge, or, as Spencer Johnson would put it, not wanting to deal with the fact that something or someone has moved the cheese.

Knowledge managers, as well as ePM managers, are leaders, and leaders lead, or colead, during times of change. To do that, they must be aware of the intricacies and inner workings of the groups they interact with or lead. Although leading can be exciting and challenging, at times of major change it can be very frustrating, as organizations are made up of people and human behavior can be very difficult to predict. Change always requires the creation of new systems; it requires innovation. Innovation is a great thing, but it demands leadership. Therefore, before ePM mangers can aid the implementation of change in a group or organization, they must understand what makes an organization tick.

Dealing with Resistance to Change

One of the primary sources of resistance to change is the organization's culture. KM professionals and ePM managers involved with organizational learning are typically aware of this. But unless senior staff and leaders understand what organizational culture entails, very little can be accomplished in dealing with resistance to change. By definition, organizational culture is a pattern of common and shared basic assumptions that the organization learned as it solved its problems of external adaptation and internal integration; it has worked well enough to be considered valid and therefore to be taught to new members as the correct way to perceive, think, and feel in relation to those challenges.

In dealing with the need to change, knowing who or what caused the need for change is important, but it is not so important if you look at it proactively. Of course, it is important to know who or what moved your cheese so that you can run after it or them and compete to get the cheese back. This is what I call a reactive approach to change, which does not necessarily lead to innovation. Chances are, your cheese was moved as a result of innovation, but that innovation was not generated by you or your organization. Thus, you must move your cheese before someone does it for you or, as Jack Welch once said, "change before you have to." Successful change must lead to innovation. Otherwise, your project organization is only playing catch-up. Often failed attempts to change are a result of lack of vision. In such cases, you find plenty of plans and programs but not vision. Success is the result of a vision in action. If your organization is pursuing change based on a vision but is not being successful, verify your action plans, as there probably is not much action in place, typically as a result of resistance or fear. By the same token, if you believe you have a good action plan, have the support of the organization, and still are not being successful in implementing changes and consequently innovating, you must check your vision or lack thereof.

Always remember that innovative success is the result of vision in action. Some immediate actions that can be taken in managing change in e-projects include the following:

- Create a new vision.
- Define a mission statement, core values, basic principles, and an operating style.

- Create a quality council of senior leaders to oversee the change process.

To ensure that changes are institutionalized in the organization's culture, knowledge about the change and the new way of doing things has to be turned into action. One way of verifying that that is happening is by consciously attempting to show employees all the positive results the new approach, behavior, and attitude have brought to the organization and its performance. It is very important that leaders make an effort to communicate such accomplishments as employees may have very inaccurate views of the results.

For instance, at Virtual Access Networks, where I was a CKO, I was asked to manage the research group working on a new wireless technology concept that had failed under the previous management. This was an unusual situation for a CKO to be in, but management understood that most of the challenges the group faced were not of a technical nature but were multicultural and motivational. It was clear that several changes had to take place in that group if it was to be successful.

As I began removing the cheese, the team members' characters began to clash with the new vision. At some point half the group threatened to resign if they were forced to change. But after much communication, group lunches, peer quality reinforcement meetings, and the development of a unique identity, the group finally began to turn around, accepting the new shape of the cheese. We were able to reposition the group, its goals, and its deliverables in record time.

However, the group members did not naturally take ownership of their success, and a few even stated that they stayed around out of consideration for me. Those team members at first clearly missed the point, as there was no way one person alone could change a group unless each element of the group did its part, beginning by believing in the new vision and doing its best to succeed. It was necessary for us to meet as a group a few times, as well as individually, to emphasize that the glory for the accomplishment was theirs individually and as a group, and not just their leaders'.

The group today is self-sufficient and successfully operates under that new vision. Furthermore, at least one successor has risen from the pack and is ready to lead the group. Leaders must breed new leaders.

G L O S S A R Y

A

Acceptance—The formal process of accepting delivery of a product or a deliverable.

Activity—The smallest self-contained unit of work used to define the logic of a project. In general, activities share the following characteristics: a definite duration; logical relationships to other activities in a project; use of resources such as people, materials, and facilities; and an associated cost.

Activity definition—Identifying the specific activities that must be performed to produce project deliverables.

Activity duration—The length of time (hours, days, weeks, months) it takes to complete an activity. This information is optional in the data entry of an activity. Workflow (predecessor relationships) can be defined before durations are assigned. Activities with zero duration are considered milestones (milestone value of 1 to 94) or hammocks (milestone value of 95 to 99).

Activity duration estimating—Estimating the number of work periods that will be needed to complete an activity.

Activity file—A file containing all the data related to the definition of activities on a project.

Activity ID—A unique code identifying each activity in a project.

Activity-on-node—A network where activities are represented by a box or a node linked by dependencies. See also *precedence diagram method*.

Activity status—The state of completion of an activity. A planned activity has not yet started. A started activity is in progress. A finished activity is complete.

Actual cost—The cost actually incurred.

Actual cost of work performed (ACWP)—The sum of costs actually incurred in accomplishing the work performed.

Actual dates—Dates that are entered as the project progresses. These are the dates when activities really started and finished as opposed to planned or projected dates.

Actual direct costs—Costs specifically identified with a contract or project, based on the contractor's cost identification and accumulation system. See also *direct costs*.

Actual finish—Date on which an activity was completed.

Actual start—Date on which an activity was started.

ACWP—See actual *cost of work performed*.

ADM project—A nonhierarchical project that uses the arrow diagram method.

Advanced material release (AMR)—A document used by organizations to initiate the purchase of long-lead-time or time-critical materials before the final release of a design.

Alternative resource—A resource that may be substituted as the requirement for an activity if the requested resource is not available.

Approval to proceed—Approval by the project board at initiation or before the beginning of the next stage.

Archive plan—A function of some computer programs that allows versions of a plan to be archived.

Arrow diagram method (ADM)—One of two conventions used to represent an activity in a project. Also known as activity-on-arrow or i/j method.

As-late-as-possible (ALAP)—An activity for which the application sets the early dates as late as possible without delaying the early dates of any successor.

As-soon-as-possible (ASAP)—An activity for which the application sets the early dates to be as soon as possible. This is the default activity type in most project management systems.

Assumptions—Statements taken for granted or as the truth.

Authorized unpriced work (AUW)—Any change in scope for which authorization to proceed has been given but for which the estimated costs have not yet been settled.

Authorized work—The effort that has been defined, plus work for which authorization has been given but for which defined contract costs have not been agreed upon.

B

Backward pass—A procedure within time analysis to calculate the late start and late finish dates of all activities in a project.

Balanced matrix—An organizational matrix in which functions and projects have the same priority.

Bar chart—A view of project data that uses horizontal bars on a time scale to depict activity information. Frequently called a *Gantt chart*.

Baseline—A copy of the project schedule for a particular time (usually before the project is started) that can be used for comparison with the current schedule.

Baseline dates—Original planned start and finish dates for an activity. Used to compare with current planned dates to determine any delays. Also used to calculate budgeted cost of work scheduled for earned-valued analysis.

Baseline review—A customer review conducted to determine with a limited sampling that a contractor is continuing to use the previously accepted performance system and is properly implementing a baseline on the contract or option under review.

Baseline schedule—A fixed project schedule. The standard by which project performance is measured. The current schedule is copied into the baseline.

Batch operations—Operations performed by the computer without the need for user intervention.

BCWP—Budgeted cost of work performed.

BCWS—Budgeted cost of work scheduled.

Benefits—The enhanced efficiency, economy, and effectiveness of future business operations to be delivered by a program.

Benefits framework—An outline of the expected benefits of the program, the business operations affected, and current and target performance measures.

Benefits management—Combined with program management, the process for planning, managing, delivering, and measuring program benefits.

Benefits management plan—Specifies who is responsible for achieving the benefits set out in the benefit profiles and how achievement of the benefits is to be measured, managed, and monitored. Part of the program definition.

Benefits profiles—Located in the program definition; describe the planned benefits to be realized by the program. Also state where, when, and how they are to be realized.

Bottom-up cost estimating—The method of making estimates for every activity in the work breakdown structure and summarizing them to provide a total project cost estimate.

Brainstorming—The unstructured generation of ideas by a group of people.

Breakdown structure—A hierarchical structure by which project elements are broken down, or decomposed. See also *organizational breakdown structure* (OBS) and *work breakdown structure (WBS)*.

Budget—The planned cost for an activity or project.

Budget at completion (BAC)—The sum total of the time-phased budget.

Budget cost—The cost anticipated at the start of a project.

Budgeted cost of work performed (BCWP)—A measure used in an earned-value management system that allows one to quantify the overall progress of the project in monetary terms. BCWP is calculated by applying a performance measurement factor to the planned cost. (By comparing BCWP with ACWP, it is possible to determine if the project is under or over budget.) Another term for BCWP is *earned value*.

Budgeted cost of work scheduled (BCWS)—The sum of the budgets for all planned work scheduled to be accomplished within a time period. Often used to designate the cumulative to-date budget.

Budget element—Budget elements are the same as resources: the people, materials, or other entities needed to do the work of the program. For example, engineer, technician, travel, and pipe can all be budget elements. These elements can be validated against a *resource breakdown structure (RBS)*. Budget elements are typically assigned to a work package but can also be defined at the cost account level.

Budget estimate—See *estimate*.

Budgeting—Time phased financial requirements.

Budget unit—The base unit for a calculation. For example, the engineer budget element might have a budget unit of hours. Since budget units are user-defined, they can be any appropriate unit of measure. For example, a budget unit might be hours, dollars, linear feet, or tons.

Burden—Overhead expenses distributed over the appropriate direct labor and/or material base.

Business assurance—Ensuring that actual costs and elapsed time are in line with plan costs and schedule times and that the business case remains available.

Business assurance coordinator—A person in the project assurance team who is responsible for planning, monitoring, and reporting on all business assurance aspects of a project.

Business case—A document used to justify the commitment of resources to a project.

C

Calculate schedule—The critical path method (calculate schedule) is a modeling process that defines all the project's critical activities that must be completed on time. The Calc tool bar button on the Gantt and PERT (found in most GUI-based PM software) windows calculates the start and finish dates of activities in the project in two passes. The first pass calculates early start and finish dates from the earliest start date forward. The second pass calculates the late start and finish activities from the latest finish date backward. The difference between the pairs of start and finish dates for each task is the float or slack time for the task (see *float*). Slack is the amount of time a task can be delayed without delaying the project completion date. A great advantage of this method is the fine-tuning that can be done to accelerate the project. One can shorten various critical path activities and then check the schedule to see how it is affected by the changes. By experimenting in this manner, one can determine the optimal project schedule.

Calendar file—A file containing calendar information for one or more calendars.

Calendars—A project calendar lists time intervals in which activities or resources can or cannot be scheduled. A project usually has one default calendar for the normal workweek (Monday through Friday, for example) but may have other calendars as well. Each calendar can be customized with its own holidays and extra work days. Resources and activities can be attached to any of the calendars that are defined.

Case structure—A breakdown of the project budget. Case numbers can be subdivided only twice to produce three levels: case, subcase, and sub-subCase.

Change control board (CCB)—A formally constituted group of stakeholders responsible for approving or rejecting changes to project baselines.

Change in scope—See *scope change*.

Change requests—May arise through changes in the business or issues in a project. Change requests should be logged, assessed and agreed on before the project can be done. Changes may be needed to the scope, design, methods, or planned aspects of a project.

Chart of accounts—Any numbering system, usually based on a corporate chart of accounts of the primary performing organization, used to monitor project costs by category.

Child—A lower-level element in a hierarchical structure.

Chunk Chart—List of prioritized project work areas for a case number and fiscal year as part of a Department of Energy (DOE) defense programs (DP) Sector Project Data Document (PDD).

Closeout—The completion of work on a project.

Code file—A file used in reporting that contains information associated with codes entered on an activity record.

Commitment—A binding financial obligation typically in the form of a purchase order. If commitments are entered as a budget, a forecast using the method retain EAC can show the open commitments.

Committed costs—Costs that will be incurred even if the project is terminated.

Communication—The transmission of information so that the recipient understands what the sender intends.

Communications planning—Determining project stakeholders' communication and information needs.

Completion date—The date calculated by which the project could finish after careful estimating.

Compound risk—A risk made up of a number of interrelated risks.

Concurrent engineering—A systematic approach to the simultaneous, integrated design of products and their related processes, such as manufacturing, testing, and supporting.

Configuration—The technical description needed to build, test, accept, operate, install, maintain, and support a system.

Configuration item—A part of a configuration that has a set function and is designated for configuration management.

Configuration librarian—Responsible for administering configuration management. May be on a project team or have system responsibilities rather than project responsibilities.

Configuration management—The process of defining the configuration items in a system, controlling the release and change of those items throughout the project, recording and reporting their status, and verifying their completeness.

Conflict management—The ability to manage conflict effectively.

Constraints—Applicable restrictions that will affect the scope of a project.

Consumable resource—A type of resource that remains available until it is consumed (for example, a material).

Contingency—The planned allotment of time and cost for unforeseeable elements in a project. Including contingencies will increase the confidence of the overall project.

Contingency planning—The development of a management plan that uses alternative strategies to ensure project success if specified risk events occur.

Contract—A mutually binding agreement in which the contractor is obligated to provide services or products and the buyer is obligated to provide payment for them. Contracts fall into three categories: fixed price, cost reimbursable, and unit price.

Contract budget base—The negotiated contract cost value plus the estimated value of authorized but unpriced work.

Contract closeout—Settlement of a contract.

Contract target cost (CTC)—The negotiated costs for the original definitized contract and all contractual changes that have been definitized but excluding the estimated cost of any authorized unpriced changes. Equals the value of the BAC plus the management or contingency reserve.

Contract target price (CTP)—The negotiated estimated costs plus a profit or fee.

Contract work breakdown structure (CWBS)—A customer-prepared breakout or subdivision of a project, typically down to level three, that subdivides the project into all its major hardware, software, and service elements; integrates the customer and contractor effort; and provides a framework for planning, control, and reporting.

Control—The process of comparing actual performance with planned performance, analyzing the differences, and taking the appropriate corrective action.

Control and coordination—Control is the process of developing targets and plans: measuring actual performance and comparing it with planned performance and taking steps to correct the situation. Coordination is the act of ensuring that work is being carried out in different organizations and places to fit together effectively in terms of time, content, and cost to achieve project objectives effectively.

Control charts—Display the results, over time, of a process. Used to determine if the process is in need of adjustment.

Controlling relationship—The early dates of an activity are controlled either by a target date on the activity or, more normally, by one of the predecessor relationships. In the latter case, the relationship is called the controlling relationship.

Coordinated matrix—An organizational structure where the project leader reports to the functional manager and does not have authority over team members from other departments.

Corrective action—Changes made to bring future project performance into the plan.

Cost—Can be divided into internal and external expenses. External costs can be controlled by contracts and budgets for each phase of a project and for each deliverable or work product. Internal cost is the cost of project resources.

Cost account—Usually defined as the intersection of the program's work breakdown structure (WBS) and organizational breakdown structure (OBS). In effect, each cost account defines what work is to be performed and who will perform it. Cost accounts are the focal point for the integration of scope, cost, and schedule. Another term for *cost account* is *control account*.

Cost account manager (CAM)—A member of a functional organization responsible for cost account performance and for the management of resources to accomplish such tasks.

Cost account plan (CAP)—The management control unit in which measurement of earned-value performance takes place.

Cost-benefit analysis—The analysis of the potential costs and benefits of a project to allow comparison of the returns from alternative forms of investment.

Cost breakdown structure—A hierarchical structure that rolls budgeted resources into elements of costs, typically labor, materials, and other direct costs.

Cost budgeting—Allocating cost estimates to individual project components.

Cost codes—Codes assigned to activities that allow costs to be consolidated according to the elements of a code structure.

Cost control point—The point in a program at which costs are entered and controlled. Frequently, the cost control point for a program is the cost account or the work package.

Cost control system—Any system of keeping costs within the bounds of budgets or standards based on work actually performed. Cost control is typically a level in the budget element breakdown structure.

Cost curve—A graph plotted against a horizontal time scale and a cumulative cost vertical scale.

Cost element—A unit of costs to perform a task or acquire an item. The cost estimated may be a single value or a range of values.

Cost estimating—The process of predicting the costs of a project.

Cost incurred—Costs identified through the use of the accrued method of accounting or costs actually paid. Costs include direct labor, direct materials, and all allowable indirect costs.

Cost management—The effective financial control of a project through evaluating, estimating, budgeting, monitoring, analyzing, forecasting, and reporting the cost information.

Cost of money—A form of indirect cost incurred by investing capital in facilities employed on government contracts.

Cost of quality—The cost of quality planning, control, assurance, and rework.

Cost overrun—The amount by which a contractor exceeds or expects to exceed the estimated costs and/or the final limitations (the ceiling) of a contract.

Cost performance index (CPI)—Ratio of work accomplished to work cost incurred for a specified time period. An efficiency rating for work accomplished for resources expended.

Cost performance report (CPR)—A monthly cost report generated by the performing contractor to reflect cost and schedule status information for management.

Cost plus fixed fee contract (CPFF)—A type of contract where the buyer reimburses the seller for the seller's allowable costs plus a fixed fee.

Cost plus incentive fee contract (CPIFC)—A type of contract where the buyer reimburses the seller for the seller's allowable costs and the seller earns a profit if defined criteria are met.

Cost reimbursement type contracts—A category of contracts based on payments to a contractor for allowable estimated costs, normally requiring only a "best efforts" performance standard from the contractor. Risk for all growth over the estimated value rests with the project owner.

Cost/schedule control systems criteria (C/SCSC)—Thiry-five defined standards that have been applied against private contractor management control systems since 1967 to insure the government that cost reimbursable and incentive contracts are managed properly.

Cost/schedule planning and control specification (C/SPCS)—The U.S. Air Force inititative in the mid–1960's that later resulted in the C/SCSC.

Cost schedule status report (C/SSR)—The low-end cost and schedule report generally imposed on smaller-value contracts that do not warrant full C/SCSC.

Cost variance—The difference between the budgeted and the actual cost of work performed.

Crashing—The process of reducing the time it takes to complete an activity by adding resources.

Critical activity—An activity that it has zero or negative float.

Criticality index—Used in risk analysis. Represents the percentage of simulation trials that resulted in the activity being placed on the critical path.

Critical path—Series of consecutive activities that represent the longest path through a project.

Critical path method (CPM)—A technique used to predict project duration by analyzing which sequence of activities has the least amount of scheduling flexibility. Early dates are figured by using a forward pass using a specific start date, and late dates are figured by using a backward pass starting from a completion date.

C/SCSC—See *cost/schedule control system criteria*.

Customer—Any person who defines needs or wants, justifies or pays for part of the project, or evaluates or uses the results.

Cutoff date—The ending date in a reporting period.

CV—See *cost variance*.

D

Dangle—An activity or network that has either no predecessors or no successors. If it has neither, it is referred to as an isolated activity.

Data type—The characteristic indicating whether a data item represents a number, date, character string, and so on.

Delaying resource—In resource scheduling, inadequate availability of one or more resources may require that the completion of an activity be delayed beyond the date on which it could otherwise be completed. The delaying resource is the first resource in an activity that causes that activity to be delayed.

Delegating—The process by which authority and responsibility are distributed from the project manager to subordinates.

Deliverable—A report or product that must be completed and delivered to ensure satisfaction of contractual requirements.

Delphi technique—A process in which a consensus view is reached by consultation with experts. Often used as an estimating technique.

Dependencies—Relationships between products or tasks. For example, one product may be made up of several other dependent products, or a task may not begin until a dependent task is complete. See also *logical relationship*.

Dependency links—Different types of links connecting activities in a precedence network.

Design and development phase—The period in which production process and facility and production processes are developed and designed.

Detailed plans—See *detailed resource plan* and *detailed technical plan*.

Detailed resource plan—A plan implemented when it is necessary to plan and control a major activity within a stage. The plan sets costs and resource usage that correspond to the detailed technical plan.

Detailed technical plan—A plan used to give a specific breakdown of major activities. It exists in all but the smallest projects.

Deterministic network—A network with no facilities to accommodate probabilistic dependencies. Precedence networks are said to be deterministic.

Direct costs—Costs (labor, material, and other direct costs) that can be consistently related to work performed on a particular project. Direct costs can be contrasted with indirect costs, which cannot be identified with a specific project.

Discontinuous activity—An activity in which the interval between the start and finish dates is allowed to exceed its duration to satisfy start-to-start and finish-to-finish relationships with other activities.

Discontinuous processing—An option that assigns the discontinuous attribute to all activities for a time analysis session except when overridden by a specific activity type.

Discrete effort—Tasks that have a specific measurable end product or end result. Ideal for earned-value measurement. See *work package*.

Discrete milestone—A milestone that has a definite scheduled occurrence in time.

Duration—The length of time needed to complete an activity.

Duration compression—Often resulting in an increase in cost; the shortening of a project schedule without reducing the project scope.

E

EAC—See *estimate at completion*.

Earliest feasible date—The earliest date on which an activity could be scheduled to start based on the scheduled dates of all its predecessors but in the absence of any resource constraints on the activity itself. This date is calculated by resource scheduling.

Early dates—Calculated in the forward pass of time analysis; the earliest dates on which an activity can start and finish.

Early finish—The early finish date is the earliest calculated date on which an activity can end. It is based on the activity's early start, which depends on the finish of predecessor activities and the activity's duration (see *Early start*). Most PM software calculates early dates with a forward pass from the beginning of the project to the end.

Early start—The earliest calculated date on which an activity can begin. It is dependent on when all predecessor activities finish. Most PM software calculates early dates with a forward pass from the beginning of the project to the end.

Earned hours—The time in standard hours credited as a result of the completion of a task or group of tasks.

Earned value—A cost control that allows one to quantify the overall progress of a project in monetary terms. Calculated by applying a performance measurement factor to the planned cost. Another term for *earned value* is *budgeted cost of work performed*.

Earned-value analysis—Analysis of project progress where the actual money budgeted and spent is compared to the value of the work achieved.

Earned-value cost control—The quantification of the overall progress of a project in dollar terms to provide a realistic yardstick against which to compare the actual cost to date.

Earned-value management—A management technique that relates resource planning to schedules and to technical cost and schedule requirements. All work is planned, budgeted, and scheduled in time-phased increments, constituting a cost and schedule measurement baseline.

Effort—The number of labor units necessary to complete the work. Effort is usually expressed in staff hours, staff days, or staff weeks and should not be confused with duration.

Effort-driven activity—Provides the option to determine activity duration through resource usage. The resource requiring the most time to complete the specified amount of work on the activity will determine its duration.

Effort remaining—An estimate of the effort remaining to complete an activity.

Elapsed time—The total number of calendar days (excluding nonwork days such as weekends or holidays) that is needed to complete an activity. Gives a "real-world view" of how long an activity is scheduled to take for completion.

End activity—An activity with no logical successors.

Engineering cost estimate—A detailed cost estimate of the work and related burdens, usually made by industrial engineering or price/cost estimating. Another term for *engineering cost estimate* is *bottom-up cost estimate*.

Enterprisewide—Across an entire sector of technology, business area, and so on.

Estimate—The prediction of the quantitative result. Usually applied to project costs, resources and durations.

Estimate at completion (EAC)—A value expressed in dollars and/or hours to represent the projected final costs of work when completed. Calculated as ETC + ACWP.

Estimate to complete (ETC)—The value expressed in dollars or hours developed to represent the cost of the work required to complete a task. You calculate the ETC by subtracting the budgeted cost of work performed from the budget at completion. The ETC is calculated as BAC − BCWP.

Estimating—The act of combining the results of postproject reviews, metrics, consultation, and informed assessment to arrive at time and resource requirements for an activity.

ETC—See *estimate to complete*.

Event—A point that is the beginning or end of an activity and is identified by the I-node or J-node, respectively.

Exceptions—Items that exceed the predefined acceptable cost and/or schedule variance.

Expected monetary value—A measure of probabilistic value. Calculated by multiplying each outcome value by its probability and adding all the results together. Can be calculated using a formula.

Expenditure—A charge against available funds evidenced by a voucher, claim, or other documents. Expenditures represent the actual payment of funds.

Extended subsequent applications review (ESAR)—A formal review performed in lieu of a full C/SCSC demonstration review when contractor conditions have changed or when programs change

External constraint—Any factor that affects the ability to complete the project on time, within budget, or within scope.

F

Fast-tracking—The process of reducing the number of sequential relationships (FS) and replacing them typically with parallel relationships (SS).

Filter—A facility allowing subsequent commands to operate only on records that conform to specified criteria.

Finish date—The actual or estimated time associated with an activity's completion.

Finish float—The amount of excess time an activity has at its finish before a successor activity must start. The difference between the start date of the predecessor and the finish date of the current activity, using the early or late schedule. (early and late dates are not mixed). May be referred to as slack time. All floats are calculated when a project has its schedule computed.

Finishing activity—The last activity that must be completed before a project can be considered finished. This activity is not a predecessor to any other activity; it has no successors. Many PM software packages allow for multiple finish activities.

Finish-to-finish lag—The minimum amount of time that must pass between the finish of one activity and the finish of its successor(s). All lags are calculated when a project has its schedule computed. Finish-to-finish lags are often used with start-to-start lags.

Finish-to-start lag—The minimum amount of time that must pass between the finish of one activity and the start of its successor(s). The default finish-to-start lag is zero. All lags are calculated when a project has its schedule computed. In most cases, finish-to-start lags are not used with other lag types.

Firm fixed price contract (FFP)—A contract where the buyer pays a set amount to the seller regardless of the seller's cost to complete the project.

Fixed date—A calendar date (associated with a plan) that cannot be moved or changed during the schedule.

Fixed-duration scheduling—A scheduling method in which regardless of the number of resources assigned to the task, the duration remains the same.

Fixed finish—See *imposed finish*.

Fixed price contracts—A generic category of contracts based on the establishment of firm legal commitments to complete the required work. A performing contractor is legally obligated to finish the job no matter how much it costs to complete it. Risks of all cost growth rest on the performing contractor.

Fixed start—See *imposed start*.

Float—The amount of time an activity can slip past its duration without delaying the rest of the project. The calculation depends on the float type. See *start float, finish float, positive float*, and *negative float*. All float is calculated when a project has its schedule computed.

Forecast at completion (FAC)—The scheduled cost for a task.

Forecast final cost—See *estimate at completion*.

Forward pass—A procedure within time analysis to determine the early start and early finish dates of activities.

Fragnet—See *subnet.*

Free float—The maximum amount by which an activity can be delayed beyond its early dates without delaying any successor activity beyond its early dates.

Functional manager (FM)—The person responsible for the business and technical management of a functional group.

Functional matrix—An organization type where the project has a team leader in each functional department and the products are passed from one team to the next.

Functional organization—The hierarchical organization of a staff members according to their specialties.

Funding profile—An estimate of funding requirements.

G

Gantt (bar) chart—A time-phased graphic display of activity durations. Also referred to as a bar chart. Activities are listed with other tabular information on the left side with time intervals over the bars. Activity durations are shown in the form of horizontal bars.

Gantt, Henry—The inventor of the Gantt chart.

General and administrative (G&A or GANDA)—A form of indirect expenses incurred for the administration of a company, including senior executive expenses. Such expenses are spread over the total direct and burden costs for the company.

Goal—A one-sentence definition of specifically what will be accomplished, incorporating an event signifying completion.

H

Hammock—Groups activities, milestones, or other hammocks together for reporting. A hammock's milestone number ranges from 95 to 99. This allows for five levels of summation. For example, two hammocks at the 95 level can be combined in a 96 level hammock. Any number of hammocks are allowed within the five levels for a project. Most PM software calculates the duration of a hammock from the early and late dates of the activities to which that hammock is linked.

Hard zeros—In resource scheduling, a distinction is made between resource availabilities that are specified as zero but can be exceeded under certain circumstances and hard zeros, which can never be exceeded. Hard zeros may cause an activity to be impossible to schedule, in which case the resource scheduling process may be aborted.

Hierarchical coding structure—A coding system that can be represented as a multilevel tree structure in which every code except those at the top of the tree has a parent code.

Highlight Report—Reviews progress to date and highlights actual or potential problems. The project manager prepares this report at intervals determined by the project board.

Histogram—A graphic display of resource usage over a period of time. Allows the detection of overused or underused resources. The resource usage is displayed in colored vertical bars.

Holiday—An otherwise valid working day that has been designated as exempt from work.

Hypercritical activities—Activities on the critical path with negative float. This can be achieved through the imposition of constraints such as target dates.

I

Immediate activity—An activity that can be forced to start on its earliest feasible date by resource scheduling even if that means overloading a resource.

Impact—The assessment of the adverse effects of an occurring risk.

Impact analysis—Assessing the pros and cons of pursuing a particular course of action.

Implementation review or visit—An initial visit by members of the customer C/SCSC review team to a contractor's plant to review the contractor's plans for implementing C/SCSC on a new contract. Such visits should take place within 30 days after contract award.

Imposed finish—A finished date imposed on an activity by external constraints.

Imposed start—A start date imposed on an activity by an external constraint.

Indirect costs—Resources expended that are not directly identified to any specific contract, project, product, or service, such as overhead and G&A.

Individual work plan—Defines the responsibilities of an individual team member; the lowest level of a technical plan.

Informal review—A less formal subset of a quality review.

Information distribution—Distributing information to stakeholders in a timely manner.

Initiation—Committing an organization to begin a project.

In progress—An activity that has been started but not yet completed.

Integrated baseline review (IBR)—The newest form of the Department of Defense C/SCSC verification review process in which the technical staff members lead the effort to verify that the entire project baseline is in place, together with a realistic budget to accomplish all planned work.

Integrated cost/schedule reporting—See *earned value.*

Integrated product development team (IPDT)—The development of new products through the use of multifunctional teams that work in unison form the conceptual idea until completion of the product. Best contrasted with the traditional form of sequential functional development. Another term for *IPDT* is *concurrent engineering.*

Integration—The process of bringing people, activities, and other things together to perform effectively.

International Project Management Association—A federation of European project management organizations. Does not include PMI or AIPM.

Invitation for bid (IFB)—Similar to a request for proposal but often with a more specific application area.

IT executive committee—The departmental top management group that is responsible for the overall direction of IT projects.

K

Key event schedule—See *master schedule.*

Key performance indicators—Measurable indicators that will be used to report progress that is chosen to reflect the critical success factors of a project.

KPI—See *key performance indicators.*

L

Labor rate variance—Difference between planned labor rates and actual labor rates.

Ladder—A sequence of parallel activities connected at their starts or finishes or both.

Lag—The time delay between the start or finish of an activity and the start or finish of its successor(s). See *finish-to-finish lag, finish-to-start lag*, and *start-to-start lag.*

Late dates—Calculated in the backward pass of time analysis; the latest dates on which an activity can start and finish.

Late event date—Calculated from the backward pass; the latest date an event can occur.

Late finish—Late finish dates are defined as the latest dates by which an activity can finish without causing delays in the project. Many PM software packages calculate late dates with a backward pass from the end of the project to the beginning.

Late start—Late Start dates are defined as the latest dates by which an activity can start without causing delays in the project. Many PM software packages calculate late dates with a backward pass from the end of the project to the beginning.

Leadership—Getting others to follow direction.

Leveling—See resource leveling.

Level of effort (LOE)—Work that does not result in a final product (such as liaison, coordination, follow-up, and other support activities) and cannot be effectively associated with a definable end product process result. Measured only in terms of resources actually consumed within a time period.

Life cycle costing—Used in evaluating alternatives; the concept of including acquisition, operating, and disposal costs.

Likelihood—Assessment of the probability that a risk will occur.

Line manager—The manager of any group that makes a product or performs a service.

Link—See *logical relationship*.

Links—See *dependency links*.

Logic—See *network logic*.

Logical relationship—Based on the dependency between two project activities or between a project activity and a milestone.

Logic Diagram—See *project network diagram*.

Logic link—See *dependency links*.

Logic loop—A circular sequence of dependency links between activities in a network.

Loop—In networks, a set of symbols indicating that one or more activities are mutually dependent.

M

Management by project—A term used to describe normal management processes that are being project managed.

Management development—All aspects of staff planning, recruitment, development, training, and assessment.

Management reserve (MR)—A portion of the contract budget base that is held for management control purposes by the contractor to cover the expense of unanticipated program requirements. It is not a part of the performance measurement baseline. Another term for *management reserve* is *contingency*.

Master schedule—A summary schedule that identifies major activities and milestones.

Material—Property that may be incorporated into or attached to an end item to be delivered under a contract or that may be consumed or expended in the performance of a contract. It includes but is not limited to raw and processed material, parts, components, assemblies, fuels and lubricants, and small tools and supplies that may be consumed in normal use in the performance of a contract.

Mathematical analysis—See *network analysis*.

Matrix organization—An organizational structure where the project manager and the functional managers share the responsibility for assigning priorities and directing the work.

Methodology—A documented process for management of projects that contains procedures, definitions, and roles and responsibilities.

Midstage assessment—An assessment in the middle of a project that can be held for several reasons: (1) at the request of the project board, (2) to authorize work on the next stage before the current one is completed, (3) to allow for a formal review in the middle of a long project, or (4) to review exception plans.

Milestone—An activity with zero duration (usually marking the end of a period).

Milestone plan—A plan containing only milestones that highlight key points of the project.

Milestone schedule—A schedule that identifies the major milestones. See also *master schedule*.

Military time—A means of representing time by using a 24-hour clock.

Mission statement—A brief summary, approximately one or two sentences, that sums up the background, purposes, and benefits of a project.

Mitigation—Working to lessen risk by lowering its chances of occurring or reducing its effect if it occurs.

Modern project management (MPM)—A term used to distinguish the difference between current broad-range project management, which encompasses scope, cost, time, quality, and risk, from more traditional project management.

Monitoring—The analyzing and reporting of project performance as opposed to the plan.

Monte Carlo simulation—The technique used by project management applications to estimate the likely range of outcomes from a complex random process by simulating the process a large number of times.

MSA—See *midstage assessment*.

Multiproject—A project consisting of multiple subprojects.

Multiproject analysis—Used to analyze the impact and interaction of activities and resources whose progress affects the progress of a group of projects or for projects with shared resources or both. Can also be used for composite reporting on projects that have no dependencies or resources in common.

Multiproject management—Managing multiple projects that are interconnected either logically or by shared resources.

Multiuser—An application that gives multiple users simultaneous access to a project and its data.

Must finish—See *imposed finish*.

Must start—See *imposed start*.

N
Near-critical activity—A low total float activity.

Negative float—The amount of time by which the early date of an activity exceeds its late date.

Negotiated contract cost—The estimated cost negotiated in a cost plus fixed fee contract or the negotiated contract target cost in either a fixed price incentive contract or a cost plus incentive fee contract. See also *contract target cost*.

Negotiation—The art of achieving what one wants from a transaction, leaving all other parties involved content that the relationship has gone well.

Network—A view of project data in which the project logic is the sole determinant of the placements of the activities in the drawing. Frequently called a flowchart, PERT chart, logic drawing, or logic diagram.

Network analysis—The process of identifying early and late start and finish dates for project activities. Done with a forward and backward pass through the project. Many PM software tools will check for loops in the network and issue an error message if one is found. The error message will identify the loop and all activities within it.

Network diagram—A view of project data in which the project logic is the sole determinant of the placements of the activities in the drawing. Frequently called a flowchart, PERT chart, logic drawing, or logic diagram.

Network logic—The collection of activity dependencies that make up a project network.

Network path—A series of connected activities in a project network.

Nonrecurring costs—Expenditures against specific tasks that are expected to occur only once in a program. Examples are such items as preliminary design effort, qualifications testing, initial tooling, and planning.

Not earlier than—A restriction on an activity that indicates that it may not start or end earlier than a specified date.

Not later than—A restriction on an activity that indicates that it may not start or end later than a specified date.

O

Objectives—Predetermined results toward which effort is directed.

Offset—See *resource offset*.

Order of magnitude estimate—See *estimate*.

Organizational breakdown structure (OBS)—A hierarchical structure designed to pinpoint the area of an organization responsible for each part of a project.

Organizational planning—The process of identifying, assigning, and documenting project responsibilities and relationships.

Organization design—The design of the most appropriate organization for a project. There are five basic kinds: functional, coordination, balanced, second, and project.

Original budget—The initial budget established at or near the time a contract was signed or a project was authorized, based on the negotiated contract cost or management's authorization.

Other Direct Costs (ODC)—A group of accounting elements that can be isolated to specific tasks other than labor and material. Included are such items as travel, computer time, and services.

Out-of-sequence progress—Progress that has been reported even though activities that have been deemed predecessors in project logic have not been completed.

Output format—In an open plan, device-specific information that governs the final appearance of a report or drawing.

Overall change control—Coordinating changes across the entire network.

Overhead—Costs incurred in the operation of a business that cannot be directly related to the individual products or services being produced. See also *indirect costs*.

Overload—The amount of required resources that exceeds the resource limit.

Overrun—Costs incurred in excess of the contract target costs in an incentive-type contract or the estimated costs in a fixed fee contract. The value of costs that are needed to complete a project, over the value originally authorized by management.

Over target baseline (OTB)—A baseline that results from formal reprogramming of an overrun; used only with the approval of the customer.

P

Parallel activities—Two or more activities that can be done at the same time. This allows a project to be completed faster than it could if the activities were arranged serially in a straight line.

Path—A series of connected activities. See *critical path method* for information on critical and noncritical paths.

Path convergence—The tendency of parallel paths of approximately equal duration to delay the completion of the milestone where they meet.

PDM—See *precedence diagram method*.

Percent complete—A measure of completion used to determine the remaining duration of a partially completed activity.

Performance measurement baseline (PMB)—The time-phased budget plan against which project performance is measured. It is formed by the budgets assigned to scheduled cost accounts and the applicable indirect budgets. For future effort not planned to the cost account level, also includes budgets assigned to higher-level CWBS elements. Does not include any management or contingency reserves, which are isolated above the PMB.

Performance measurement techniques (PMTs)—Methods used to estimate earned value. Different methods are appropriate to different work packages because of the nature of the work or the planned duration of the work package. Another term for *performance measurement techniques* is *earned-value methods*.

Performance reporting—Collecting project performance information and distributing it to ensure project performance.

Performing—A team-building stage where the emphasis is on the work currently being performed.

Performing organization—The organizational unit responsible for the performance and management of resources to accomplish a task.

Period of performance—The time interval of contract performance that includes the effort required to achieve all significant contractual schedule milestones.

Pessimistic duration—The longest duration in the three duration technique.

Phase—See *project phase*.

Physical percent complete—The percentage of the work content of an activity that has been achieved.

Placements—The ability to direct aspects of a network view.

Plan—An intended future course of action; the basis of project controls.

Planned activity—An activity not yet started.

Planned cost—Costs set when the schedule becomes the plan or baseline plan.

Planning—The process of identifying the means, resources, and actions necessary to accomplish an objective.

Planning package—A logical aggregation of far-term work within a cost account that can be identified and budgeted but not yet defined into work packages. Planning packages are identified during the initial baseline planning to establish the time phasing of the major activities in a cost account and the quantity of the resources required for their performance. Are placed into work packages consistent with the rolling wave concept before the performance of the work.

Planning stage—The stage before the implementation stage when product activity, resource, and quality plans are produced.

PMI—See *Project Management Institute*.

PMP—See *Project Management Professional*.

Pool resource—A group of resources related by skill, department, or function.

Positive float—The amount of time an activity's start can be delayed without affecting the project completion date. An activity with positive float is not on the critical path and is called a noncritical activity. Most software packages calculate float time during schedule analysis. The difference between early and late dates (start and finish) determines the amount of float.

Postimplementation review—A review 6 to 12 months after a system in a project has met its objectives and the system continues to meet user requirements.

Postproject appraisal—An evaluation that provides feedback for future use and education.

Precedence diagram method (PDM)—One of the two methods of representing a project as networks, in which the activities are represented by nodes and the relationships between them are represented by arcs. (The other method, the *arrow diagram method*, is rarely used.)

Precedence notation—A means of describing project workflow. Sometimes called activity-on-node notation. Graphically, precedence networks are represented by using descriptive boxes and connecting arrows to denote the flow of work.

Predecessor—An activity that must be completed or partially completed before a specified activity can begin. The combination of all predecessor and successor (see *successor*) relationships among the project activities forms a network that can be analyzed to determine the critical path and other project scheduling implications.

Predecessor activity—In the precedence diagramming method, the "from activity," or the activity that logically precedes the current activity.

Presenter—A person with the responsibility of making sure that those at a quality review have the information needed to carry out the review.

Priority rule—A rule used to determine the order of processing in resource scheduling algorithms.

Probability—The likelihood of a risk occurring.

Process—A set of interrelated work activities in which value is added to the inputs to provide specific outputs.

Procurement planning—Determining what to procure and when.

Product breakdown structure—Identifies the products that are required and must be produced. Describes the systems in a hierarchical way.

Product description—The description of the purpose, form, and components of a product. Should always be used as a basis for acceptance of the product by the customer.

Product flow diagram—Represents how the products are produced by identifying their derivation and the dependencies between them.

Product realization team (PRT)—A multidisciplinary team that is responsible for the definition, development, delivery, and support of a product through concurrent engineering methods.

Program—A broad effort encompassing a number of projects.

Program benefits review—A review to assess whether targets have been reached and measure the performance levels in the resulting business operations.

Program benefits review report—A report produced at the end of a program that describes the findings, conclusions, and recommendations in the program benefit review.

Program brief—Produced in the program identification phase; sums up the program and gives the terms of reference for the work to be carried out and the program director's terms of reference.

Program definition phase—Program management's second phase, including a feasibility study, a full definition, and funding approval.

Program director—The senior manager with the responsibility for the overall success of the program. Drawn from the management of the target business area.

Program directorate—A committee that directs the program when circumstances arise where there is no individual to direct the program.

Program evaluation and review technique (PERT)—A project management technique for determining how much time a project needs before it is completed. Each activity is assigned a best, worst, and most probable completion time estimate. These estimates are used to determine the average completion time. The average times are used to figure the critical path and the standard deviation of completion times for the entire project.

Program execution phase—The phase in program management where project portfolio management and transition activities are undertaken.

Program executive—A group of individuals that supports the program director.

Program identification phase—Program management's first phase. All high-level change proposals from available strategies and initiatives are considered, and their objectives and directions are translated into achievable programs of work.

Program management—The effective management of several individual but related projects to produce an overall system that works effectively.

Program management office—The office responsible for the business and technical management of a specific contract or program.

Program plan—A term that refers to all the following: benefits management plan, risk management plan, transition plan, project portfolio plan, and design management plan.

Program status date—The date up to which all program information is complete.

Program support office—A group that gives administrative support to the program manager and the program executive.

Progress—The partial completion of a project or a measure of the same thing. Also, the act of entering progress information for a project.

Progress payments—Payments made to a contractor during the life of a fixed price contract on the basis of an agreed-to formula, for example, BCWP or simply costs incurred on most government-type contracting.

Progress reporting—The act of collecting information on work done and revised estimates, updating the plan, and reporting the new revised plan.

Project—A set of activities directed toward an overall goal. Also, the collection of data relating to the achievement of that goal. More specifically, a network of activities or files containing such a network.

Project appraisal—The discipline of calculating the viability of a project.

Project assurance team—A three-member team composed of the business assurance coordinator, the technical assurance coordinator, and the user assurance coordinator, whose roles cross stage boundaries and through whom continuity of project development and technical product integrity is maintained.

Project board—The body to which the project manager is accountable for achieving the project objectives. Should be viewed as representing the stakeholders. For example, on a small project the sponsor may represent the interests of the executive, the senior user, and the technical authority, whereas in a large project, the project board may be larger than the three or four usual members.

Project boundary—The boundary of a project defined to indicate how the project interacts with other projects and nonproject activity in and outside the organization.

Project brief—A statement of reference terms for a project.

Project calendar—A calendar that defines global project working and nonworking periods.

Project champion—A senior manager who is above the project manager and who gains support and resources for the project.

Project charter—Clearly defines a project to bring a project team into necessary agreement. Consists of a mission statement, including background, purpose, and benefits; a goal; objectives; scope; and assumptions and constraints.

Project closure—The formal end of a project. Requires the project board's approval.

Project communications management—A subset of project management that includes communications planning, information planning, information distribution, performance reporting, and administrative closure in an effort to disseminate project information correctly.

Project cost management—A subset of project management that includes resource planning, cost estimating, cost control, and cost budgeting in an effort to complete the budget within its approved proposal.

Project culture—The general attitude toward projects within a business.

Project data document (PDD)—A summary of the project plan for the business office.

Project Director—The manager of a very large project that requires senior-level responsibility or the person at the board level in an organization who has the overall responsibility for project management.

Project directory—A file containing a record for each project maintained by the system.

Project environment—The context within which a project is formulated, assessed, and realized. Includes all external factors that have an impact on the project.

Project evaluation—A documented review of a project's performance, that is produced at project closure. It ensures that the experience of the project is recorded for the benefit of others.

Project file—A file containing the overall plans of a project and any other important documents.

Project initiation—The beginning of a project, at which point certain management activities are required to ensure that the project is established with clear reference terms and a substantial management structure.

Project initiation document—A document approved by the project board at project initiation that defines the terms of reference for the project.

Project issue report—A report that raises either technical or managerial issues in a project.

Project life cycle—The events, from beginning to end, necessary to complete a project.

Project logic—The relationships between the various activities in a project.

Project logic drawing—A representation of the logical relationships in a project.

Project management—Approach used to manage work within the constraints of time, cost, and performance targets.

Project management body of knowledge—An inclusive term that describes the sum of knowledge within the profession of project management. As with other professions, such as law and medicine, the body of knowledge rests with the practitioners and academics who apply and advance it.

Project Management Institute—The American professional body for project managers.

Project management professional (PMP)—An individual certified by the Project Management Institute.

Project management software—A computer application designed to help with the planning and controlling resources, costs, and schedules of a project.

Project management team—Members of the project team who are directly involved in its management.

Project manager—The individual responsible for the day-to-day management of a project.

Project matrix—An organization matrix that is project-based and in which the functional structures are duplicated in each project.

Project network diagram—Drawn from left to right to show project chronology; displays the logical relationships between project activities.

Project organization—A term that refers to the structure, roles, and responsibilities of the project team and its interfaces with the outside world.

Project phase—A group of related project activities that come together with the completion of a deliverable.

Project plan—A document for management purposes that gives the basics of a project in terms of its objectives, justification, and the ways the objectives are to be achieved. Used as a record of decisions and a means of communication among stakeholders.

Project plan development—The process of putting the results of other planning processes into a consistent document.

Project plan execution—The act of carrying out activities as stated in the project plan.

Project planning—Developing and maintaining a project plan.

Project portfolio—The constituent projects within a program.

Project portfolio plan—A plan within the program definition statement that defines a schedule of work that includes the timing, resourcing, and control for the program's projects.

Project procurement management—A subset of project management that includes procurement planning, solicitation and solicitation planning, source selection, contract administration, and contract closeout in an effort to obtain goods and services from outside organizations.

Project quality management—A subset of project management that includes quality planning, quality assurance, and quality control in an effort to satisfy the needs and purpose of the project.

Project risk management—A subset of project management that includes risk identification, risk quantification, risk response development, and risk response control in an effort to identify, analyze, and respond to project risks.

Project schedule—Planned dates for starting and completing activities and milestones.

Project scope management—A subset of project management that includes initiation, scope planning, scope definition, scope verification, and scope change control in an effort to ensure that the project has all the necessary work required to complete it.

Project sponsor—A person or group concerned with the definition of project objectives in the context of the sponsoring organization.

Project status report—A report on the status of accomplishments and any variances to spending and schedule plans.

Project strategy—A comprehensive definition of how a project will be managed.

Project success/failure criteria—The criteria on which the success or failure of a project may be based.

Project support office—The central location of planning and project support functions that has the responsibility of managing resources across projects and maintaining planning standards.

Project team—Those who report to the project manager.

Project technical plan—A plan produced at the beginning of a project that addresses strategic issues related to quality control and configuration management.

Project time management—A subset of project management that includes activity definition, activity sequencing, activity duration estimating, schedule development, and schedule control in an effort to complete the project on time.

PROMS-G—The project management special-interest group in the British Computer Society.

Public—Individuals who have an interest in a project's outcome but are not directly involved in it.

Public relations—An activity meant to improve a project organization's environment in order to improve project performance and reception.

Q

QA—See *quality assurance.*

Qualitative Risk Analysis—A generic term for subjective methods of assessing risks.

Quality—A trait or characteristic used to measure the degree of excellence of a product or service.

Quality assurance (QA)—The process of evaluating overall project performance on a regular basis to provide confidence that the project will satisfy the relevant quality standards.

Quality assurance plan—A plan that guarantees a quality approach and conformance to all customer requirements for all activities in a project.

Quality control (QC)—The process of monitoring specific project results to determine if they comply with relevant standards and identifying ways to eliminate causes of unsatisfactory performance.

Quality criteria—The characteristics of a product that determine whether it meets certain requirements.

Quality file—Contains records of quality reviews and technical exceptions procedures on a project.

Quality guide—Describes quality and configuration management procedures and is aimed at people directly involved with quality reviews, configuration management, and technical exceptions.

Quality planning—Determining which quality standards are necessary and how to apply them.

Quality review—A review of a product against an established set of quality criteria.

R

Readiness assessment—A meeting or series of meetings of selected members of the customer C/SCSC review team at a contractor's plant to review contractor plans and progress in implementing C/SCSC in preparation for a full demonstration review.

Recurring costs—Expenditures against specific tasks that would occur on a repetitive basis. Examples are sustaining engineering, production of operational equipment, tool maintenance, and so forth.

Relationship—A logical connection between two activities.

Relationship float—Relationship free float is the amount by which the lag on a relationship would have to be increased to delay the successor activity. Relationship total float is the amount by which it would have to be increased to cause a delay in the completion of the project as a whole or the violation of a late target.

Remaining duration—Time needed to complete the remainder of an activity or project.

Replanning—Actions performed for any remaining effort within project scope. Often the cost and/or schedule variances are zeroed out at this time for history items.

Report specification file—A set of codified instructions that defines the layout of a report.

Reprofiling—In resource scheduling it is possible to indicate that the specified resource requirement profile may be modified to fit the availability without changing the total amount required.

Request for change—A proposal by the project manager for a change to the project as a result of a project issue report.

Request for proposal (RFP)—A bid document used to solicit proposals from prospective sellers of products or services.

Request for quotation—Equivalent to a *request for proposal* but with more specific application areas.

Requirements—A negotiated set of measurable customer wants and needs.

Resource—An item required to accomplish an activity. Can be people, equipment, facilities, funding, or anything else needed to perform the work of a project.

Resource analysis—A term for resource leveling and resource smoothing.

Resource assignment—The work on an activity related to a specific resource.

Resource availability—The level of availability of a resource, which may vary over time.

Resource breakdown structure—A feature of hierarchical resources that facilitates both roll-up reporting and summary resource scheduling by enabling one to schedule at the detailed requirements level and roll up both requirements and availabilities to a higher level.

Resource calendar—A calendar that defines the working and nonworking patterns for specific resources.

Resource-driven task durations—Task durations that are driven by the need for scarce resources.

Resource histogram—A view of project data in which resource requirements, usage, and availabilities are shown against a time scale.

Resource level—A specified level of resource units required by an activity per time unit.

Resource leveling—The resource scheduling process of determining scheduled dates so that neither the project completion date nor any target finishes are jeopardized while minimizing the maximum extent to which resource availability is exceeded.

Resource-limited resource scheduling—The production of scheduled dates in which the resource constraints are considered as absolute and project completion is delayed as necessary to avoid exceeding resource requirements.

Resource offset—In the definition of resource requirements, the number of work periods between the start of an activity and the time when a resource is first required.

Resource optimization—A term for resource leveling and resource smoothing.

Resource period—In the definition of a resource requirement, the number of work periods for which a resource is required.

Resource planning—Evaluating what resources are needed to complete a project and determining the quantity needed.

Resource pool—A higher-level resource in a resource breakdown structure.

Resource profile—The multiple specification of a single resource requirement or availability to indicate a variation over a period of time.

Resource requirement—The requirement for a particular resource by a particular activity.

Resource scheduling—The process of determining dates on which activities should be performed to smooth the demand for resources or avoid exceeding stated constraints on these resources. See also *resource leveling, time-limited resource scheduling,* and *resource-limited resource scheduling.*

Resourcing plan—Part of the definition statement; states how the program will be resource loaded and what supporting services, infrastructure, and third-party services are required.

Responsibility assignment matrix (RAM)—Correlates the work required by a contract work breakdown structure (CWBS) element with the functional organization responsible for accomplishing the assigned tasks. The responsibility assignment matrix is created by intersecting the CWBS with the program organizational breakdown structure (OBS). This intersection identifies the cost account.

Responsibility chart—See *responsibility assignment matrix.*

Responsibility matrix—See *responsibility assignment matrix.*

Responsible organization—A defined unit within the contractor's organization structure that is assigned responsibility for accomplishing specific tasks or cost accounts.

Retainage—A part of payment withheld until the project is completed to ensure satisfactory performance completion of contract terms.

Reviewers—Those responsible for ensuring that a product is completed and fault-free at a quality review.

RFC—See *request for change.*

Risk—The probability of an undesirable outcome.

Risk analysis—A technique designed to quantify the impact of uncertainty. Usually but not necessarily associated with the Monte Carlo simulation technique.

Risk analysis histogram—A view in which the results of risk analysis are displayed as vertical bars, S curves, or tables against a date scale.

Risk avoidance—Planning activities to avoid risks that have been identified.

Risk event—A discrete occurrence that affects a project.

Risk identification—Determining which risk events will affect a project.

Risk management—The art and science of identifying and assessing the risk factors during a project and responding to them in the best interests of the project objectives.

Risk management plan—Part of the program definition statement; contains a record of all the risks in the business environment and risks to the program itself.

Risk matrix—A matrix with risks located in rows and with impact and likelihood in columns.

Risk prioritizing—Ordering of risks according first to their risk value and then by which risks need to be considered for risk reduction, risk avoidance, and risk transfer.

Risk quantification—Evaluating the probability of a risk event's effect and occurrence.

Risk ranking—Allocating a classification to the impact and likelihood of a risk.

Risk reduction—Action taken to reduce the likelihood and impact of a risk.

Risk register—A file that holds all information on identifying and managing a risk.

Risk response control—Responding to changes in risk during a project.

Risk response development—Developing a plan of action to enhance opportunities and decrease threats.

Risks—Events that, if they occur, can jeopardize the successful completion of a project. Should be identified and assessed for probability of occurrence and impact on the project.

Risk transfer—A contractual arrangement between two parties for delivery and acceptance of a product where the liability for the costs of a risk is transferred from one party to the other.

Risk value—The number obtained when numerical impact and likelihood values are multiplied.

Rubber baselining—An attempt by a contractor to take a far-term budget and move it into the current period in an attempt to disguise cost problems. Moving the budget, but without a corresponding value of work, to mask cost difficulties. An indicator of a likely cost overrun condition.

S

Schedule—The timetable for a project. Shows how project tasks and milestones are planned out over a period of time.

Schedule compression—See *duration compression.*

Schedule control—Controlling schedule changes.

Schedule dates—The start and finish dates calculated by the resource scheduling program with regard to resource constraints as well as project logic.

Schedule development—Developing a project schedule based on activity sequences, activity durations, and resource requirements.

Scheduled finish—The date calculated by the resource scheduling program as the earliest date on which an activity can finish with regard to resource constraints as well as project logic.

Scheduled start—The date calculated by the resource scheduling program as the earliest date on which an activity can start with regard to resource constraints as well as project logic.

Schedule performance index (SPI)—The ratio of work accomplished to work planned for a specified time period. An efficiency rating for work accomplishment, comparing work accomplished to what should have been accomplished.

Schedule variance—The difference between the budgeted cost of work performed and the budgeted cost of work scheduled at any point in time (BCWP − BCWS).

Scheduling—The process of determining when project activities will take place depending on defined durations and preceding activities. Schedule constraints specify when an activity should start or end based on duration, predecessors, external predecessor relationships, resource availability, and target dates.

Scope—The sum of the work content of a project.

Scope baseline—See *baseline*.

Scope change—Any change in project scope that requires a change in the project's cost or schedule.

Scope change control—Controlling changes to the scope.

Scope definition—Breaking down a deliverable into smaller manageable parts to ensure better control.

Scope of work—A chronological description of the work to be accomplished or the resources to be supplied.

Scope verification—Ensuring that all identified project deliverables have been completed satisfactorily.

S curve—A display of cumulative costs, labor hours, or other quantities plotted against time.

Security plan—A plan to abide by security measures related to the project.

Semi-time-scaled logic drawing—A drawing in which the positioning of activities is modified somewhat by some date. Unlike true time-scaled drawings, in which all horizontal positions correspond to a point in time, semi-time-scaled logic drawings simply group activities whose dates fall within a specific time period.

Senior technical—A member of the project board who represents the interests of the development and operational organizations.

Senior user—A member of the project board who represent the interests of users and others affected by the project.

Sequence—The order in which activities will occur with respect to one another. This establishes the priority and dependencies between activities. Successor and predecessor relationships are developed in a network format, allowing those involved in the project to visualize the workflow.

SF link—See *start to finish*.

Should-cost estimate—An estimate of the cost of a product or service that is used to provide an assessment of the reasonableness of a prospective contractor's proposed cost.

Skill groups—Some computer packages allow the definition of resources by their skills. The scheduling algorithm then chooses the most appropriate resource for an activity on the basis of its availability and skill.

Skills—A feature of hierarchical resources that allows one to assign an attribute to a resource and define the resource requirement for an activity in terms of that attribute.

Slippage—The amount of slack or float time used up by the current activity owing to a delayed start. If an activity without float is delayed, the entire project will slip.

Smoothing—A resource scheduling option that modifies the way time-limited scheduling (and resource-limited scheduling with thresholds) works. The objective of time-limited scheduling is to minimize the maximum extent to which each resource availability needs to be exceeded, and the standard algorithm provides the maximum flexibility to achieve this by making use of any excess already incurred. The smoothing option modifies this so that it will not use the excess for a particular activity unless that is necessary to schedule that activity within its total float.

Soft project—A project that is intended to bring about change and does not have a physical end product.

Soft skills—Include team building, conflict management, and negotiation.

Solicitation—The process of obtaining quotes, bids, or proposals.

Solicitation planning—Identifying targets for quotes, bids, or proposals.

Source selection—Choosing from potential contractors.

Span activity—See *hammock*.

Spending plan—The total budgeted funds, based on the same subcategories as the cost plan, for a given task area over a given fiscal year.

Spending plan adjustments form—A form used to change and authorize a spending plan adjustment during a fiscal year. Explains why the spending plan and the cost plan do not match.

Splitting—In resource scheduling, it is possible to specify that an activity may be split if this results in an earlier scheduled finish date. This means that the specified duration may be divided into two or more pieces while retaining the specified profile for resource requirements relative to this split duration.

Stage—A subsection of a project that has its own organizational structure, life span, and manager.

Stage assessment—See and *midstage assessment*.

Stage file—A file with detailed management plans and reports for the stage.

Stage manager—The person responsible for the management and successful completion of a stage.

Stage resource plan—A plan with all the details of the required resources for a stage.

Stage team—A team built to complete a stage.

Stage technical plan—A plan that states all the technical products, activities, and quality controls of a stage.

Stakeholders—The people who have a vested interest in the outcome of a project.

Start to finish—See *logical relationship*.

Start float—The amount of excess time an activity has between its early start and late start dates.

Starting activity—An activity that has no predecessors; does not have to wait for any other activity to start. Many PM software packages permit multiple start activities if needed.

Start-to-start lag—The minimum amount of time that must pass between the start of one activity and the start of its successor(s). May be expressed in terms of duration or percentage.

Statement of work (SOW)—A description of products and services to be procured under contract; a statement of requirements.

Status date—See *time now*.

Status reports—Written reports given to both the project team and to a responsible person on a regular basis, stating the status of an activity, work package, or whole project. Should be used to control the project and keep management informed of project status.

Stretching—In resource scheduling it is possible to specify that an activity may be stretched if this results in an earlier scheduled finish date. This means that the specified duration may be increased while the specified profile is reduced proportionally.

Subcontract—A contractual document that legally defines the effort of transferring services, data, or other hardware from one firm to another.

Subnet—A division of a project network diagram representing a subproject.

Subnetwork—See *subnet*.

Subproject—A group activities represented as a single activity in a higher level of the subproject.

Subsequent application review (SAR)—A review by customer personnel to determine whether the contractor has properly applied the C/SCSC to a new contract.

Successor—An activity whose start or finish depends on the start or finish of a predecessor activity. See *predecessor* for related information.

Sunk costs—Unavoidable costs.

Supercritical activity—An activity that is behind schedule is considered supercritical. It has been delayed to a point where its float is calculated to be a negative value. The negative float is representative of the number of units an activity is behind schedule.

System—The complete technical output of a project, including technical products.

System acceptance letter—A letter signed by the senior technical member of the project board after ensuring that the project has completed system test requirements and is ready for user acceptance.

Systems and procedures—Detail the standard methods, practices, and procedures for handling frequently occurring events within a project.

Systems management—Management that includes the prime activities of systems analysis, systems design and engineering, and systems development.

T

Target completion date—A date contractors strive toward for completion of an activity.

Target date—The date imposed on an activity or project by the user. There are two types of target dates: target start dates, and target finish dates.

Target finish activity—The user's imposed finish date for an activity. A target finish date is used if there are predefined commitment dates. Most PM software will not schedule a late finish date later than the target finish date. PM software may alert one to negative float that occurs when a late finish date is later than a target finish date. This is caused by the duration of predecessors, which makes it impossible to meet the target finish date. The negative float can be eliminated by reducing the duration of predecessors, increasing parallelism, or extending the target finish date.

Target finish date—The date planned to finish work on an activity.

Target finish project—A user's target finish date can be imposed on a project as a whole. A target finish date is used if there is a predefined completion date. Most PM software will not schedule any late finish date later than the target finish date. See *target finish activity* for how to deal with negative float.

Target schedule—See *baseline*.

Target start activity—An imposed starting date for an activity. Most PM software will not schedule an early start date earlier than the target start date.

Target start date—The date planned to start work on an activity.

Task—Also called an activity. Tasks take place over a period of time and generally consume resources.

Team—Made up of two or more people working interdependently toward a common goal and a shared reward.

Team building—The ability to gather the right people to join a project team and get them to work together for the benefit of a project.

Team development—Developing skills as a group and individually that enhance project performance.

Team leader—The person responsible for managing a stage team.

Team members—Individuals, reporting to the project manager, who are responsible for some aspect of a project's activities.

Technical assurance—The monitoring of the technical integrity of products.

Technical assurance coordinator—A member of the project assurance team who is responsible for reporting the technical assurance aspects of a project.

Technical exceptions—Unplanned situations relating to an end product.

Technical file—A file that holds all the end products to be delivered at the end of a project.

Technical guide—A document that guides stage managers, team leaders, and technical assurance coordinators in planning the production of products.

Technical products—Products produced by a project for an end user.

Three duration technique—A method to reduce estimating uncertainty.

Time analysis—The process of calculating the early and late dates for each activity on a project based on the duration of the activities and the logical relations between them.

Time-limited resource scheduling—The production of scheduled dates in which resource constraints may be relaxed to avoid delays in project completion.

Time now—The time at which all remaining work starts. Sometimes referred to as the status date because all progress information entered for a project should be correct as of this date. No work will be scheduled by the time analysis or resource scheduling programs before this date.

Time recording—The recording of effort done on each activity to update a project plan.

Time recording software—Software packages that build a time sheet from project planning software files and feed actual effort back to the project plan.

Time-scaled logic drawing—A drawing that allows one to display the logical connection between activities in the context of a time scale in which each horizontal position represents a point in time.

Time-scaled network diagram—Any project network diagram drawn so that the positioning of an activity represents the schedule.

Time sheet—A means of recording the actual effort expended against project and nonproject activities.

To complete performance index (TCPI)—The projected performance that must be achieved on all remaining work to meet a financial goal set by management.

Tolerability—An level of risk accepted to achieve certain benefits.

Tolerance—The permitted cost and time scale limits set by the executive committee for the project or set by the project board.

Top-down cost estimating—The total project cost subdivided for individual activities based on historical costs and other project variables.

Total allocated budget (TAB)—The sum of all budgets allocated to the contract. This value is the same as the contract budget base (CBB) unless an over target baseline (OTB) has been established.

Total float—The maximum number of work periods by which an activity can be delayed without delaying project completion or violating a target finish date.

Total quality management (TQM)—A strategic, integrated management system for customer satisfaction that guides all employees in every aspect of their work.

Tracking—Collecting actual time, cost, and resource information and putting it back into the project plan.

Transition plan—The part of the program definition statement that describes how the transition from the current business operation to the new environment of the blueprint will be managed.

Triple constraint—Accomplishing performance specifications, time schedules, and monetary budgets simultaneously.

Turnaround report—A report created especially for the various responsible managers to enter their progress status against a list of activities that are scheduled to be in progress during a particular time window.

U

Undistributed budget (UB)—A budget applicable to contract effort that has not yet been identified to specific cost accounts or work packages.

User acceptance letter—A letter prepared by the project or stage manager after ensuring that the system complies with the user's acceptance criteria.

User assurance coordinator—The individual who represents the users on a day-to-day basis and is responsible for reporting and monitoring the user assurance components of a project.

V

Validation—A term used in C/SCSC for approval or compliance with the criteria.

Value—A standard, principle, or quality considered worthwhile or desirable.

Value management—A structured means of improving business effectiveness that includes the use of management techniques such as value engineering and value analysis.

Variance—A discrepancy between actual and planned performance on a project in terms of schedule or cost.

Variance at completion (VAC)—The algebraic difference between budget at completion and estimate at completion.

Variance threshold—The amount of a variance that will require a formal problem analysis report as agreed to by the contractor and the customer. Variance parameters will differ depending on the function, level, and stage of the project.

Variation order—A term used in the construction industry for an approved technical change to a project.

W

WBS dictionary—A document that describes each element in the WBS, including a statement of work (SOW) describing the work content of the WBS element and a basis of estimate (BOE) describing how the budget for the element was developed. Additional information about each WBS element might include the responsible organization, the contract number, and so on. Will often result in the project or contract statement of work (SOW).

What-if analysis—The process of evaluating alternative strategies.

Work—The total number of hours, people, or effort required to complete a task.

Workaround—An unplanned response to a negative event.

Work breakdown code—A code that represents the family tree of an element in a work breakdown structure.

Work breakdown structure (WBS)—A tool for defining the hierarchical breakdown and work in a project. Developed by identifying the highest level of work in the project. These major categories are broken down into smaller components. The subdivision continues until the lowest required level of detail is established. These end units of the WBS become the activities in a project. Once implemented, the WBS facilitates summary reporting at a variety of levels.

Workflow—The relationship of the activities in a project from start to finish. Takes into consideration all types of activity relationships.

Workload—The amount of work units assigned to a resource over a period of time.

Work item—See *activity*.

Work package—Detailed short-span tasks or material items identified by the performing contractor for accomplishing work required to complete a project. Represents a further breakdown of the work defined by the cost account. In traditional cost/schedule systems, the criteria for defining work packages is as follows: (1) Each work package is clearly distinguishable from all other work packages in the program. (2) Each work package has a scheduled start and finish date. (3) Each work package has an assigned budget that is time-phased over the duration of the work package. (4) Each work package has a relatively short duration or can be divided into a series of milestones whose status can be measured objectively. (5) Each work package has a schedule that is integrated with higher-level schedules.

Work products—The results or deliverables that need to be produced to complete the project and deliver the necessary changes. May range from a new building to a completed training course.

Work units—The measurement of resources. For example, people as a resource can be measured by the number of hours they work.

Z

Zero float—A condition where there is no excess time between activities. An activity with zero float is considered a critical activity. If the duration of any critical activity is increased (the activity slips), the project finish date will slip.

B I B L I O G R A P H Y

Barkley, B., and J. Saylor. *Customer-Driven Project Management*. New York: McGraw-Hill Professional, 2001.

Block, Thomas R., and J. Davidson Frame. *The Project Office*. Menlo Park, CA: Crisp Publications, 1998.

Cobb, Nancy. *The Project Management Workbook*. New York: McGraw-Hill, 2003.

Davidow, William H., and Michael S. Malone. *The Virtual Corporation: Structuring and Revitalizing the Corporation for the 21st Century*. 1992.

DeWeaver, Mary F., and Lori C. Gillespie. *Real-World Project Management: New Approaches for Adapting to Change and Uncertainty*. New York: Quality Resources, 1997.

Dinsmore, Paul C. *Human Factors in Project Management*. New York: AMACOM, 1990.

Esque, Timm J. *No Surprises Project Management: A Proven Early Warning System for Staying on Track*. Mill Valley, CA: ACT Publishing, 1999.

Freedman, Mike. *The Art and Discipline of Strategic Leadership*. New York: McGraw-Hill, 2003.

Fuller, Jim. *Managing Performance Improvement Projects*. San Francisco: Pfeiffer (Jossey-Bass), 1997.

Gates, Bill. *Business @ the Speed of Thought*. New York: Warner Books, 1999.

Ghoshal, Sumantra, and Christopher A. Bartlett. *The Individualized Corporation: A Fundamentally New Approach to Management*. New York: 1999.

Gilbert, Shayne. *90 Days to Launch: Internet Projects on Time and on Budget*. New York: Wiley, 2001.

Goldratt, Eliyahu M. *Critical Chain*. 1997.

Goncalves, Marcus. *The Knowledge Tornado: Bridging the Corporate Knowledge Gap*. Dublin: Blackhall Publishing, 2002.

Gray, C., and E. Larson. *Project Management: The Managerial Process*. New York: McGraw-Hill/Irwin, 2003.

Harbour, Jerry L. *Cycle Time Reduction: Designing and Streamlining Work for High Performance*. New York: Quality Resources, 1996.

Kostner, Jaclyn. *Bionic eTeamwork: How to Build Collaborative Virtual Teams at Hyperspeed*. New York: Dearborn, A Kaplan Professional Company.

Lewis, James. *Project Leadership*. New York: McGraw-Hill, 2003.

Lewis, James P. *Fundamentals of Project Management*. 1997.

Lyneis J. M., K. G. Cooper, and S. A. Els. "Strategic Management of Complex Projects: A Case Study Using System Dynamics" *System Dynamics Review*, Vol. 17, No. 3, Fall 2001.

Maxwell, John C. *The 21 Irrefutable Laws of Leadership: Follow Them and People Will Follow You*. New Jersey: 1991.

Maxwell, John C. *The 17 Indisputable Laws of Teamwork*. Nashville, TN: Tom Nelson Publishers, 2001.

McMahon, Paul E. *Virtual Project Management: Software Solutions for Today and the Future*. New York: CRC Press, 2000.

Mourier, Pierre, and Martin Smith. *Conquering Organizational Change: How to Succeed Where Most Companies Fail*. New York: CEP Press, 2001.

Peters, Tom. *Thriving on Chaos: Handbook for a Management Revolution*. New York: Harper & Row, 1988.

Phillips, Joseph. *IT Project Management: On Track from Start to Finish*, 2d ed. New York: McGraw-Hill, 2004.

Pinkerton, William. *Project Management*. McGraw-Hill, 2003.

Project Management Institute. *A Guide to the Project Management Body of Knowledge*. Philadelphia.

Project Management Institute. *People in Projects*, Project Management Institute, 2001.

Rad, Parviz F., and Ginger Levin. *The Advanced Project Management Office: A Comprehensive Look at Function and Implementation*. New York: CRC Press, 2002.

Robert E. and Randy Schwartz. *The Self-Defeating Organization*. 1996.

Slader, R. *Jack Welch on Leadership*. New York: McGraw-Hill, 2004.

Verzuh, Eric. *The Fast Forward MBA in Project Manaagement*. New York: Wiley, 1999.

E N D N O T E S

CHAPTER 1

1. For more information on this section, contact Peter W. G. Morris, Professor of Project Management, UMIST, at PWMorris@netcomuk.co.uk.
2. www.247customer.com/newsandeventarticle-so.com

CHAPTER 2

1. Stevie Peterson and Velda Stohr, "Management Assistance Programs for Non-Profits." Available at http://www.mapnp.org/library/grp_skll/virtual/virtual.htm.
2. Betty Cooper, "Systems Thinking: A Requirement for All Employees," CSWT Papers, Center for the Study of Work Teams, University of North Texas (1998). Available at http://www.workteams.unt.edu/reports/bcooper.htm.
3. Gabriele Sandhoff, "Virtual Organizations as Power-Asymmetrical Networks," *Project Management Journal*, March 2000, pp 24–34.
4. Marcus Goncalves *The Knowledge Tornado*, Blackhall Publishing, Dublin, Irelands, 2002.

CHAPTER 3

1. Jeffrey Pinto, and Diane Parent, *SimProject*, McGraw-Hill, 2003.
2. Vijay Kanabar, *Project Risk Management*. Acton, MA: Copley Custom Publishing, 1997.
3. http://e-meetings.mci.com/meetingsinamerica/pdf/MIA3.pdf.

CHAPTER 4

1. The Labour party relied on RetrievalWare search and retrieval software from the Viennese company Convera (www.convera.com).
2. Project Avalanche, http://www.psgroup.com/doc/products/2004/4/PSGP4-15-04CC/PSGP4-15-04CC.asp.
3. J. P. Donlon, "The Virtual Organization," *Chief Executive* (U.S.), July 1997, p. 58.
4. Evan I. Schwartz, *Digital Darwinism*, Broadway Books, New York, 1999.

CHAPTER 5

1. *PMBOK Guide*, 2000, p 127. PMI, Newton Square, PA.

CHAPTER 7

1. HBS Press, 2000, Cambridge, MA.

CHAPTER 8

1. McGraw-Hill, 2001, New York.
2. McGraw-Hill/Irwin, 1984, New York.

CHAPTER 9

1. This case is fully described in Marcus Goncalves, *The Knowledge Tornado: Bridging the Corporate Knowledge Gap.* (Dublin, Blackhall Publising, 2002).

CHAPTER 10

1. www.IDA.ORG/IDANEW/RESEARCH/RESOMM.HTML
2. This section was written by Carla Carter, of Carla and Associates. For additional information on the theme, contact Ms. Carter at CarlaCarter@ChangeExcellence.com or visit http://www.changeexcellence.com/.
3. www-CSL.MTY.ITESM.MY/CGI.BIN/CSC
4. Putnam, 1998.
5. John Kotter, "Leading Change: Why Transformation Efforts Fail," *Harvard Business Review on Change*, 1998, p. 48.

I N D E X

NOTE: Boldface numbers indicate illustrations or code listing; *t* indicates a table.

ABOUT THE AUTHOR

 Marcus Goncalves has more than 14 years of management consulting experience and practices in the United States, Central and South America, and Europe and the Middle East. He is the former CTO and earlier a CKO of Virtual Access Networks, a start-up that under his leadership and project management skills and with the use of his Knowledge Tornado methodology was awarded the best enterprise product award at the International Comdex Fall 2000 only 13 months after the company's inception. This led six months later to the acquisition of the company by Symantec.

Marcus is also the former CEO of iCloud, Inc., which was later acquired by GenExpo, and the former COO of Parking Access.com, a successful online parking reservation company. He holds a master's degree in computer information systems and a BA in business administration. He has had more than 32 books published and is often invited to speak on these subjects worldwide. As president of MGCG, Inc., he specializes in knowledge, project, and risk management practices. Marcus is a member of the Project Management Institute (PMI) and lectures on that subject and a few other management topics in Boston University's graduate programs.

In 1989, Marcus was selected for Who's Who in the U.S. Executives and was recognized in the computer industry by the Rockefeller and Carnegie foundations.